PRAISE FOR WHITE HAND SOCIETY

"Peter Conners has given us a wondrous tale of picaresque adventure and authentic friendship—b⸱⸱⸱⸱ explorer-scientist and Ginsberg th⸱ two seminal figures who pioneered cultural maelstrom of the Sixties."
    —Ralph Metzner, co-author, wi⸱
                        of Birt⸱   ⸱⸱⸱⸱⸱⸱⸱ Culture

"The Psychedelic Revolution of the Sixties began with the meeting of two visionary explorers into the unmapped regions of inner consciousness—Timothy Leary and Allen Ginsberg. In *White Hand Society* Peter Conners charts the course from the earliest dirt roads of laughing gas to the superhighways of LSD in one compelling story. It is a thrilling ride on what Ginsberg called the Trackless Transit System, going where no one else had dared venture. Take this as a new kind of guidebook into the mystery of the mind."
    —Bill Morgan, author of *Beat Atlas: A State by State Guide to the Beat Generation in America* and *The Typewriter Is Holy: The Complete, Uncensored History of the Beat Generation*

"Peter Conners' *White Hand Society* is a gripping account of a key event in twentieth-century history, the decision to actively promote strong psychedelics to the population at large. Conners tells the Timothy Leary story from the traditional perspective of the West Coast counterculture, but he emphasizes the egalitarian influence that the Beat movement had on him and, in particular, the huge Blakean personality of Allen Ginsberg. The result is a portrait of two remarkable figures who came together and changed our culture forever."
    —John Higgs, author of *I Have America Surrounded: The Life of Timothy Leary*

"Through the years City Lights has brought us seminal work by Allen Ginsberg, Gregory Corso, and now, this detail-rich double bio of Allen Ginsberg and Timothy Leary. I knew both these men pretty well, and the times intimately, and Peter Conners has been true to it all. I don't know how he amassed the trunks of data he must have used to find the jillions of details which were new to me, but I'm certainly glad that he did. This book wins a well deserved spot on my shelf, and belongs with anyone who wants an intimate view of the Sixties-Seventies spinning of the Great Wheel of the Dharma."

— Peter Coyote, actor/author, *Sleeping Where I Fall*

White Hand Society

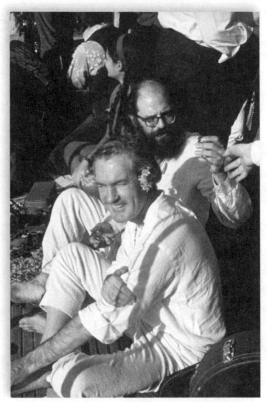

Allen Ginsberg and Timothy Leary
at the Human Be-In, Golden Gate Park, 1967.
Photographer: Gene Anthony,
© www.wolfgangsvault.com

White Hand Society

The Psychedelic Partnership of Timothy Leary and Allen Ginsberg

Peter Conners

City Lights Books ▪ San Francicsco

Cover and book design by Linda Ronan.
Cover photograph of Allen Ginsberg by Christa Fleischmann, 1971,
© The Poetry Center and American Poetry Archives, San Francisco State University.
Cover photograph of Timothy Leary, 1967 © Lisa Law.

Excerpts of letters from Timothy Leary to Allen Ginsberg, courtesy of Department
of Special Collections and University Archives, Stanford University Libraries. All
content by Timothy Leary used with permission of the Leary estate.

Excerpt on pp. 171–172 is from Tom Wolfe's epic of literary journalism, *The
Electric Kool-Aid Acid Test*, published by Farrar, Straus and Giroux in 1968,
and reissued by Picador, 2008.

The Houseboat Summit, which took place in Sausalito, CA, in February 1967,
was recorded and transcribed by the staff of the *Oracle* and is reprinted here
with permission of Ann Cohen.

Library of Congress Cataloging-in-Publication Data

Conners, Peter H.
  White hand society : the psychedelic partnership of Timothy Leary and Allen
Ginsberg / Peter Conners.
     p. cm.
  Includes bibliographical references.
  ISBN 978-0-87286-535-8
  1. Leary, Timothy, 1920-1996. 2. Psychologists—United States—Biography. 3.
Leary, Timothy, 1920-1996.—Friends and associates.
  4. Hallucinogenic drugs. I. Title.
  BF109.L43.C36 2010
  150.92—dc22
  [B]
                            2010036074

City Lights Books are published at the City Lights Bookstore
261 Columbus Avenue, San Francisco, CA 94133

www.citylights.com

Contents

Turn On

Tune In

Drop Out

"Technology has produced a chemical which catalyzes a consciousness which finds the entire civilization leading up to that pill absurd."
—Allen Ginsberg

"We have statisticians who systematize the static—how about ecstatisticians who systematize the ecstatic?"
—Timothy Leary

Turn On

Blakean Vision in Harlem

July 1948. Allen Ginsberg lay in bed reading William Blake. He was 23 years old, heartbroken and lonely.

> *Ah, Sunflower, weary of time,*
> > *Who countest the steps of the sun,*
> *Seeking after that sweet golden clime*
> > *Where the traveler's journey is done;*
>
> *Where the youth pined away with desire,*
> > *And the pale virgin shrouded in snow,*
> *Arise from their graves and aspire*
> > *Where my Sunflower wishes to go!*

It was a hot summer day in Spanish Harlem. The window was open beside Allen's bed and the slightest of breezes ruffled the pages of the book that was open on his chest, *Songs of Innocence and Songs of Experience* by William Blake. His closest friends were scattered, far away. William Burroughs was living with his wife Joan in New Orleans. Jack Kerouac was living with his mother in Long Island and rarely came to visit Allen in Harlem. Allen's "psycho-spiritual sexo-cock jewel fulfillment" lover, Neal Cassady, was on the West Coast running his usual sixteen-ring circus of girls, girls, cars, and girls. In fact, in April Allen had received a letter from Neal saying that he had just married Carolyn, the woman with whom Allen had been involved in a tug-of-war for Neal's affections. Carolyn had won. When Allen wrote back with blatant disgust and resentment, Neal lashed back at him, saying, "You and I are now farther apart than ever. Only with effort can I recall you." And further, "Let's stop corresponding—I'm not the N.C. you knew. I'm not N.C. anymore."

> O Rose, thou art sick!
> The invisible worm,
> That flies in the night,
> In the howling storm,
>
> Has found out they bed
> Of crimson joy:
> And his dark secret love
> Does thy life destroy.

Allen's pants were open and he half-heartedly touched himself while reading Blake. He had read Blake's poems so often that he barely gave them any attention at all. The words puffed easily through his brain, a pretty-sounding daisy chain that no longer demanded interpretation. His mind wandered from the poems to the window, to his cock, to his loneliness and isolation, to the Harlem skyline reaching out and up into the sunny beyond. It was a meditative, peaceful loop that even allowed Allen to distance himself from his mother's horrifying situation.

Allen's mother, Naomi, was schizophrenic. Her mental state had been on a downward trajectory for years. However, in recent months her mind had taken a decisive plummet. Naomi had already become so paranoid and abusive of Allen's father, the poet and teacher Louis Ginsberg, that she had moved out of the family's house and in with her sister, Eleanor. But now Eleanor was at wits' end with Naomi as well. Naomi was regularly accusing Eleanor of being a spy. Eventually, Eleanor called Allen in desperation, saying she could no longer house Naomi in the state that she was in. By the time Allen got to Eleanor's to pick her up, Naomi was completely out of touch with reality. The rooms were full of wires, her brain was full of wires, and everyone was a spy taking orders from dark, sinister forces. She was too far gone. Allen had no choice. He called the police and they took her to the police station, a final stop before committing her to a psychiatric ward.

At twenty-three years old, Allen was feeling the first pangs of a lonely adulthood. As with all youths, he had depended on his friends and family for reassurance that he was doing, thinking, reading, writing, learning the right things. He was still far from the bearded, freewheeling hippie-poet whose image would dominate the media (underground as well as mainstream) during the Sixties. His face still held the doughy softness of adolescence and his already penetrating gaze was magnified by thick black glasses. He looked like every other student of the era: short hair parted to the right, jacket, tie, and pressed pants. At Columbia, he had been part of a close circle of like-minded friends, but now those friends were far away. His mother was insane, and lobotomized. His father had reacted horribly when Allen came out of the closet to him, and their relationship was more strained than ever before. Allen was truly alone.

And then the world opened up to him.

Allen had just ejaculated when he heard a deep voice intoning Blake's "Ah, Sunflower" poem. This was not the proverbial *voice in your head* or any sort of inner-monologue voice that Allen had ever heard before. At first, he thought it must be the voice of God. Who else could command the naked air to reverberate with such a solemn, commanding tone? But then he quickly decided that it was the voice of the poet himself, William Blake. Allen was convinced that he was receiving a spiritual vision directly from William Blake through the incanting of Blake's "Ah, Sunflower."

While Allen had read the poem dozens of times, it now made sense to him in new and wondrous ways. He looked out the window, into the vast, blue sky where the radiating flares of the sun scorched into his eyes, *"Ah, Sunflower, weary of time, / Who countest the steps of the sun,"* and then back out across the rooftops and cornices of Harlem, *"Seeking after that sweet golden clime / Where the traveler's journey is done."* He sensed the ancient wisdom, and he understood, through Blake's words and the pure, unearthly sound of Blake's voice, the tender, mortal, grave, and spiritual nature of his own life, and all the creation that surrounded him. *"Where the Youth pined away with desire, / And the pale virgin shrouded in snow, / Arise from their graves, and aspire / Where my Sunflower wishes to go!"*

In a flash of insight known to Buddhists as "satori," Allen understood that this was his initiation into the world of the visionary. The great poet-artist-prophet William Blake was anointing Allen by bestowing upon him the ability to see the true nature of existence. And what was the true nature of existence? "Looking out at the window, through the window at the sky, suddenly it seemed that I saw into the depths of the universe, by looking simply into the ancient sky. The sky suddenly seemed very *ancient.* And this was the very ancient place that he was talking about, the sweet golden clime, I suddenly realized that *this* existence was *it*! And, that I was born in order to experience up to this very moment that I was having this experience, to realize what this was all about—in other words that this was the moment I was born for."

Had Allen's insight ended with a deeper understanding of his own flashing, ancient moment in the universe, that would have been enough to alter his perspective. However, the vision didn't end there. Allen now saw the world as alive and purposeful in ways he had never perceived. "What I was speaking about visually was, immediately, that the cornices in the old tenement building in Harlem across the back-yard court had been carved very finely in 1890 or 1910. And were like the solidification of a great deal of intelligence and care and love also. So that I began noticing in every corner where I looked evidences of a living hand, even in the bricks, in the arrangement of each brick. Some hand placed them there—that some hand had placed the whole universe in front of me. That some hand had placed the sky . . . that the sky was the living blue hand itself. Or that God was in front of my eyes—existence itself was God."

These hallucinatory insights launched Allen outside of his own life, outside of his temporary body, beyond the pull of his desires, beyond the tragic comedy of his existence, and bestowed upon him "a cosmic consciousness, vibrations, understanding, awe, and wonder and surprise. And it was a sudden awakening into a totally deeper real universe that I'd been existing in."

Allen turned back to *Songs of Innocence and Songs of Experience* and tried another poem. This time he heard Blake's voice intoning lines from "The Sick Rose."

While the insights of "Ah, Sunflower" were filled with lightness and joy, "The Sick Rose" is a darker poem. Again, Allen heard Blake's solemn, sacred voice chanting lines, "O Rose, thou art sick! / The invisible worm, / That flies in the night, / In the howling storm, / Has found out thy bed / Of crimson joy, / And his dark secret love / Does thy life destroy." Allen was transported into a heavier, albeit no less inspired view of the universe; a realization of his own mortality and, indeed, the mortality of the universe; a flash into the true meaning of nothingness, complete emptiness forever and ever. While Allen had appreciated the poet Blake before, he now saw Blake's words as "a prophecy, as if Blake had penetrated the very secret core of the entire universe and had come forth with some little magic formula statement in rhyme and rhythm that, if properly heard in the inner inner ear, would deliver you beyond the universe."

Allen read on, this time "Little Girl Lost," and once again Blake spoke to him.

Sweet sleep, come to me,
Underneath this tree;
Do father, mother weep?
Where can Lyca sleep?

Lost in desert wild
Is your little child.
How can Lyca sleep
If her mother weep?

If her heart does ache,
Then let Lyca wake
If my mother sleep,
Lyca shall not weep.

"I suddenly realized that Lyca was me, or Lyca was the self; father, mother seeking Lyca, was God seeking, Father, the Creator; and 'If her heart does ache / Then let Lyca wake'—wake to what? *Wake* meaning wake to the same awakeness I was just talking about—of existence in the entire universe. The total consciousness then, of the complete universe. Which is what Blake was talking about."

Again, Allen turned to the world outside his window. And again, each and every detail of that world crackled with cosmic energy and revealed the fingerprints of a compassionate intelligence. It all fit together, and it was purposefully beautiful. However, the beauty and essence of existence was hidden deep within the details of our quotidian world. Allen made a vow right then that he would honor this vision throughout his entire life. "My first thought was this was what I was born for, and second thought, never forget—never forget, never renege, never deny. Never deny the voice—no, never *forget* it, don't get lost mentally wandering in other spirit worlds or American or job worlds or advertising worlds or war worlds or earth worlds. But the spirit of the universe was what I was born to realize."

But how can one sustain such insight throughout a lifetime? How can one even hope to achieve *flashes* of such powerful, ancient truths while living in a world that seems intent on concealing its true nature? How, or what, could assist him in following through on his vow to "never forget, never renege, never deny" the illuminations that his Blake visitations had bestowed upon him?

A New Game

"My Darling, I cannot live without your love. I have loved life but have lived through you. The children will grow up wondering about their mother. I love them so much and please tell them that. Please be good to them. They are so dear."

With those words, Marianne Leary took her life. Nine-year-old Susan Leary and seven-year-old Jack Leary lost their mother. It was Timothy Leary's thirty-fifth birthday. October 21, 1955. His first wife had just killed herself.

For two years prior to Marianne's death, Leary had been carrying on an affair with a project manager at the Kaiser Foundation Hospital named Mary Della Cioppa. Her nickname was Delsey. While Marianne and Timothy never discussed the affair, the dalliance was an open secret among their cocktail party crowd—a crowd that Leary had dubbed the International Sporting House Set. As sophisticated and enlightened as this may sound through the gauzy romantic light of history, there was no such veil over the situation for Marianne. Since young adulthood, Marianne had demonstrated a weakness for alcohol. Tim—with more than a trace of defensiveness—retold a story of Marianne falling down drunk outside the swank St. Moritz Hotel in New York City on their honeymoon. Now, as her husband's afternoon trysts with Delsey at his rented apartment on Telegraph Avenue became the fodder for cruel party gossip, Marianne relied more and more on alcohol to soften the sting. She had also begun seeing a psychiatrist and taking tranquilizers.

However, none of the therapy or stupor-inducing booze and pills could bury the fact that Marianne Leary was losing her husband. The couple had already agreed to a period of informal separation during which Marianne planned to take the kids to Switzerland. She had always felt eclipsed by Tim's outsize personality, charisma, and professional accomplishments, and the trip to Switzerland was meant to give her an opportunity to assert her independence away from him.

But they both knew the real score. The marriage was ending.

Tim and Marianne had spent the evening before his 35th birthday at a martini-fueled cocktail party with the International Sporting House Set. After they returned home, spun out on booze and at frayed ends, Delsey had stopped by the Leary house to quickly wish Tim a happy birthday before she boarded a plane to Reno for the weekend. Marianne saw the couple outside and stumbled out the door to intervene. It was a hideous situation for all involved. Leary shushed Marianne from the driveway and tried to send her back inside. Marianne began protesting but lost her footing and tumbled down a long flight of wooden stairs. To Delsey's horror, Tim was unfazed by his wife's fall. Perhaps recalling other such drunken falls, Tim assured Delsey that Marianne would be all right.

While Delsey had seen the couple's discordant escapades up close many times, this was ugliness at a new level. She extracted herself from the situation as quickly as possible and drove off to the airport. Meanwhile, Tim shambled back inside, his steps heavy with booze and the scorn of two women.

According to Leary, he tried to make temporary amends with his wife. Nobody will ever know what truly transpired between the couple that evening in the privacy of their home. Either way, the outcome is the same.

When Tim awoke the next morning, Marianne was gone. She had written her note, then made her way out to the garage, started the car and waited for the noxious fumes to end her life.

Tim rolled out of bed and started searching through the house calling his wife's name. No reply. As Tim's search continued without success, he grew more frantic. His yells got louder, and Susan and Jack were stirred awake. Tim made his way out to the driveway. The garage door—always left open—was now closed. He heard the car running inside. Tim pulled open the heavy redwood door just as Jack rushed in beside him. Together, father and son discovered Marianne's body. Tim sent Susan to call an ambulance, but the trip to the hospital was a formality. Nothing could be done for Marianne. As they loaded her body into the ambulance the dissipating clouds of exhaust floated into the Berkeley morning.

Within a year of Marianne's death, Tim and Delsey were married. Another year later, they were divorced. Tim made a promise to Delsey not to discuss their marriage publicly, and he kept that promise throughout his life. The best insights into their short-lived, ill-conceived, and often violent relationship come from Delsey: "When we were married, we had a big fight one morning and I ran out of the house.

We both had to go to work and he chased me all over the hills and found me and I was fighting him in the car and I hit him on the nose and broke it and he never got it fixed. So the shape of his nose is my handiwork." Their relationship steadily disintegrated, "He was trying to make me into Marianne and the very thing that attracted him to me in the first place was that I was unlike her."

Leary's romantic relationships were exploding in the most dramatic, tragic ways. His professional life as Director of Psychology Research at the Kaiser Foundation Hospital was wavering too. The flow of grant money was starting to trickle out due, in part, to Leary's neglect of his duties there. His reputation as a golden boy, the hit of the party, the charismatic captain of the ship, was turning green with tarnish. It was time for Tim to perform the disappearing act he would eventually perfect.

In the summer of 1958, attempting to put two marriages and an increasingly uncomfortable social and professional life behind him, Tim whisked Jack and Susan away to Spain. His plan was to write his next psychology book, a follow-up to his renowned *Interpersonal Diagnosis*, and also work on a novel. The family started out living in a rented villa in Torremolinos on the Costa del Sol in Spain. By January, 1959, they had moved to a hotel, then into an apartment. By day, Tim sweated with little success over piles of statistics, numerical indices, and test scores. He was trying to wrangle the mass of information he had gathered in Berkeley into a coherent statement about the failings of the current psychotherapeutic model. Meanwhile, Susan and Jack attended school. Tim had attempted to lighten the kids' situation by buying Jack a puppy. But the puppy (as puppies do) defecated all over their little apartment. The kids were increasingly subjected to Tim's darkening moods.

Susan and Jack were also subjected to the strange, gloomy physical confines of the apartment itself. As Tim described it, the apartment was "tunneled into the rock at the foot of Calle San Miguel" and was a "cave with oozing stone walls. The beds were always damp."

Mentally, spiritually, and physically, Tim was falling apart. In addition to clear-cut clinical depression, his body had started turning against him. As Tim describes it, "There the break-through-break-down started. It began in the head. One morning my scalp began to itch. By noon it was unbearable. Each hair root was a burning rod of sensation. My hair was a cap of fire. I ran down the beach and cut my feet on rocks to keep from ripping my fingers through my scalp. By evening, my face began to swell and huge water blisters erupted from my cheeks. A young Danish doctor came, injected me with a huge needle, and gave me sleeping pills. . . . In the morning I was blind—eyes shut tight by swollen tissue and caked with dried pus. I felt my way to the bathroom, lit a candle, and pried open one eye before the mirror. . . . In the oblong glass I saw the twisted, tormented face of an insane stranger."

In a 1953 exchange between two figures who would play important roles in Leary's psychedelic future, Aldous Huxley wrote to Dr. Humphry Osmond, "Disease, mescaline, emotional shock, aesthetic experience and mystical enlightenment have the power, each in its different way and in varying degrees, to inhibit the functions of the normal self and its ordinary brain activity, thus permitting the 'other world' to rise in consciousness." While mescaline was not yet a part of his vocabulary, Tim certainly believed that the "disease" he was suffering provided access to the "other world," ultimately raising his consciousness. "By the time I wrenched back to the room. . . . I was weak and trembling. I slumped in the chair for the rest of the dark night, wrapped in a Burberry mackintosh.

"I died. I let go. I surrendered."

At this point, Leary describes a massive transformation taking place, a sloughing away of his old values, ambitions, drives, and guilt. The transformation continues to the point that Leary describes his entire identity melting away. Later in his career, Tim would translate the Tibetan Book of the Dead into psychedelic terms and come to view it as a guide-book to the "other world" of consciousness travels that of-ten led to the sort of ego disintegration that he was currently experiencing. But in Spain, Tim had no such guidebook. He was on his own. "With a sudden snap, all the ropes of my social self were gone. I was a thirty-eight-year-old male ani-mal with two cubs. High, completely free."

By morning, Tim understood that he had undergone a radically life-altering experience. In his words, it was "the first of some four hundred death-rebirth trips I have expe-rienced since 1958." Not only was he mentally altered, but his physical crisis was now abating too. The swelling in his face and extremities was subsiding. When he looked in the mirror, he once again recognized the face looking back at him. In many ways, it was the same old Tim. But it was Tim on a new mission. "I found a pen and paper. I wrote three letters. One to my employers, telling them that I was not returning to my job. A second to my insurance agent to cash in my policies. And a third long manuscript to a colleague, spelling out certain revelations about the new psychology, the limiting artifactual nature of the mind, the unfolding possibilities of mind-free consciousness, the liberating effect of the ancient rebirth process that comes only through death of the mind." His illness had, at least momentarily, emptied him of his past, and radically altered his perspective on the future.

Two years later, Leary would take his first dose of hallucinogens in the form of seven psychedelic mushrooms. By that time he would be employed as a lecturer at Harvard. That dose of psychedelics would pick up where this first "death-rebirth trip" had left him, and Dr. Leary was on his way to becoming the Timothy Leary the world would come to know.

3 The Father, Son, and the Holy Ghost

In his book *Leviathan*, published in 1651, the political philosopher Thomas Hobbes famously summed up humankind's existence: "The life of man, solitary, poor, nasty, brutish, and short." Three hundred years later, author and philosopher Aldous Huxley, in his essay *Heaven and Hell*, would extend Hobbes' bleak observation into a rationalization for the timeless, universal quest to self-medicate: "That humanity at large will ever be able to dispense with Artificial Paradises seems very unlikely. Most men and women lead lives at worst so painful, at the best so monotonous, poor and limited, that the urge to escape, the longing to transcend themselves if only for a few moments, is and has always been one of the principal appetites of the soul."

Interestingly enough, Huxley, though a passionate believer in the value of psychedelics for unlocking human intellectual and spiritual potential, never believed that the masses should be encouraged to use the drugs. For a man who valued psychedelics so much that his wife, Laura Huxley, injected him with 200 micrograms of LSD on his deathbed, Aldous Huxley was more concerned about what these drugs could do *to* the majority of people than what they could do *for* them. Huxley was Timothy Leary's role model and his early advocate, but this was always a sticking point in their relationship. Huxley had faith in Leary, but he fretted over Leary's overzealous attitude toward LSD. It was Tim who delivered Huxley's dying dose to Laura on November 20, 1963. Huxley would die two days later, the same day John F. Kennedy was killed in Dallas. In his final visit with Aldous that day, the old master instructed Tim, "Be gentle with them, Timothy. They want to be free, but they don't know how. Teach them. Reassure them." Aldous Huxley died while Laura whispered into his ear, "You are going forward and up; you are going towards the light. Willing and consciously you are going, willing and consciously, and you are doing this beautifully; you are doing this so beautifully—you are going towards the light; you are going towards a greater love; you are going forward and up. . . ."

Perhaps, in his concerns on the impact that widespread psychedelic use could have on the general populous, Huxley was following Hobbes' lead. After all, Huxley understood that LSD was a revolutionary drug, and Hobbes put forth that, as part of the social contract, people should put aside their "right of revolution." In any event, Huxley was not alone in his concern. In fact, the intellectual, scientific, and psychological community that supports LSD has always—to this day—publicly argued against its widespread, unregulated use.

That argument started with LSD creator and user #1: Dr. Albert Hofmann.

In 1943 Albert Hofmann was a chemist employed by Sandoz Pharmaceuticals in Basel, Switzerland. He was at work on a research project to create a new analeptic using the synthesized molecules of ergot. Ergot—scientifically known as *Claviceps purpurea*—is a fungus that grows on diseased kernels of rye. Because the fungus was used for a variety of purposes in folk medicine, Sandoz felt that therein might lie the basis for the world's next wonder drug. For the past several years, Hofmann had been methodically working his way through ergot, synthesizing and testing the properties of each molecule before moving on to the next. On Friday, April 16, 1943, for some reason that he would later describe as "a peculiar presentiment," he decided to revisit a synthesis that he had done back in 1938. The twenty-fifth compound of the lysergic acid series.

Hofmann spent all day on April 16 synthesizing LSD-25 into a crystalline form that could be dissolved in water. Little did he know that there was no need to directly ingest the chemical for it to take effect. While working with the compound, he inadvertently absorbed some of the substance through his fingertips.

He began to feel woozy and wrote a memo to his boss explaining, "I had to leave work for home because I was suddenly hit by a feeling of unease and mild dizziness." He went home, climbed into bed, and spent the rest of the day mildly hallucinating. "At home I lay down and sank into a not unpleasant intoxicated-like condition, characterized by an extremely stimulated imagination. In a dreamlike state, with eyes closed (I found the daylight to be unpleasantly glaring), I perceived an uninterrupted stream of fantastic pictures, extraordinary shapes with intense, kaleidoscopic play of colors. After some two hours this condition faded away."

Hofmann was, rightfully, stupefied, but certainly not put off by the experience. He marched back into Sandoz the following Monday, put together a new batch of LSD-

25, and promptly dosed himself again with 250 millionths of a gram. In common scientific terms, 250 millionths of a gram is an infinitesimal dosage. But that is not the case with LSD.

As the acid kicked in, Hofmann told his fellow scientists that he wanted to go home. He asked them to send a doctor to his house, and then—accompanied by an assistant—he climbed onto his bicycle for the most famous ride in psychedelic lore; a ride that is still celebrated by psychedelic enthusiasts as "Bicycle Day." Hofmann began pedaling, but even while he rode he "had the sensation of being unable to move from the spot. Nevertheless, my assistant later told me that we had traveled very rapidly." Hofmann made his way home through a familiar landscape made surreal, hysterical, foreboding, and strange. He went on to describe how that day he was "filled with an overwhelming fear that I would go crazy. I was transported to a different world, a different time." Indeed, much of Hofmann's description of his first LSD experiments would be considered, by later parlance, "bad trips." He was paranoid, tortured by hallucinations of demons, and terrified that the drug had permanently driven him insane.

In his book *LSD: My Problem Child*, Hofmann recounts the dark side of that Bicycle Day trip. "Even worse than these demonic transformations of the outer world were the alterations that I perceived in myself, in my inner being. Every exertion of my will, every attempt to put an end to the disintegration of the outer world and the dissolution of my ego, seemed to be wasted effort. A demon had invaded me, had taken possession of my body, mind, and soul. I jumped up and screamed, trying to free myself from him, but then sank down again and lay helpless on the sofa.

The substance, with which I had wanted to experiment, had vanquished me. It was the demon that scornfully triumphed over my will. I was seized by the dreadful fear of going insane. I was taken to another world, another place, another time. My body seemed to be without sensation, lifeless, strange. Was I dying? Was this the transition?"

However, later that day, after the most intense part—the peak—of the acid trip was past, Hofmann quite enjoyed himself. "The horror softened and gave way to a feeling of good fortune and gratitude, the more normal perceptions and thoughts returned, and I became more confident that the danger of insanity was conclusively past."

Hofmann eventually went to sleep and awoke refreshed. Not only refreshed, but feeling that "a sensation of well-being and renewed life flowed through me. Breakfast tasted delicious and gave me extraordinary pleasure. When I later walked out into the garden, in which the sun shone now after a spring rain, everything glistened and sparkled in a fresh light. The world was as if newly created. All my senses vibrated in a condition of highest sensitivity, which persisted for the entire day."

Thus, Hofmann experienced the dark and the light of acid. Over time (in fact, a lifetime of use), Hofmann would pursue the renewing properties of LSD many times. Ultimately, he came to believe that—when used correctly—LSD could play a major role in the spiritual development of mankind. In a 1996 interview, Hofmann, then 90 years old, said, "This is a very, very deep problem of our time in that we no longer have a religious basis in our lives. Even with religion, with the churches, they are no longer convincing with their dogma. And people need a deep spiritual foundation for their lives." He encouraged young people to go out into nature, where they would gain an appreciation for the fleeting, ephemeral character of our existence; where they could look beyond our Hobbesian solitary, poor, nasty, brutish, and short lives and "experience the beauty and deep meaning which is at the core of our relation to nature." He emphasized that these experiences, these understandings, had to be gotten firsthand. Not simply through reading books or going to church—not by substituting other people's words for firsthand experience. "Aldous Huxley taught us not to simply believe the words, but to have the experience ourselves. This is why the different forms of religion are no longer adequate. They are simply words, words, words, without the direct experience of what it is the words represent." Hofmann then mingled wisdoms from William Blake and Aldous Huxley with the Eastern practices that have always been inextricably linked to psychedelic culture: "We must have the experience directly. And the experience occurs only by opening the mind, and opening all of our senses. Those doors of perception must be cleansed. And if the experience does not come spontaneously, on its own, then we may make use of what Huxley calls a gratuitous grace."

However, despite Hofmann's advocacy of the drug, he always made sure to emphasize that it must be used in what he deemed appropriate ways, and always under proper guidance. He and Huxley were certainly of like mind in those beliefs. And, despite outward appearances and effects, Timothy Leary also took this lesson to heart. He spent countless hours trying to figure out the best ways to communicate the importance of "set and setting" to LSD users. In his essay "Using Psychedelics Wisely" Myron J. Stolaroff describes "set" as "the contents of the personal unconscious, which is essentially the record of all one's life experience. It also includes one's walls of conditioning, which determine the freedom with which one can move through various vistas. Another important aspect of set consists of one's values, attitudes, and aspirations. These will influence the direction of attention and determine how one will deal with the psychic material encountered." "Setting" refers to the physical environment where the trip is taking place. That is the most easily controllable factor and one that Leary took great pains to arrange and outfit accordingly. However, Leary was also Leary. As Hofmann summed it up, "He was a very intelligent man, and quite charming; I enjoyed our conversations very much. However, he also had a need for too much attention. He enjoyed being provocative, and that shifted the focus from what should have been the essential issue."

In many ways, the groundwork of the Sixties psychedelic-spiritual movement was laid by the trinity of Albert Hofmann (the Father of psychedelics), Aldous Huxley (the Son who would spread the word), and William Blake (the Holy Ghost). The groundwork set, Timothy Leary and Allen Ginsberg took up the mission of easing the movement out of its rarefied space and bringing LSD to the people. Of course, there were other key figures on a similar mission, most visibly Ken Kesey and his band of Merry Pranksters. Operating out of California's Bay Area, Kesey, LSD chemist Owsley Stanley, and a Leary-inspired group called The Brotherhood of Eternal Love were responsible for a huge quantity of per capita dosing. However, Kesey—the most public of the West Coast psychedelic advocates—was more about—as visionary poet Arthur Rimbaud would put it—"a systematic derangement of the senses." There was an aspect of the Jackson Pollock approach to Kesey's LSD experimentalism: use psychedelics to splatter people's consciousness at the canvas and, eventually, a living artwork will emerge. Those living artworks were called The Acid Tests, and, to largely negative and sensationalistic effect, they brought LSD to national attention. The Acid Tests were LSD-fueled sensory assaults of music, dance, art, and extravagant weirdness that were meant to, as the title implies, "test" the trippers' psyches under extreme conditions. Unlike Leary's experiments, the Acid Tests weren't about visionary revelation or self-realization for the participants; they were more about releasing cosmic tension and upending the confines of constricting societal mores. It is arguable, but not terribly important, whether Kesey or Leary influenced more people to drop acid. (Both received enormous help from the media.) More important were their very different approaches. Ken Kesey was a pure populist and unrepentant wild-man with regard to LSD use. But Leary and Ginsberg were the gentler bridges between the "holy trinity" of visionary consciousness expansion and the 1960s psychedelic movement.

Immovable If Not Immortal

True to his oath, Allen didn't forget, deny, or renege on the insights he gained that afternoon in Harlem in 1948. After years of poetic apprenticeship—studying, writing, searching for the unique poetic vibration that would be particular to him and also honor the enormous visionary shoes he intended to step into—Allen had crafted a long master poem called "Howl." As the title would imply, "Howl" was, among other things, a cathartic burst of "telling." Allen had spent his entire young life trying to tell something—everything!—to someone—anyone! Lawrence Ferlinghetti, the poet and publisher who launched Allen Ginsberg's career, once said, "The first thing a poet has to do is to live that type of life which doesn't compromise himself." By the time Allen publicly revealed "Howl," he had cast off the last vestiges of a straight life and embraced his role as a bohemian poet. There would be no compromise. It was in this role that he would "tell" the world everything. It is fitting that he would begin his watershed poem with the words, "I saw" and then proceed with a harrowing, hallucinatory recounting of all he had seen, heard, and experienced during his young adulthood. Of course, his Blakean vision would figure immediately into "Howl" in the form

of "Mohammedan / angels staggering on tenement roofs illuminated, / who passed through universities with radiant
cool eyes hallucinating / Arkansas and Blake-light tragedy
among the scholars of war." And true to Ginsberg's nature,
if he was going to tell it, he was going to tell it all, including
the great Columbia University underwear bust with Jack
Kerouac.

> *who were expelled from the academies for crazy &*
> *publishing obscene*
> *odes on the windows of the skull,*
> *who cowered in unshaven rooms in underwear . . .*

In March, 1945, Allen Ginsberg was suspended from
Columbia. The ostensible reason was that a university
cleaning woman had found the phrases "Fuck the Jews"
with a skull and crossbones under it and "Butler has no
balls" (Nicholas Murray Butler being the university president) scrawled into the dust on Allen's dorm window.
However, it couldn't have helped that when the assistant
dean of student-faculty relationships burst into Allen's
room at 8AM to confront him about the dust-graffiti, he
found Jack Kerouac and Allen in bed together. They were
in their underwear, not naked, and—although Allen pro-
fessed his love for Jack a year later (to which Jack simply
let out a groan, "Ooooooh, no. . . .")—this encounter had
been chaste.

Still, when the assistant dean entered the room, it
didn't look good to him. Jack Kerouac, the former star full-
back for the Columbia football team, hopped out of bed in
his underwear and ran to Allen's roommate's vacant bed
in the next room. He pulled the covers over his head and
stayed there waiting for the situation to resolve itself. Jack

had dropped out of Columbia when his football career was ended by a broken leg. As far as he was concerned, this university scene was Allen's problem now.

Allen's suspension was relatively brief. He was re-admitted to Columbia for the fall 1946 semester, and six years—and a lifetime of drama—later, he received his BA in English. Aside from the mentoring relationship he formed with renowned literary critic Lionel Trilling, Allen's most formative experiences while at Columbia undoubtedly occurred outside the classroom. Incidents like the stabbing death of David Kammerer at the hands of Allen and Jack's close friend Lucien Carr and Allen's adventures with William Burroughs and junkie guru Herbert Huncke around Times Square are the stuff of Beat legend. These incidents reappear in both Allen's and Jack's writing and in numerous retellings of their lives. For Allen, the most primal energy of this heady period burst through in "Howl," a long poem that fused the frenetic energy of Times Square's hustlers with a barrage of apocalyptic imagery delivered in an impassioned, incantatory burst of language.

Allen debuted "Howl" at a group reading on Fillmore Street in San Francisco on October 7, 1955. The reading was held at the Six Gallery, a small art gallery that had been converted from a car repair shop. The reading was billed as "Six Poets at Six Gallery," and the handbills promised a "remarkable collection of angels on one stage reading their poetry. No charge, small collection for wine, and postcards. Charming event."

Jack Kerouac was also present at the Six Gallery. When Allen told Jack that he loved him in 1946, he was clumsily voicing his desires—coming out of the closet—for the first time. Throughout his life, Allen remained grateful for Jack's delicate handling of this sensitive admission. "His tolerance gave me *permission* to open up and talk, you know 'cause I felt there was space for me to talk, where he was. He wasn't going to hit me. He wasn't going to reject me, really, he was going to accept my soul with all its throbbings and sweetness and worries and dark woes and sorrows and heartaches and joys and glees and mad understandings of mortality, 'cause that was the same thing he had."

Now, at the Six Gallery, Kerouac emboldened Allen to release his full bardic potential. Kerouac had declined to participate as a reader, but he was the most active audience member at the event. He passed a hat around to collect money and then rushed out to buy gallon jugs of California Burgundy. The jugs were also passed communally around the audience. As Ginsberg really got cooking while reading "Howl" and the audience got deeper into their cups, Kerouac led the crowd in chants of "Go! Go! Go!"

Among those shouting encouragement from the audience were Ginsberg's old love, Neal Cassady, and his new love, Peter Orlovsky.

Neal Cassady had been Ginsberg's first full-fledged, adult affair. Neal was, by all accounts, a born hustler. He was also handsome, athletic, and darkly brooding. He was a world-class talker and self-educated street philosopher, the hero of the Beat gang.

Particularly at first meeting, Neal's mixture of fast friendship, good looks, passion, energy, and pure unadulterated hustle was irresistible to most. That was particularly the case with Allen. Allen met Neal in December 1946, during Neal's first trip to New York City. Neal was in New

York visiting Hal Chase, one of his boyhood chums from Denver who was attending Columbia. Neal was married to a girl named LuAnne at the time, and she accompanied him on his trip. Hal Chase was friends with both Jack and Allen and had told them many stories about his wild, free-wheeling buddy from Denver. Still, Allen was unprepared when he met Neal at the West End Bar. He was completely love-struck. As luck would have it, Cassady's relationship with LuAnne—as with all women—was volatile. The rowdy young Neal Cassady, turned loose in New York City, quarreled often with the naïve bride he trailed behind him. Soon LuAnne was on a bus back to Denver, alone. It took only days after that for Allen and Neal to start a sexual relationship.

On January 21, 1947, Allen wrote a journal entry following the start of his affair with Neal. "Having spent a wild weekend in sexual drama with Cassady, I am left washed up on the shore of my 'despair' again. . . . I think that I should approach Neal and propose to him that we live together for a season, short or long as it may be; I need to catch the ways of his personal power, his lack of some fears. I have not much to offer him in return except what he seems to think that I have, intellectual polish, learning, subtlety of thought. All of this is so childish and useless. Everything that is dust and ashes in my mouth—and everything that I do not possess: I shall offer these to him in return for the secret of existence?"

As always, Allen doubted himself, while immediately leaping to fantasies of dramatic soul-entwinement with his new love. There would be no slow, yielding process of falling in love for Allen. Cassady's sexual energy had Ginsberg's mind spinning in his braincase and his emotionally heightened, theatric tendencies immediately kicked into high gear.

The windshield's full of tears
rain wets our naked breasts
we kneel together in the shade
amid the traffic of night in paradise.

Allen Ginsberg, excerpted
from "The Green Automobile"

Allen was prepared to dedicate himself to Neal, but Neal was too manic to settle for one lover. Eventually, Neal would marry—and stay married—to Carolyn Cassady (née Carolyn Robinson). However his numerous trysts would continue for years to come. Neal was Allen's early poetic muse and his model for a peculiarly American masculinity. It took years of pining, lamenting, reuniting, and separating again, until Allen finally put Neal behind him.

In 1954, Allen met the true love of his life: Peter Orlovsky. The couple was introduced in San Francisco by the painter Robert LaVigne, but Allen was smitten with Peter before they even met. LaVigne had already shown Allen a naked portrait that he had painted of Peter. So when Allen met Peter, it was as if this sexy, potent, erotic image had walked off the canvas and assumed flesh. Allen and Peter moved in together in San Francisco, and soon after they would pledge their lives and souls to each other. In Foster's Cafeteria, at 3AM, Allen and Peter "made a vow to each other that he could own me, my mind and everything I knew, and my body, and I could own him, and all he knew, and his body. Neither of us would go into heaven unless we could get the other one in."

Each of the poets who participated at the Six Gallery reading that night—Michael McClure, Gary Snyder, Philip Whalen, and Philip Lamantia, as well as the night's master of ceremonies and guiding figure of the San Francisco literary scene, Kenneth Rexroth—could claim their own solid reputations as poets. But the Six Gallery reading was Allen's night. It was, simultaneously, the debut of a great American poem, the first public reading by a major American poet, and the beginning of what would be known as the San Francisco Literary Renaissance.

Lawrence Ferlinghetti, poet and bookstore owner, was one of the people present at the Six Gallery reading. Like everyone else in attendance, he was jolted and inspired by Allen's reading. He had also recently founded a poetry publishing house using the same name as his bookstore: City Lights. In acknowledgment of the Whitmanic tradition in which Ginsberg was working, Ferlinghetti went home after the reading and wrote Allen a letter. The letter paraphrased what Ralph Waldo Emerson had written to Walt Whitman upon reading *Leaves of Grass*. "I greet you at the beginning of a great career." Followed immediately by the publisher's come-on, "When do I get the manuscript?"

For any writer, publishing your first book is an exhilarating, nerve-wracking milestone that snaps the world into sharper focus. Most poets achieve this milestone out of public view; only a handful of people regularly read poetry, and of those, even fewer read a poet's first book. That was not the case with *Howl and Other Poems*.

Howl started out as inauspiciously as any poetry book. The applause of the Six Gallery lingered, but it seemed the impact of the poem would be confined to the poetry community. While *Howl* was going through the production stages toward publication, Allen had taken work as a yeo-man-storekeeper on a ship headed for the Arctic Circle. Shortly before he shipped out, Allen received a telegram informing him that his mother, Naomi, had died.

As when any loved one dies after years of illness and suffering, there was relief mixed with sadness in his reaction to Naomi's passing. In San Francisco, Allen was comforted in his grief by Peter and Jack. The long trip to the Arctic aboard the USNS *Sgt. Jack J. Pendleton* also afforded Allen an abundance of time to reflect on Naomi's tragic life. In a letter to his brother, Eugene, Allen wrote, "I've been thinking a lot. We all die, life's a short flash. Standing on the prow of ship with roaring ocean and stars and force of wind in sleeves, great majesty and tenderness to life, at its heart, a kind of instantaneous universal joy at creation, at everything in the ocean moves."

The Arctic trip also allowed Allen time to proof the galleys of *Howl and Other Poems*. He corresponded by mail with Ferlinghetti along the way, and finally, one day in August, the printed copies of the book arrived. Allen was elated, but also slightly embarrassed to see his words in print; immovable if not immortal. He fretted to Ferlinghetti, "I wonder if we will actually sell the thousand copies." Ferlinghetti—as his publisher—no doubt wondered the same thing. As it turned out, neither need have worried.

Bolstered by good reviews and tremendous curiosity within the literary community *Howl and Other Poems* sold through its first printing. The book was reprinted and, at that point, would have already been considered a "successful" poetry book. By this time, Allen had covered thousands more miles. He returned from the Arctic to San Francisco in September. On September 2, 1956, Richard Eberhart published an article in the *New York Times* titled "West Coast Rhythms." The article elucidated on the new San Francisco poetry scene as a whole, but emphasized, "The most remarkable poem of the young group, written during the past year, is 'Howl' by Allen Ginsberg."

As the saying goes, you can't *buy* publicity like that. Book sales continued to swell, and Eberhart's praise was echoed in numerous other reviews and in poet-to-poet gossip across the country. Meanwhile, Ginsberg traveled from San Francisco to Mexico City where Kerouac was living and writing. After that, he was off with Jack and Peter to New York City.

On May 21, 1957, City Lights Bookstore employee Shige-yoshi Murao was arrested for selling a copy of *Howl* to undercover officers. Earlier that spring, customs officials had confiscated a shipment of copies entering the United States from the printer in England. In both cases, the argument was that the book—Allen's poetry—was obscene. The trial commenced in August and was a cause célèbre for America's literati. Between the *New York Times* article by Richard Eberhart, the book's foreword written by William Carlos Williams, and shows of support from noteworthy authors and distinguished professors, the case appeared to be a slam-dunk. The trial was a straightforward First Amendment cause, and, though it generated plenty of column inches, no one on the defense side entertained thoughts of losing. In fact, Ginsberg himself didn't even stick around to participate in the trial. While the case was pending, he slipped out of the country to travel with Peter through Europe.

In October 1957, in an impressively considered statement, Judge W.J. Clayton Horn pronounced, "I do not believe that 'Howl' is without redeeming social importance."
He went on to analyze *Howl* in its isolated components.
"The first part of 'Howl' presents a picture of a nightmare
world; the second part is an indictment of those elements
in modern society destructive of the best qualities of human
nature; such elements are predominantly identified as materialism, conformity, and mechanization leading toward
war. The third part presents a picture of an individual who
is a specific representation of what the author conceives as
a general condition. 'Footnote to Howl' seems to be a decla-
mation that everything in the world is holy, including parts
of the body by name. It ends with a plea for holy living. . . .
The theme of 'Howl' presents 'unorthodox and controversial ideas.' Coarse and vulgar language is used in treatment
and sex acts are mentioned but unless the book is entirely
lacking in 'social importance' it cannot be held obscene."

The charges were overturned. *Howl and Other Poems*
had been declared, by law, to have redeeming "social importance." Meanwhile, *Life* magazine published an article
on the *Howl* trial. The book was into its fourth printing.
It had become a national best-seller. Allen Ginsberg had
become a notorious, national celebrity.

The first psychedelic session Allen Ginsberg had with
Timothy Leary took place at Leary's house in November,
1960. While not nearly as public, the time between Tim's
Spanish "death-rebirth trip" and his first meeting with
Allen had also been dramatic.

In spring 1959, following Leary's massive breakdown,
Tim's colleague Frank Barron visited the Leary family in

Europe. By then, Tim had recovered sufficiently to complete his new manuscript (which was never published) and move the family to Florence, Italy. Barron brought with him two important bits of information.

First, Barron told Tim about his recent trip to Mexico. Frank had been researching the nature of creativity, which led to an interview with a psychiatrist in Mexico who had been using and studying psychedelic mushrooms. The psychiatrist boasted of the visions the mushrooms induced and their creativity-enhancing value. Intrigued, Barron took some mushrooms back to Berkeley, where he ingested them to—unsurprisingly—cosmic effect.

As Tim told the story in later years, Barron's raving about the mushroom trip turned him off. "At this point Frank lost me with his talk about William Blake revelations, mystical insights, and transcendental perspectives produced by the strange fungi. I was a bit worried about my old friend and warned him against the possibility of losing his scientific credibility if he babbled this way among our colleagues."

Secondly, Barron passed along the information that Professor David McClelland, director of the Center for Personality Research at Harvard University, was currently in Florence. Barron had been in touch with McClelland and told him about Marianne Leary's suicide and Tim's subsequent tough times. McClelland had read Leary's acclaimed first book, *The Interpersonal Diagnosis.* He was also familiar with "the Leary Circle" which is a self-report test related to anxiety and self-esteem that is still used by some psychologists today.

Barron facilitated a meeting between Leary and McClelland in Florence. Tim brought his new manuscript to the meeting and proceeded to charm McClelland over a bottle of Chianti. Harvard had recently been denied accreditation for its clinical psychology program by the American Psychology Association, and McClelland had been charged with beefing up the program and bringing in some new mavericks in the field. Leary had already established his position in the vanguard of clinical psychology, and McClelland saw an opportunity to put Harvard where he thought it belonged—at the forefront of the discipline. He extended an invitation for Leary to become a lecturer at Harvard.

Leary may have initially been turned off by Frank Barron's proselytizing about mushrooms, but a stay in Cuernavaca, Mexico, in the summer of 1960 changed that opinion forever. Tim was about to turn forty. For a year, he had been a lecturer at Harvard, where—even before psychedelics—he had quickly managed to polarize both colleagues and students. As was often the case with Leary, people either loved him or couldn't stand him; individuals certainly moved from camp to camp, but there was seldom middle ground. At Harvard, Tim pushed for his students to get away from Freudian approaches, which he felt created distance between patient and therapist and eliminated the potential for therapeutic transaction that was the key to helping patients. Tim insisted on the experiential over the abstract. He came to call this his "existential-transactional" theory. He encouraged his students to go to where their patients were—ghettos, jails, community centers, police stations, schools, orphanages— rather than pushing them into the sterile environment of a clinical office. Naturally, Leary's maverick approaches and theories, coupled with the magnetic Leary personality, intrigued and captivated many students. On the flip side, these same approaches (and, no doubt, his popularity among students) frustrated some colleagues, including, at times, the man who had hired him, David McClelland.

As he'd done in Berkeley, Tim founded a drinking group at Harvard. He dubbed it the White Hand Society. It consisted of himself and a twenty-six-year-old assistant professor named Charles Slack sitting around bars in Harvard Square arguing about psychology and anything else that came up. As was common in that era, neither bothered to separate their drinking from their professional lives—office hours, and even student lectures, were often well lubricated by booze. Perhaps the biggest difference between Leary's White Hand Society and the old International Sporting House Set was the lack of spousal involvement. The polite veneer of well-dressed young newlyweds playing cocktail party games was gone. At Harvard, Leary was single and partying with (and like) a twenty-six-year-old.

Leary was also hanging out with another young assistant professor, a Stanford Ph.D. named Richard (Dick) Alpert whose father was a wealthy lawyer who had served as president of the New Haven Railroad. The Alpert family connections had helped Dick overcome a mediocre academic record to become an assistant professor at Harvard with a clear line to a tenured faculty position. But Dick—an outsider at Harvard by way of religion (Jewish) and sexual orientation (gay)—never felt as though he fit in on campus. So, naturally, he was drawn to the other outsider among the elite—Timothy Leary. Alpert was also a heavy drinker, and alcohol helped strengthen the friendly bond.

Another key ally at Harvard was a gifted graduate student named George Litwin, who was already giving mescaline to people at the Massachusetts Mental Health Center when he met Tim. But—just as with Barron—Litwin had been unable to convince Tim of the potentialities that the drug held for psychological advances. Rather, Tim warned Litwin of the dangers of using chemicals as a short cut to mental health. In no uncertain terms, he called Litwin's advocacy of mescaline tests, "foolishness."

So it was with pleasant surprise that Litwin met Tim on his return to campus in the fall of 1960 only to learn of Tim's Mexican mushroom experiences. Rather than criticizing Litwin for his "foolishness," Tim was now set on throwing his oversize efforts behind initiating psilocybin tests at Harvard. It seems that in Mexico, Tim and a group of his friends had managed to acquire a batch of Sacred Mushrooms from a *curandera* (a shaman, folk healer, and spiritual guide) named Juana. The group had choked down the black, moldy fungus and then sat around poolside watching each other closely and waiting to see what would happen. Roughly thirty minutes later, they had their answer.

It is telling that in his first autobiography, *High Priest*, published eight years later in 1968, Timothy Leary fractures the narrative about his first mushroom trip until it becomes a free verse poem. In his essay *The Research Enterprise and Its Problems* Richard Blum, Ph.D., wrote, "A different sort of problem in our study has to do with the communication of content of personal experiences. It is hardly a new problem to psychology, but its presence requires discussion and leads us to now consider some of our findings. Many persons who have taken hallucinogens make the statement that their experience is ineffable; that is, what has gone on in their minds cannot be communicated to others; that no such words exist to describe these internal events, and, even if there were such words, they would be devoid of significance unless the listener had himself gone through the same experiences."

Indeed, how to describe an acid trip? Particularly in a way that makes sense to the uninitiated? Or, even more unlikely, makes the information clinically useful as a research tool?

Leary always appreciated high culture, but under the influence of psychedelics, and in close association with Allen Ginsberg, he began to see the poet and artist in himself and in those around him. After their initial meeting and the start of their partnership, he wrote often to Ginsberg about the ways that psychedelics could turn convicts and squares into contemplative poets and art aficionados. "Work is booming. Getting prisoners out of jail, prisoners writing visionary poems. Words as colored chips. Put words of same color in pail and dip brush in and paint with words. No writers. Anyone can paint with words."

While at Harvard, he also struggled constantly with the difficulty of communicating hallucinatory experiences and revelations to straitlaced psychologists who preferred to keep their patients—and their patients' psychoses—at a distance. In short, the vocabulary for discussing, and, certainly, for quantifying psychedelic trips had not yet been invented. But Leary was working in academia and science—realms that demanded explanation.

Thus, we have Leary presenting a paper on his prison testing to his professional peers: "After three orientation meetings with the prisoners the drug was given. I was the first one to take the drug in that bare hospital room behind barred windows. Three inmates joined me. Two psychologists and two other inmates served as observers—taking the drug three hours later. This psilocybin session was followed by three discussions. Then another drug session. Then more discussions. At this point the inmates have taken the drug an average of four times. There has been not one moment of friction or tension in some forty hours of ego-less interaction. Pre-post testing has demonstrated marked changes on both objective and projective instruments. Dramatic decreases in hostility, cynicism, depression, schizoid ideation. Definite increases in optimism, planfulness, flexibility, tolerance, sociability."

And we have Leary describing the same prison tests in a letter to Ginsberg: "Big deal at the prison. Convicts love it. Hoodlums have satori, deciding to devote rest of life to keep JD's out of jail etc. Administration is puzzled but goes along with Harvard and the word of this swinging psychiatrist who has joined the team. Tremendous amount of time, tho. Unforgettable scenes—convicts lying around high, digging jazz records etc. One con controls the locked door and when the guards knock to announce lunch he lets them in etc. There's a colored cat in for heroin, a tenor sax man. Imagine his reaction. Comes these doctors from Harvard and suddenly he is turned on hi her [sic] than ever in his life understanding Rollins sax chains like never before. He has a dazed worshipful look in his face everytime [sic] we meet."

Just as psilocybin had given Leary access to artistic realms that he had revered but never experienced, Ginsberg's hip poetic slang gave Leary a language—aside from the rigid, confining language of his profession—in which he could discuss his psychedelic experiences. While at Harvard, Leary was constantly trying to balance the flash and jive of psychedelic satori with the professional communication and contact that would ensure his professional validation, and thus continued employment and support for his testing. But by the time he got around to publishing *High Priest* in 1968, Leary had already chosen the hip over the straight world. As a result, we read about his first mushroom trip in Mexico in an innovative literary mix of parallel narratives, quotations, prose poetry, and free verse.

> *Suddenly*
>   *I begin*
>   *to feel*
> *Strange.*
> *Going under dental gas. Good-bye.*
> *Mildly nauseous. Detached. Moving away*
>   *away*
>   *away*
> *From the group in bathing suits.*
> *On a terrace*
>   *under the bright*
>   *Mexican sky.*

Leary's choice of "dental gas" as the nearest comparable sensation to slipping under the spell of psilocybin is also telling. Before meeting Leary, Ginsberg often used the experience of being anesthetized in the dentist's office as an early touchstone hallucinatory experience. He spent years working on fragments that eventually came together in the 1958 poem *Laughing Gas.*

> *It's the instant of going*
> *into or coming out of*
> *existence that is*

important—to catch on
to the secret of the magic
     box.

Stepping outside the universe
    by means of Nitrous Oxide
anesthetizing mind-consciousness

      the chiliasm was an impersonal dream—
one of many, being mere dreams.

Later in *High Priest*, Leary also evokes the name of the Ginsberg's early guru, William Blake, in visionary prose poem form: "Then begins Blake's long red voyage EVERY TIME LESS THAN A PULSATION OF THE ARTERY down the blood stream IS EQUAL IN ITS PERIOD AND VALUE TO SIX THOUSAND YEARS floating, bouncing along labyrinthian tunnels FOR IN THIS MOMENT THE POET'S WORK IS DONE artery, arteriole and ALL GREAT EVENTS OF TIME START FORTH through every capillary AND ARE CONCEIVED IN SUCH A PERIOD through pink honeycomb tissue world with A MOMENT. . . ."

Yes, Dr. Leary had gone on the fantastic voyage. And, as he said of that first trip, "I learned more in the six or seven hours of this experience than in all my years as a psychologist." Allen Ginsberg would later help him to find the language and metaphors to explain it.

Fortunately George Litwin was already "initiated." So when Tim ran into him on campus in September 1960 and started talking to him about his Mexican mushroom trip, he was able to cut right to it. No jargon or reaching for words necessary. Leary *got it* now. As the jazz musicians and Beat poets said, he was *hip*. And he wanted, immediately, to get a batch of psilocybin onto campus so that he could start experimenting with subjects. And on himself. But he had no intention of making these tests into some big party. This would be a true scientific investigation into the higher levels of human consciousness, creativity, and, eventually, criminal rehabilitation. Leary's studies would be professional and psychological. They would quantify while they explored.

Once Leary knew that he wanted to use psilocybin in his campus experiments, the problem became—where to get it? There weren't exactly well-stocked curanderas wandering around Harvard Square. Fortunately for Leary, Dr. Albert Hofmann—the same Swiss chemist who first created LSD in 1938—had also developed synthetic psilocybin pills in the 1950s.

This is where George Litwin's experience came into play. Litwin knew that the company Hofmann worked for—the Sandoz Company in Switzerland—was providing psilocybin pills to qualified experimenters. Tim and George sent Sandoz Laboratories a letter using Harvard stationery, explaining the testing they wanted to undertake and requesting a supply of psilocybin. A short time later, Litwin recalled, "they just sent us back a big bottle and said, 'We appreciate your request and we are interested in sponsoring work in this area. Here's a starter kit to get going and please send us a report of the results.'"

The Road to November

Before Timothy Leary came on the scene, two British psychiatrists, Dr. Humphry Osmond and Dr. John Smythies, were for years the most influential medical figures in early psychedelic research. Their assertion in 1952 that schizophrenia could be caused by the body producing its own hallucinogenic compounds was an unprecedented and bold statement, which they supported with research and presented through the proper medical channels. The theory that drove their research was called the "adrenochrome theory."

The adrenochrome theory began taking shape when Osmond and Smythies were both young, ambitious and intellectually curious psychiatrists working their first jobs at the famous London teaching hospital, St. George's. Osmond had become involved with the roots and, perhaps more important, the symptoms of schizophrenia during his internship. He had worked with a schizophrenic girl who, whenever she looked in the mirror, saw herself as an elephant. This was Osmond's first encounter with schizophrenia, and he was thoroughly fascinated by its singular hold on the mind. As he asked among colleagues and consulted books on the illness, he realized that schizophrenia had not been thoroughly researched. Aside from a compelling first-person account in a book called *The Witnesses* by Thomas Hennell, Osmond found almost nothing of use in understanding this strange illness.

John Smythies was raised in India and sent to Cambridge for his intellectual training. He was an upper-class Englishman following the proper path through British society. However, he was also deeply interested in philosophy and—more troubling to the psychiatric community that he had elected to join—parapsychology. It seemed that his main interest lay in plumbing the speculative possibilities of the mind rather than in understanding how its functions impacted his patients' daily lives.

One day, Smythies came across a book written by Alexandre Rouhier titled *Le Peyotl*, which contained the molecular formula for mescaline. The molecule reminded both Smythies and Osmond of another molecule, but they couldn't identify which one. Eventually they consulted a biochemist who told them that the molecular structure of mescaline was closest to that of adrenaline.

Buoyed along by the thrill of discovery, Smythies and Osmond began hypothesizing on the link between adrenaline, schizophrenia, and the effects of mescaline. In botany, a phenomenon called transmethylation exists whereby certain plants are capable of metabolic transformation. Smythies and Osmond hypothesized that in a human version of transmethylation—which had never been confirmed as physically possible—an abundance of adrenaline in the body could transform into something akin to mescaline. This transformation could then account for the symptoms of schizophrenia, including a girl seeing herself as an elephant or any number of the extreme hallucinations described by Thomas Hennell in *The Witnesses.*

Taking the same bold leap that Albert Hofmann had taken upon glimpsing the scientific possibilities of hallucinogens, Smythies and Osmond got their hands on some mescaline (from Lights Chemical, not Sandoz) and promptly dosed themselves. Again, similar to Hofmann, Osmond felt menaced on his first trip. Common things—a tape recorder, a door, a light—took on sinister qualities. Once he had come down, Osmond realized that what he had experienced were, at very least, cousins to the symptoms of schizophrenia.

These self-administered mescaline sessions coupled with their professional observations of schizophrenic patients, their research in the field, and the close molecular structure between adrenaline and mescaline led Smythies and Osmond to co-author an essay called "A New Approach to Schizophrenia." In the essay, the authors argued that there was a cycle at play leading a patient deeper into the throes of schizophrenia. The cycle started with stress, and this stress lead to the creation of a naturally occurring hallucinogen, which in turn disoriented the sufferer. The more disorientation, the more stress, the more hallucinogen was produced and the further disoriented the schizophrenic became. Eventually the body's only way of insulating itself from the devastating cycle was to completely withdraw from reality. They called this cycle "the M factor theory."

The M factor theory was complex, well researched, and elegant. Since little research had been done on schizophrenia, and since hallucinogens were still legal and considered fair scientific game, Smythies and Osmond found themselves at the cutting edge of important psychiatric research. Shortly after the publication of "A New Approach to Schizophrenia," Osmond accepted a job as Clinical Director of Weyburn Hospital in Saskatchewan, Canada. The hospital was a small outpost on the Saskatchewan prairie. It was Osmond's job to update and clean up the facility. No doubt, he also saw this as a perfect Petri dish for carrying out his research.

John Smythies soon joined Osmond at the hospital, and another Weyburn Hospital psychiatrist named Abram Hoffer, who was also interested in mescaline, joined the duo in their research. One of Osmond's first experiments after arriving in Saskatchewan was to dose himself with adrenochrome, a compound that is formed when adrenaline decomposes, and which has a molecular structure similar to that of mescaline. Osmond took a dose of adrenochrome at the hospital under the watchful eyes of his colleagues, and sure enough, he was soon tripping.

Smythies and Osmond, bolstered by their continued success, co-published another essay in a quarterly called the *Hibbert Journal*. In this essay, they made the assertion that "no one is really competent to treat schizophrenia unless he has experienced the schizophrenic world himself," followed closely by "This is possible to do quite simply by taking mescaline." They even went so far as to chide the psychiatric community: "One would have thought that anyone, concerned in devising systems of psychology based on the concept of the unconscious mind, would have utilized such a prolific source of material as mescaline offers, but no one has yet done so, although Rouhier made this suggestion as long ago as 1922."

This essay further established the duo of John Smythies

and Humphry Osmond as being on the cutting edge of psychiatry and hallucinogen research. Now their work had taken a turn in support of the psychomimetic potential (the power to mimic psychosis) of hallucinogens and toward dismantling the wall between patient and therapist. This got the attention—both positive and negative—of a great many psychiatrists. It also got the attention of an influential non-psychiatrist, a British intellectual and author with an increasingly public interest in hallucinogens, Aldous Huxley.

Aldous Huxley wrote to Osmond and Smythies, praising their work and expressing interest in their research. Huxley's famous 1931 novel *A Brave New World* had described a totalitarian world in which the citizens are controlled—quite willingly—by a drug called Soma. Huxley, a scholar of world cultures, knew that a drug called Soma appeared in ancient Hindu scriptures, and he used it as a symbolic warning about relinquishing control to so-called leaders. But he also understood that the right drugs might open up new vistas of human consciousness. Thus, he offered himself as a willing participant in Smythies and Osmond's mescaline tests.

Osmond was a little concerned about doing tests on such a famous figure. He said, "I did not relish the possibility, however remote, of being the man who drove Aldous Huxley mad." Yet the opportunity for gathering feedback from such a preeminent thinker and writer was too good to pass up.

In May 1953, Humphrey Osmond visited Aldous Huxley at his home in the Hollywood Hills of California. As Huxley describes it in *The Doors of Perception*: "By a series of, for me, extremely fortunate circumstances I found myself, in the spring of 1953, squarely athwart that trail. One of the sleuths had come on business to California. In spite of seventy years of mescalin [*sic*] research, the psychological material at his disposal was still absurdly inadequate, and he was anxious to add to it. I was on the spot and willing, indeed eager, to be a guinea pig. Thus it came about that, one bright May morning, I swallowed four-tenths of a gram of mescalin [*sic*] dissolved in half a glass of water and sat down to wait for the results."

Two things happen when a figure of Huxley's stature takes on hallucinogenic drugs as his muse. One, the drugs are taken more seriously. Two, the drugs become part of the larger discourse, thus opening up a veritable Pandora's box of potential troubles. Thankfully, Osmond, Smythies, and Huxley were all aware that psychedelic drugs could be a hotbed of trouble. None of them were looking to stir up conflict. They were all sincerely interested in the spiritual (Huxley) and the medical (Osmond and Smythies) value of hallucinogens. Even though the CIA had taken note of Osmond and Smythies' work in Saskatchewan around the same time that Huxley had, the duo hadn't yet run afoul of the authorities. In fact, their work was running parallel to the CIA's own hallucinogen tests in their MK-Ultra program. The MK-Ultra program's most famous patient, Ken Kesey, used his psychedelic experiences and work in a mental health facility as the jumping-off point for his famous novel *One Flew over the Cuckoo's* Nest. The CIA was also covertly funding hallucinogen research through a front organization called the Society for the Study of Human Ecology. After leaving Weyburn in 1963, Osmond took a position at the Princeton Neuropsychiatric Institute, where his work was funded by the Society for the Study of Human Ecology. In other words, Osmond spent the most influential part of his career doing work that was either closely monitored or directly funded by the CIA.

But in the early 1950s, neither Osmond, Smythies, nor Huxley had any idea that the CIA was monitoring their output. Even if they had, they might not have been overly concerned. They were not looking to stir up any trouble or fight the government; they were only interested in their studies. So when Huxley recommended Timothy Leary to Osmond as someone who would continue their work in the halls of Harvard, they both took it in good faith that Leary would do so ethically.

Tim first met Huxley in October 1960, while Huxley was serving as a distinguished visiting professor at MIT. Huxley accepted Leary's invitation to have lunch at the Harvard Faculty Club, and the two bonded over an inside joke about "mushroom" soup. Initially, Huxley felt confident that Leary was capable of, as the elder philosopher was fond of saying, "doing good stealthily." After all, Leary was now working in the same department where William James had used nitrous oxide to pursue visions and psychological insight. If anything, upon their first meeting, both Osmond and Huxley expressed concerns that Leary seemed a little too conventional to carry out the research. But they were both willing to take a chance and trust Leary. It was in that same spirit that Osmond suggested to Allen Ginsberg that he pay Leary a visit at Harvard and participate in his psilocybin tests. He'd met Allen at a conference and had been impressed with his ability to describe his mescaline experiences.

Without his international renown and the notoriety the Beats had received, there would be no rational reason for Allen Ginsberg to be asked to give a poetry reading to the Group for the Advancement of Psychiatry. Why would psychiatrists sit for a reading by a formal psychiatric in-patient whose insistence on flouting social conventions hinted at a less-than-complete recovery? According to biographer Bill Morgan, Allen had even been refused inclusion in out-patient mescaline experiments following his 1949 stint in Columbia Presbyterian Psychological Institute (depicted in *Howl* as "Rockland"). But Allen Ginsberg was famous. And, after all, he did have firsthand knowledge of psychiatric illness—his own and his mother's—and used that knowledge in some of his most famous poems. So it is to their credit that the group brought Ginsberg in to address their gathering in Boston in 1960. It is to Ginsberg's credit that he was willing to stand up in front of such a conventional, and no doubt intimidating, audience and read his poems "Laughing Gas," "Mescaline," and "Lysergic Acid."

> It is a multiple million eyed monster
> it is hidden in all its elephants and selves
> it hummeth in the electric typewriter
> it is electricity connected to itself, if it hath wires
> it is a vast Spiderweb
> and I am on the last millionth infinite tentacle of the spiderweb, a
>   worrier
> lost, separated, a worm, a thought, a self
> one of the millions of skeletons of China
> one of the particular mistakes
> I allen Ginsberg a separate consciousness
> I who want to be God
> I who want to hear the infinite minutest vibration of eternal harmony

I who wait trembling my destruction by that aethereal music in the
  fire
I who hate God and give him my name
I who make mistakes on the eternal typewriter
I who am Doomed

excerpted from "Lysergic Acid"
Collected Poems 1947–1980

The overall reception to Ginsberg's presentation was chilly. Most of the doctors thought he was, in a word, nuts—and were willing to tell him as much. However, Dr. Humphry Osmond was also in the crowd in Boston that day. With nearly a decade of hallucinogen research under his belt, Osmond was not so quick to dismiss Ginsberg. Perhaps Ginsberg's line *"it is hidden in all its elephants"* brought Osmond back to the schizophrenic patient who saw herself as an elephant and started him down this road of psychomimetic study. At the very least, Osmond—through his association with Aldous Huxley—knew the value of having a writer as a guinea pig. Writers have the ability to convey details and nuances of their experiences in ways that non-writers could never express. In the cases of Huxley and Ginsberg, both men were also well connected within the arts and literary communities that were natural breeding grounds for hallucinogenic testing. After Ginsberg's presentation, Osmond recommended that the poet look into the psilocybin tests being done at Harvard. He passed along Leary's contact information, and the two men parted ways. Dr. John Spiegel, an organizer of the conference who served on the founding board of the Harvard Psilocybin Project and eventually served as president of the American Psychiatric Association, also recognized the value of pairing Ginsberg with Leary. He wrote to Leary describing Ginsberg's presentation. On November 8, 1960, Leary wrote Ginsberg the first missive in what would become a voluminous, worldwide, and lifelong correspondence.

"Dear Mr. Ginsberg: Dr. John Spiegel has told me (he spoke very glowingly about your contribution, by the way) about your participation in his psychiatric conference and about your experience with 'consciousness-expanding' drugs. This news interested me."

Leary goes on to explain to Allen that his testing is "very different" from traditional studies. That he was approaching the tests in a more "naturalistic" way that would generate more authentic, less skewed results. He offered to pay Allen's expenses and "a token fee of fifty dollars" if Allen was willing to come to Cambridge to discuss his experiences with hallucinogens. He also emphasized that he had "strong feelings about not accepting money from Foundations for 'research' which means our resources are human rather than financial." If Allen was unable to come to Cambridge, Tim offered to visit him in New York City. "Needless to say if you are interested in trying out the synthetic mushrooms this could be arranged." Tim closed the letter by emphasizing that his interest in Allen's perspective was "increased by my considerable respect for your work."

So it was that Tim came to visit Allen for the first time in Allen's East Village apartment. The two men, both natural born talkers, spent the afternoon smoking pot and getting acquainted. Tim was, of course, familiar with Ginsberg's legend and background, referring to him as "the secretary general of the world's poets, beatniks, anarchists, socialists, free-sex/love cultists." However, Tim was not yet the famous Dr. Timothy Leary. He was an interesting character, no doubt, but not a famous one.

If anything—much as with Osmond's first impression—Allen found Tim a bit square and naïve. Tim obviously had no idea how prevalent drug use was in Allen's artistic circles. By the time these two met, Allen had already been through numerous hallucinogen trips (peyote, mescaline, and yagé) and interacted with more than his fair share of shrinks. In fact, after years of aesthetic searching, it was a combination of a potent peyote vision he'd had in San Francisco ("The root skullface of Moloch . . . Moloch whose eyes are a thousand blind windows") and an empathic psychiatrist who gave Allen permission to live as a free, openly gay bohemian poet, that juiced his mind into the first blush of "Howl." Among Allen's crowd, drugs flowed as easily as Shelley's "Ode to the West Wind," and undergoing psychoanalysis was often held as a badge of honor. Freudian psychoanalysis was still at the top of the heap, but Ginsberg's friends were also at the cutting edge of New Age philosophies promoted by Edgar Cayce (Neal Cassady was an early, fanatic devotee) and Wilhelm Reich (William Burroughs would spend a substantial part of his adult life sitting inside of one of Reich's "Orgone Accumulators," which were said to promote health and vitality).

Allen was fluent in the languages of psychedelics and psychotherapy. He had been seeking out, experimenting, contemplating, and debating their various attributes for more than a decade when he met Leary. He had seen the revelations drugs could bring, but had also lost several friends to madness, addiction, and drugged misadventure. In the sedate world of 1950s America, he was also aware of how society treated nonconformists. Women in particular were vulnerable to systemic abuse for nontraditional be-havior. Because no one was sure how or why it worked, electroshock therapy was used with chilling regularity in the 1950s; for women, it was even used for premarital pregnancy or failure to fulfill expected gender roles (duti-ful wife, mother, and so forth). By the late 1950s and early '60s, doctor-prescribed tranquilizers and stimulants (Mick Jagger's famed "Mothers Little Helpers") began to be mass-marketed to address "female problems." But in the late '40s and early '50s, flouting convention was no joke for women or for men: nonconformity, not fitting in, could get you locked up and maybe even cost you your life.

Allen was taken aback by how cavalierly Leary treated his psilocybin experiments. When he showed up at Harvard he remarked that "Leary had this big beautiful house, and everybody there was wandering around like it was some happy cocktail party. They were all so cheerful and opti-mistic and convinced that their kind of environment would be welcomed as a polite, scholarly, socially acceptable, perfectly reasonable pursuit and would spread through the university and automatically be taken on as part of the cur-riculum. Like Leary couldn't conceive of meeting any aca-demic opposition. I kept saying, 'You have no idea what you're going to meet or what you're up against.'"

Ironically, it is possible that without Ginsberg's influ-ence, Leary could have carried on his testing at Harvard without the type of confrontations that Ginsberg foresaw. By the time that Allen, Peter Orlovsky, and Peter's brother Lafcadio (on leave from a mental hospital) arrived at Har-vard in November 1960, Leary had largely escaped the Harvard administration's scrutiny. He had undertaken the psilocybin project with planning and preparation and had

made promises to document it all appropriately, scientifically. His raffish demeanor certainly ruffled some tweed
feathers, but if William James, the founder of Harvard's
psychology department and brother of writer Henry James,
could conduct the experiments with nitrous oxide that led
to his watershed book *The Varieties of Religious Experience*, then how could Harvard quash this brilliant and cre-
dentialed new psychologist and his bold project?

Without a doubt, Leary had already administered (including self-administered) psilocybin pills in ways that
most at Harvard would have frowned on if they had known
about them. The most harrowing so far had been an incident
at Newton Centre, only a month prior to Ginsberg's arrival.
In *High Priest*, Leary calls the two men involved in this incident "Charlie" and "O'Donell." Charlie was the husband
of the housekeeper at Newton Centre, who was otherwise
uninvolved in the Project. Less clear is the identity of
O'Donell, who is at the heart of the controversial incident.
It now seems likely that O'Donell was, in fact, the man who
had originally told Leary about psychedelic mushrooms:
Frank Barron. Leary writes about Frank Barron by name
in other parts of *High Priest*, but always in a positive light.
Since "O'Donell" appears as an erratic, menacing character
in the book, but also one who is very close to Leary and the
experiments, Leary was apparently shielding his friend and
colleague from his own darker behavior, while still recounting incidents that were seminal in the early experiments.
Leary's colleague Ralph Metzner recalls, "I had heard vague
rumors of a rift between Frank and Leary, who were old
friends, because of Barron's inappropriate behavior with
the teenage girls. He and Leary remained friends and I also
became friends with him and we spent time together at

various other gatherings—though not involving psychedelics. I think that session scared Leary a lot."

On the night of the incident "O'Donell" and "Charlie" drank copious amounts of Scotch and then took large doses of psilocybin. At that point, Leary was tired of holding the "ring of power." As the faculty member in charge of the project, it was up to Leary to dole out the psilocybin pills, and, so he claimed, the weight of that responsibility was getting to be a drag. So on this particular night, Leary decided to drop this role. "Look, Charlie, let's stop all the playing around for the mushroom power. I have the ring of power. But I don't want it. I'm getting rid of it. I'm giving the precious mushroom bottle to you. Here, take it. Now you're stuck with it. Now you decide who gets them and how many and when. Let them come to you for the word. You decide. You dispense them. You take responsibility."

The night before, O'Donell had gone on a bum trip during which he had slashed a lamp cord with a kitchen knife and demanded more pills. Rather than cutting off O'Donell, Leary had him over the next night for more Scotch and psilocybin. However this time, Leary would not be the one doling out the goods. This time it would be left up to Charlie. To make the strange brew even more potent, it was Halloween night and Leary's teenage daughter Susan was hosting a combination sleepover–costume party. Now, after a bad-trip scene and only a few hours sleep the night before, Leary and O'Donell held out their hands and Charlie split up the entire quantity of the pill bottle between the three of them: ten pills for Leary and O'Donell, eleven for Charlie. The three men washed the pills down with Scotch as adolescent teen girls dressed in costume played around them.

Leary reflected on the massive dose, "From all the

literature I had read on the subject, we had just surpassed the world's record for psilocybin consumption. The psychiatric people had been using 8 to 10 milligrams (that is, four to five pills), and I had just consumed 20 milligrams (ten pills), and so had O'Donell, and Charlie had wolfed down 22 milligrams."

Leary described the early stages of that trip as similar to their usual drinking rituals. All the booze is shared, and one is expected to keep pace with the others in the group. In the initial stages, just after consumption, all was jovial in the kitchen. The men were locked in a close bond through their roles in the new psilocybin experiments, and they had plenty to talk about, complain about, and plan out over their Scotch glasses. They had also all helped contain and corral the girls from the slumber party upstairs just before they split up the mushroom pills. And that was no small task. The party had started out as a combination of ten teenage boys and nine teenage girls, all in costume. Between the games of tag, the sugary treats, and their newly raging hormones, the air was charged with hyper electricity, much of it sexual, and the adults in charge could only shake their heads, refill their Scotch glasses, and smile as the kids played out pre-sexual courting games. Eventually the boys went home, and the girls were sent upstairs to Susan Leary's room, where they were to spend the night. That's when the three men went downstairs and started taking mushrooms.

Shortly after the mushrooms took hold, Tim started to ruminate on the girls upstairs. Were they okay? Were they having fun? Should he be checking on them? Every once in a while, Susan's door opened and loud music reached the men downstairs in the kitchen. That flared Tim's curiosity even more, and even though the girls seemed to be existing on another time-space plane, he couldn't help wondering what his duties were in this situation. But Tim was also an experienced tripper. He knew that no good could come of interacting with the girls at this point. They were all better off keeping their fun separate for the rest of the night. Unfortunately, O'Donell had no such sense of responsibility. The deeper he went into his trip, the more the girls upstairs became potential sex partners.

Leary tried different ways to distract and dissuade O'Donell from going upstairs. As a last resort, he went to the kitchen sink to rinse dishes and asked the guys to help him. But it was too late. Charlie came over to the sink and told Tim that O'Donell had gone upstairs.

"Upstairs? I thought of upstairs and I thought of the girls and the slumber party. Waves of guilt washed over me for having dragged my kids around from country to country, school to school, house to house, and Susan missing friends and the warm cozy routine schedule and this was her first party, her first social event. . . . Upstairs? Where did he go upstairs?"

But Leary and Charlie both knew where O'Donell was headed. Straight for the slumber party. By the time they got upstairs, he was sprawled out across the bed like the guest of honor. The girls stood around the bed, away from him, unsure what to make of this strange adult intruding on their small, playful space. Leary and Charlie tried every argument they could to get him out of there—*This isn't your party. You don't belong here. You don't want to ruin Susan's party, do you? Don't you love Susan?*—but O'Donell resisted. Not only resisted, but became more aggressive about his right to be at the party. Leary describes his vision of

O'Donell at that moment as being pure evil—the man was a snarling, cornered rat full of malice.

Finally Tim and Charlie managed to wrestle O'Donell out of the room physically, but they knew this was only a temporary solution. They couldn't hold him off this way all night. O'Donell was now lashing out at them, saying that he was just what these girls needed to jolt them out of their pampered, suburban existence. Part of Leary—the ribald, nontraditional explorer—couldn't help but agree with O'Donell. Maybe he was right. Maybe Tim was being a prude and a conformist. Maybe O'Donell had just as much right to be there as any of the girls. Maybe he could even help the girls.

Thankfully, Tim's paternal instincts were stronger. He knew he had to keep O'Donell away from the party. But he also knew that—even in this extreme case—force was not the answer. Wrestling the man out of the room had worked in the short term, but the restraint had only made O'Donell more determined to break away and intrude on the party. There had to be a key, a reason, a single statement that O'Donell (or, for that matter, Tim and Charlie) would immediately recognize as the reason why O'Donell couldn't be in there.

Finally, Tim hit on it. A statement that would not only cut through their confusion about this situation, but would serve as a guide for all future psilocybin experiments as well. "I'll tell you why you can't go into Susan's room. Because it's her trip, her territory, her party, and *because she doesn't want you there.*"

That was it. That was the key. Do what you want, explore, experiment, probe your own internal and external environment however you want—but don't force your will on someone else. Don't fuck up their trip so you can take yours. As Leary wrote in *High Priest*: "The first ethical rule had been forged. Moses smiles."

Unfortunately, the logic did not penetrate O'Donell's desire. He was still being physically restrained and thrashing around, trying to get back to the party. Frustrated, Tim chastised Charlie for misusing the "ring of power" and not doing a better job of controlling the psilocybin doses. If he had only done his job, Leary argued, they wouldn't be in this situation in the first place. Both men knew that this argument was futile as well. Perhaps the implications could be sorted out and learned from later, but that still didn't solve their problem now. There was only one thing left to do. Charlie's wife, Rhona, was asleep in the house. She would have to be woken up and brought in to help. They needed a straight, sober mind to tackle this situation. They were out of ideas.

Charlie walked sheepishly down the hall to fetch her while Leary watched him, feeling slightly superior, as if the need to bring Rhona into the situation gave him the victory in their argument. Rhona—rubbing her eyes and blinking at the light—listened as they gave her the rundown on the situation. Her judgment was sharp, clear-eyed, and final: "Grown-ups don't join pajama parties! It just isn't done."

Rhona was only twenty-one herself. She knew all the rules of pajama parties—and strange men crashing them was not part of the program. "O'Donell was stunned. You could see his tense squirming body begin to relax. Looking down at the floor. Nodding his head. We stood for a long time and then Rhona, briskly, case dismissed, no-nonsense voice said 'All right. All of you come down to the kitchen and I'll brew up some tea and cookies.'"

This time, O'Donell listened. He pouted—in fact, he continued acting out aggressively for the rest of the night— but he followed them down the stairs. The crisis was dissolved. The girls were safe. Another psychedelic lesson had been learned.

In these early stages of the Psilocybin Project, such incidents were still kept within the inner circle. Eventually, rumors about questionable behavior by students and faculty around the project would evolve into headline-grabbing scandal, but Leary's tenuous foothold as a visiting lecturer at Harvard was initially safeguarded by the relatively small and close-knit circle surrounding the experiments. It was only when the circle expanded, and particularly when famous, and infamous, figures such as Allen Ginsberg got involved, that these incidents could no longer be contained.

6 Ambassador of Psilocybin

Allen Ginsberg, Peter Orlovsky, and Peter's brother Lafcadio shambled into Leary's house in Newton Centre just like they shambled into everywhere: Beat. Lafcadio was on leave from his latest mental hospital. Peter was still beautiful, spacey, trailing a stream of non sequiturs and spontaneous poetic observations. Ginsberg sported heavy black eyeglasses with a cracked left lens. However—Ginsberg being Ginsberg—the crack wasn't simply a crack. The crack had a story of its own. The crack paralleled a five-month-old fissure in Ginsberg's consciousness. The crack was hard won and carried its own symbolism, which Allen was only just starting to assimilate into his ever evolving worldview. Allen felt that it was important for Tim to know where the crack—figurative and literal—had come from. If Tim was going to act as their tripping guide, their curandero, then Allen wanted to inform him about his "set" and the battering it had taken in Pucallpa, Peru.

The morning after the Beat group arrived, Allen sat at the kitchen table across from Tim and told him the abridged story. He wanted to give enough information for Leary to appreciate what he had just experienced. But properly told, fully told, the story of the cracked eyeglasses begins with

William S. Burroughs in 1951 and winds like an ayahuasca vine through pre-Leary Harvard.

Among many other influences, William S. Burroughs is credited with turning the Beats on to drugs. Born in 1914 to a prominent St. Louis family, Burroughs attended Los Alamos Ranch School in New Mexico for part of high school until a series of conflicts with the authorities who ran the school, as well as with his schoolmates, landed him back in St. Louis. While at Los Alamos, he also kept track of his first homosexual crushes in his journals. Burroughs finished high school back in St. Louis and, still living out the blue-blood plot, entered Harvard University in 1932. He graduated Harvard in 1936 and began receiving a $200 monthly allowance from his parents. While the amount was by no means extravagant, it did allow Bill some freedom from constant financial pressures. One might even speculate that the freedom allowed him the leisure time to become bored. And, as Geoffrey Chaucer wrote in 1386, "Idleness is the root of mischief."

By the time Allen met him, the older Burroughs was already a fixture around the junkie hangouts of Times Square. Allen, still a student at Columbia, was fascinated by Burroughs' outlaw lifestyle and impressed by the depth and breadth of his reading and intellect. Soon Burroughs took on the role of mentor to Allen and Jack Kerouac. He turned them on to new books and philosophies, even going so far as to psychoanalyze each of them in his apartment. Burroughs also turned them on to speed by way of Benzedrine inhalers and to the internal slow-down of heroin. Burroughs was a lifelong opiate user and was always fascinated by drugs. He also studied anthropology at Harvard and Columbia, and later added courses on archaeology and ethnology at Mexico City College in 1950. Somewhere along the way, most likely through the book *Phantasica* by the German pharmacologist Louis Lewin, Burroughs learned about yagé, also known as ayahuasca.

Yagé was "discovered" for Western science in 1851 by naturalist Richard Spruce, who wrote about it in his 1908 book *Notes of a Botanist on the Amazon and Andes*. In the most basic sense, yagé is a vine that grows in the jungles of South America. However, the people who call the South American jungles home had long ago figured out the key to unleashing the psychotropic potential of yagé. When yagé is mixed with the vine *Diplopterys carerana* and the evergreen shrub *chacruna*, the combination produces a substance with intense hallucinatory properties. Richard Evans Schultes, considered the "father of ethnobotany," who took up Richard Spruce's passionate investigations, wrote in his book *Where the Gods Reign: Plants and Peoples of the Colombian Amazon*: "Both of these plants have in their leaves a different hallucinogenic chemical—tryptamine—from the active principles—beta-carbolines—found in Banisteriopsis. Addition of these leaves greatly enhances and lengthens the intoxications through a kind of synergistic activity. How, one wonders, did these Indians find from the 80,000 species around them these two additives with such extraordinary effects."

Regardless of how this magical combination was derived, the effects are staggering. Once again leading the way for the Beats, William Burroughs trekked into South America in 1953 in search of yagé. In a stroke of synchronicity, he connected with Richard Evans Schultes while on this trip. Schultes was in the midst of a twelve-year-long fieldwork study in the Northwest Amazon and, when he and Burroughs met up, he was part of the Anglo-Colombian Cacao Expedition traveling from Bogotá to Puerto Leguízamo. The two Harvard men connected in the jungles of South America, and Burroughs was folded into the expedition. Burroughs recorded some fictionalized impressions of Schultes and other brief travel sketches in letters to Ginsberg along the way. Those letters would eventually be collected and published as *The Yage Letters* by City Lights in 1953. In the book, an early yagé session is retold with typical Burroughs drama and intrigue: "In two minutes a wave of nausea swept over me and the hut began spinning. It was like going under ether, or when you are very drunk and lie down and the bed spins. Blue flashes passed in front of my eyes. The hut took on an archaic far-Pacific look with Easter Island heads carved in the support posts. The assistant was lurking there with the obvious intent to kill me. I was hit with violent, sudden nausea and rushed for the door hitting my shoulder against the door post. I felt the shock but no pain. I could hardly walk. No coordination. My feet were like blocks of wood. I vomited violently leaning against a tree and fell down on the ground in helpless misery. I felt numb as if I was covered with layers of cotton. I kept trying to break out of this numb dizziness. I was saying over and over 'All I want is out of here.'"

Three months later, he writes another, more promising—but equally Burroughsian—yagé entry, "Yagé is space time travel. The room seems to shake and vibrate with motion. The blood and substance of many races, Negro, Polynesian, Mountain Mongol, Desert Nomad, Polyglot Near East, Indian—new races as yet unconceived and unborn, combinations not yet realized pass through your body. Migrations, incredible journeys through deserts and jungles

and mountains (stasis and death in closed mountain val-
leys where plants sprout out of your cock and vast crusta-
ceans hatch inside and break the shell of the body), across
the Pacific in an outrigger canoe to Easter Island. The Com-
posite City where all human potentials are spread out in a
vast silent market."

Burroughs' experiences and his belief in the otherworldly potential of yagé inspired Allen. He decided to
make his own expedition in search of yagé and to send his
own "field reports" back to Bill along the way. In a letter
dated June 10, 1960, from Pucallpa, Peru, Allen relates a
harrowing encounter with yagé.

As with Burroughs, Allen's first yagé experiences were
not pure enough to get the full effect. But when Allen eventually drank the potion and found himself face-to-face with
"The Vomiter" he knew he was in the full throes of a yagé
trip: "The whole fucking Cosmos broke loose around me,
I think the strongest and worst I've ever had it nearly. . . .
I felt faced by Death, my skull in my beard on pallet on
porch rolling back and forth and settling finally as if in re-
production of the last physical move I make before settling
into real death—got nauseous, rushed out and began vomiting, all covered with snakes, like a Snake Seraph, colored
serpents in aureole all around my body, I felt like a snake
vomiting out the universe—or a Jivaro in head-dress with
fangs vomiting up in realization of the Murder of the Universe—my death to come—everyone's death to come—all
unready—I unready—all around me in the trees the noise
of these spectral animals the other Drinkers vomiting (normal part of the cure sessions) in the night in their awful
solitude in the universe. . . ."

Allen had already experienced peyote, LSD, mescaline,

and an array of other drugs. But yagé felled him like no other. The universe in the form of "The Vomiter" came to Allen as a horrible, destructive, dark, uncaring force. This was no peace and love trip. Much as with his early Blake visions, this yagé trip would stalk Allen for the rest of his life.

And in addition to the mental and spiritual terrors, Allen had also managed to crack the lens of his eyeglasses on that trip.

This was the Allen Ginsberg that Leary sat with in his kitchen. Inspired and informed by the intrepid work of two other Harvard men—Schultes and Burroughs—and fully aware that he was on the historical turf of William James, Ralph Waldo Emerson, Henry David Thoreau, and numerous other radical intellectuals, Ginsberg looked out at Leary through the cracked lens of his eyeglasses and told him about The Vomiter and his other yagé and hallucinatory experiences. Tim understood—and appreciated—that Allen was explaining his particular "set" in the hope that it would help Leary act as a better curandero to him. Once the "set" was clear, it was time to prepare the "setting" for Allen's trip.

Leary's home at Newton Centre was an unlikely spot to conduct psychedelic sessions. By purely superficial standards, it appeared to be quintessentially suburban: the three-story house sat on a hill surrounded by other houses of its ilk, with a three-car garage, manicured lawns, and 185 stone steps that led visitors to the front door. Inside, the house was filled with beautiful woodwork and metalwork lamps spotting the end tables. Thick carpets and a staircase winding up from the spacious foyer completed the picture of wealth and leisure. This was certainly a fitting house for a Harvard professor. But Allen was there to

take psychedelic mushrooms, not to attend a polite cocktail party. He was coming off a long, arduous trek through
the jungles of South America. Even when he was back
in New York, Allen's apartment was more of a temporary
crash pad for him and his Beat friends than any sort of
"home" in the formal sense. He was certainly dubious
about the almost frivolous gaiety with which Leary and
his colleagues treated their psychedelic tests. Allen had
stared down The Vomiter. He knew that inner exploration
was no joke. Still, this was Harvard. Leary was a respected
psychologist and he seemed to know how to run a session.
Either way, he had a big bottle of psilocybin pills that he
was willing to share.

Tim shook out a handful of pink psilocybin pills into
Allen's palm. Allen swallowed them down. Allen and Peter followed the winding staircase up to the room Tim had
assigned them. Tim had already outfitted the room with
his daughter Susan's record player. Allen selected Wagner
and Beethoven as the sound track for this trip. He put on
Wagner first. Then Allen took off all his clothes, turned
off the lights, and lay down in bed. Peter lay down next
to him, snuggled up against Allen's side, and closed his
eyes. Once they were settled, Tim left Allen and Peter
alone and told them he'd be back every fifteen minutes to
check on them.

Along with Allen, there was also a painter named
Donald tripping at the house that night. Frank Barron, on
his best professional behavior, was also on hand to help
out. Tim had given Donald, far less experienced than
Allen, a smaller dose. Donald had also brought along a
friend, a Harvard anthropology student, to observe his trip.
Leary liked the idea of having someone to help supervise

Donald; however, he made it explicitly clear that the budding anthropologist was not to take any mushrooms. While
Tim did serve as a guide to Donald throughout his trip, the
presence of this friend freed him up to focus more attention on Allen.

No sooner had Tim offered some guidance to Donald
on his trip (which already included a renunciation of technology, materialism, and American culture in general) than
it was time to check on Allen again. But first, Tim greeted
his daughter Susan. Susan had been at a friend's house, and
now she was headed upstairs to do her homework. Tim followed her up the winding staircase and then split off to
check on Allen.

Allen was tripping and in a shaky state. No doubt filled
with visions of The Vomiter, he felt himself choking back
vomit once again. He was still flat on his back in bed with
Peter resting calmly beside him. But Allen was anything
but calm. He was trembling, filled with fear, fighting back
paranoia, darkness, and trying not to return to the state he'd
struggled with in Pucallpa.

Tim leaned over the bed and peered into Allen's eyes.
Allen had taken off his cracked glasses and his pupils were
dilated, appearing to Tim as "black liquid eyes, faun's eyes,
man's eyes." Allen asked Tim what he thought of him. Tim
replied that he thought Allen was a great man and that it
was good to know him. Ginsberg later wrote, "Professor
Leary came into my room, looked into my eyes, and said I
was a great man. That determined me to make an effort to
live here and now." Tim asked if Allen needed anything,
but Allen said no. Tim left with the promise he'd be back
again in fifteen minutes.

The brief visit from Leary reassured Allen. He choked

back the vomit and told himself that all the figures he had been so haunted by were only ways to distract himself from his true fear: the fear of being Allen Ginsberg. Perhaps he was a great man after all. Perhaps he was capable of great things. Wagner's *Götterdämmerung* hit a crescendo, thundering through the bedroom, and Allen spotted a flash of light through the window that reminded him of the Star of Bethlehem. "Suddenly out of the window saw image as of the Bethlehem star, heard great horns of *Götterdämmerung*-Wagner on the phonograph I'd arranged to hear in the room. Like the horns of judgment calling from the ends of the cosmos—called on all human consciousness to declare itself the end of consciousness. Seemed as if all the world of human consciousness were waiting for a messiah, someone to take on the responsibility of being the creative god and seize power over the universe. Milton's Lucifer flashed through my mind. *Paradise Lost*, a book I'd never understood before—why Milton sided with Lucifer the rebel in heaven. I got up out of bed and walked downstairs naked Orlovsky following me curious what I would do and willing to go along in case I did anything interestingly extravagant. Urging me on in fact, thank god."

Leary was checking on Susan—actually, he was scolding her that reading without proper light would damage her eyesight—when he heard the patter of naked feet on the wooden floorboards in the hallway. He looked up just in time to see Peter's naked ass go undulating past the doorway. Tim told Susan that Allen and Peter were walking around the house naked. She gathered up all her things—books, hairbrush, curlers, hairpins—and went up to the third floor to wait it out. By the time Tim caught up with the naked poets downstairs, Allen was excitedly telling Frank Barron what was on his mind. "I'm the Messiah," Allen declared, waving a finger in the air. "I've come down to preach love to the world. We're going to walk through the streets and teach people to stop hating."

Tim and Frank, both professionally trained at maintaining an unflappable demeanor despite whatever a patient might say, told Allen that his idea was a good one.

Still, the budding Messiah was prepared to do something more convincing.

While Tim was in basic training at Fort Eustis, Virginia, he had contracted chronic bronchitis. The bronchitis coupled with hours of exposure to ninety-millimeter artillery fire at close range had caused Leary to go deaf in one ear. Thus, while it is not well known and seldom appeared in pictures, the ever youthful and smiling Timothy Leary wore a hearing aid. "Do you believe I'm the Messiah?" Allen asked. "Look, I can prove it. I'm going to cure your hearing. Take off your hearing machine. Your ears are cured. Come on, take it off, you don't need it."

Tim played along. He took out his hearing aid and placed it on the desk.

"But Allen, one thing."

"What?"

"Your glasses. You're still wearing them. Why don't you cure your own vision?"

Allen was momentarily startled. Of course, his own vision—those cracked lenses were still on his face. "Yes, you're right. I will."

Allen took off his glasses and set them on the desk beside Tim's hearing aid. Then—one half-deaf, one half-blind—they proceeded to the next challenge.

"Come on," Allen said, squinting at the two psychologists. "We're going down to the city streets to tell the people about peace and love. And then we'll get lots of great people onto a big telephone network to settle all this warfare bit."

Here was a larger problem. One hard, fast rule at Leary's was that no one could leave the house while on mushrooms. Nothing would derail their experiments quicker than a wild, tripping madman wandering naked down Beacon Street. In fact, Leary had already had one such scare with Donald earlier in the night. Just before Allen had come, bringing the holy word to the study area, the anthropology student had informed Tim that Donald was outside. Tim was chilled by the information. He scrambled onto the front porch and flicked on the two rows of spotlights that illuminated the front lawn and the stone steps leading down to the street. Tim started down the steps, calling out for Donald as he went. Fortunately, he found Donald halfway down the lawn. The tripping man had been waylaid by a majestic oak tree—he stood, barefoot, looking up at it appreciatively. Donald asked Tim to take off his shoes. While Tim squatted down to untie his trademark white tennis sneakers, Donald reprised his earlier rap about the danger of humankind isolating itself from nature. It seemed that Donald was on a nature trip. By the time he left him on the lawn, Tim was confident that the oak tree was a better curandero for Donald than the anthropology student.

Now Allen was talking about taking his trip into the outside world too. Once again, Frank Barron reacted with cool instincts instilled by his professional training. "Fine," Frank said, "but why not do the telephone bit first, right here in the house."

Peter was excited. "Who we gonna call?"

"Well," answered Allen, "we'll call Kerouac on Long Island, and Kennedy and Khrushchev and Bill Burroughs in Paris and Norman Mailer in the psycho ward in Bellevue. We'll get them all hooked up in a big cosmic electronic love talk. War is just a hang-up. We'll get the love-thing flowing on the electric Bell telephone network."

At that time, Norman Mailer had been committed to Bellevue for stabbing his wife Adele. Burroughs had already shot and killed his wife Joan during a drunken game of William Tell in Mexico City, a crime that precipitated his flight into the jungles in search of the "time-traveling" drug yagé. Ginsberg decided to start with Kerouac instead.

"Hello, operator, this is God. I want to talk to Kerouac. To whom do I want to talk? Kerouac. What's my name? This is God. G.O.D." Allen tried to expedite the process by giving the operator the number to call. Unfortunately, it was the number of the house where he'd lived as a child. He was forced to go upstairs to get his address book. He returned and got Kerouac on the phone. "Take a plane up here immediately," he ordered Jack. "The revolution is beginning. Gather all the dark angels of light at once. It's time to seize power over the universe and become the next consciousness!"

Kerouac laughed. "Whazzamatter, are you high?"

"I am high and naked and I am King of the Universe. Get on a plane. It is time!"

"But I got my mother. . . ."

"Bring your mother!"

"Aw, I'm tired."

Allen was growing agitated at his friend's reluctance. "What do you want to do?"

"Lay down and die," Kerouac sighed.

"What's the matter with you?" Allen bellowed. "Are you *afraid*?"

Allen hadn't spoken to his old friend with such passion in years. While Kerouac was not on Allen's current plane of thought, he was certainly amused by the conversation. Allen listened as much as he talked. Jack was undoubtedly seated in a comfortable chair beside the phone in his mother's house, drunk, melancholy. He also seemed to be agreeing with Allen's notion that everyone was God. "Who else but us is *it*, the life force, is God?"

Before hanging up, Allen made one last request of Jack. He made Jack promise not to die.

The phone call with Jack had only further excited Allen. He was now pacing around the room, still naked, ready to call Mailer at Bellevue. With one eye on their swelling phone bill, Tim and Frank Barron tried to casually dissuade him. "I don't think they'd let a call go through to him, Allen."

"Well, it all depends on how we come on."

"I don't think coming on as Allen Ginsberg would help in that league. I don't think coming on as the Messiah would either."

"Well," Allen said, almost out of steam, "you could come on as big psychologists and make big demanding noises about the patient."

Finally, Tim and Frank wore Allen down. They managed to get him seated and onto a different mental track by playing a record of James Joyce reading *Finnegans Wake*. Allen had lost the small battle to use the phone system to get the revolution started, but, in making his argument, he had spontaneously hit upon the key to jump-starting the psychedelic revolution: *you could come on as big psychologists and make big demanding noises about the patient.*

Allen and Peter went upstairs and put on robes while Tim started warming milk for them on the stove. The group reconvened around the kitchen table. Allen already felt the righteous rush of mushroom empowerment siphoning away—"[I] saw control of the universe slipping out of my hands"—but he was still inspired by the drug.

One revelation Allen had that night—one that was bound to fail—was that he was now going to be heterosexual. Despite his passionate love for Peter Orlovsky, Allen would still question his sexual orientation to the extent that he was willing, and often eager, to renounce his homosexuality. Allen had a big pile of baggage to fight against in accepting his homosexuality, including social stigma, a middle-aged desire to procreate (after the trip, Allen wrote to Neal and Carolyn Cassady, "I will have babies instead of jacking off into limbo"), and the acute awareness that Peter had strong heterosexual leanings.

In an interview published by *Playboy* magazine in 1969, Allen was asked about his renunciation of homosexuality following this first Harvard trip. Focusing on the American social stigma against homosexuality, Allen replied, "Well, I get those feelings every time I take acid. On a trip, you enter corridors inside, and into the heart. Naturally, you come upon old feelings you didn't know were there and were ashamed of. . . . In much the same way, the heterosexual man may discover during a trip the *natural* homosexual identity in himself—an identity suppressed by our culture but not by many others. As Whitman observed, if the natural love of man for man is suppressed, men won't be good citizens and democracy will be enfeebled. What Whitman prophesied was an adhesive element between comrades—the 'sane, healthy love of man for man.' But because of suppression of feelings in America, the overemphasis on competition and rivalry—a tough guy, *macho*, hard, sadistic police-state mentality—American men are afraid of relationships with each other."

Nevertheless, Allen's sexual pseudo-revelation was bound to fail. He was, and always would be, homosexual. But the other revelation of that night would alter the direction of the coming decade. Contrary to Huxley's belief that hallucinogens should be used quietly, by a select group, Ginsberg—in all his Whitmanic democracy—believed that everyone should have access to psilocybin. Poets, priests, doctors, students, housewives, workers, executives, musicians, soldiers, truck drivers . . . everyone should be given the option of experiencing the state of being "beshroomed." But Ginsberg also knew that hallucinogens were an inherent threat to the U.S. power establishment, starting with the government. Hallucinogens are, by nature, non-conformist. In his book *Alternating Currents* (1967), Nobel laureate Octavio Paz reflected on his government's fear of hallucinogens: "We are now in a position to understand the real reason for the condemnation of hallucinogens and why their use is punished. The authorities do not behave as though they were trying to stamp out a harmful vice, but behave as though they were stamping out dissidence. Since this is a form of dissidence that is becoming more widespread, the prohibition takes on the proportion of a campaign against a spiritual contagion, against an *opinion*. What authorities are displaying is *ideological* zeal: they are punishing a heresy, not a crime."

Although he was writing about Mexico, Paz's statements were equally true about the United States. By 1967 the government would go to great lengths to outlaw and demonize hallucinogens—and anyone who stood up publicly in their favor. In 1960, Allen Ginsberg, sipping warm milk in Leary's kitchen at Harvard, saw that future ahead. But he still believed that mushrooms must be made available to everyone.

As Allen saw it, the solution was sitting right across the table from him: Dr. Timothy Leary. Or, more important, everything that Timothy Leary represented. Leary was an ivy-league academic, a certified Ph.D., a well-respected psychologist, a clean-cut unknown with—and here was the kicker—access to mass quantities of psilocybin. On the other hand, Ginsberg was a known Beatnik poet with a history of drug use and mental illness. He wasn't just famous, he was infamous. American culture had already punched his ticket. As Ginsberg put it, "I'm too easy to put down."

No, what they needed to give hallucinogens a shot at safe passage into mainstream America was a respectable front. "Big serious scientist professors from Harvard." But the key would be to build up a base of supporters for the drug first. If they could combine Leary's scientific credentials with a roster of influential supporters, it would be much harder for the government to suppress the drug. That was their logic, anyway. Once again, this logic was based on democratic principles, the belief that the government would honor the will of the people. In 1960, this was an ideal that still had legs.

For Leary's part, he saw a key ally in Ginsberg, who had arrived at just the right time to boost the Harvard Psilocybin Project to the next level. As he wrote in *High Priest*,

"And so Allen spun out the cosmic campaign. He was to line up influentials and each weekend I would come down to New York and we'd run mushroom sessions. This fit our Harvard research plans perfectly. Our aim there was to learn how people reacted, to test the limits of the drug, to get creative and thoughtful people to take them and tell us what they saw and what we should do with the mushrooms. Allen's political plan was appealing, too. I had seen enough and read enough in Spanish of the anti-vision crowd, the power-holders with guns, and the bigger and better men we got on our team the stronger our position. And then too, the big-name bit was intriguing. Meeting and sharing visions with the famous."

Allen Ginsberg may have been a media-scarred icon, but he was a well-connected one. He ran up Leary's stairs and came back into the kitchen with his address book. And then, as Leary says in *High Priest*, "we started planning the psychedelic revolution." Robert Lowell, Thelonious Monk, Dizzy Gillespie, Jack Kerouac, William Burroughs, Charles Olson, Willem de Kooning, Franz Kline, Barney Rosset, Muriel Rukyser, LeRoi Jones . . . Allen Ginsberg's address book was a who's who of New York City, and U.S., artistic leaders. As famous as he would become, it must be remembered that at this time Timothy Leary was completely unknown beyond the small, academic psychology community. Although he loved the idea of running tests on gifted and accomplished artists, to this crowd, he would have been just some square Harvard professor. His access would have been severely limited. But with an introduction from Allen Ginsberg, Timothy Leary would become a player. He would have the blessings of the King Bohemian.

The partnership would be thus: Allen Ginsberg would

give Timothy Leary entrée to the influential world of artistic America. Timothy Leary would give Allen Ginsberg an opportunity to expose America to powerful hallucinatory visions. Ginsberg put it this way, "The idea was to give it to respectable and notable people first, who could really articulate the experience, all the while keeping it under the august auspices of Harvard. I could act as the go-between, keeping as much of a low profile as possible considering my visibility as America's most conspicuous beatnik. Really, it was a perfect role for me to play: Ambassador of Psilocybin."

In *High Priest*, Leary said, "From this moment on my days as a respectable establishment scientist were numbered. . . . [My] energies were offered to the ancient underground society of alchemists, artists, mystics, alienated visionaries, drop-outs and the disenchanted young, the sons arising. . . . Allen Ginsberg came to Harvard and shook us loose from our academic fears and strengthened our courage and faith in the process."

Tune In

Dear Mr. Monk

January 3, 1961

Mr. Thelonious Monk
243 West 63rd Street, Apt. 20
New York, New York

Dear Mr. Monk

Allen Ginsberg tells me that he has spoken to you about our mushroom research. We find that they do great things for talented people and we are going to continue giving them to people in the arts and learned professions.

   I should like very much to talk to you about our research, and tell you about our results so far. I'll be in New York the weekend of January 14th and shall give you a ring.

   I have followed your work with respect and pleasure and look forward to talking with you.

Sincerely yours,
Timothy Leary

While Leary's colleagues Richard Alpert and Frank Barron and a growing cadre of Harvard graduate students were busy analyzing data from individual report forms given as follow-ups to each psilocybin session, Leary was taking cues and introductions from Ginsberg that would forward the cultural portion of their research. Thelonious Monk was only one of the artists they would pull in—they would eventually give psilocybin to Dizzy Gillsepie's whole band.

Ginsberg gave Leary addresses and references for a rich cross-section of artists, writers, musicians, publishers, bohemians, and intellectually engaged New Yorkers. Leary sent out letters to these people on Harvard University stationery, and Ginsberg eased the way with more casual conversation and correspondence. Between the two of them, they framed the mushroom sessions with an air of scientific (and Ivy League) legitimacy as well as the furor of cutting-edge artistic and spiritual urgency. It was a powerful one-two punch, and most who were approached were interested in taking a whirl on the mushroom-go-round.

On January 13, 1961, Jack Kerouac took psilocybin along with Leary at Ginsberg's apartment on the Lower East Side. Peter Orlovsky and Bob Donlin—a poet friend of Ginsberg and Kerouac who appears in Kerouac's writing as Bob Donnelly—also ate the mushroom pills. It was decided that Ginsberg would abstain so that he could be their curandero.

Kerouac was fresh off his last major journey through America. His zeitgeist-setting 1957 masterpiece, *On the Road*, had, for better and worse, already made him a major American celebrity. The progression from being lauded in the *New York Times* to being parodied and mocked on television and in print was a rapid, jarring one and had deepened Kerouac's dependency on alcohol. In June 1960 Jack had endured the movie adaptation of his novel *The Subterraneans*. Predictably, Jack's raw, lyrical and powerful account of a true episode from his life had been turned into a cheesy, sensationalistic Hollywood movie in which Kerouac was portrayed by a lackluster George Peppard. Jack responded to the movie by shutting himself away in his mother's house for two months and drinking. In July, he decided to make a last-ditch effort to right himself both physically and mentally. Lawrence Ferlinghetti had offered Jack use of his little cabin near Big Sur in a serene ocean-side setting called Bixby Canyon. Kerouac was to go there and gather himself by chopping wood, meditating, staying away from booze, and writing. Instead, the trip turned into a harrowing personal hell alternating between drunken forays into San Francisco and alcoholic horrors and hallucinations in the woods. Kerouac would record the trip in his most heart-wrenching book, *Big Sur.*

When Leary met him at Ginsberg's apartment roughly six months after his Big Sur trip, Kerouac was already drunk. Their shared New England upbringings and passion for sports (Kerouac would dub Leary "Coach") created an immediate bond between the two men. However, Leary also detected a deep sadness in Kerouac. "Jack Kerouac was scary. Behind the dark good looks of a burly lumberjack was a New England mill-town sullenness, Canuck-Catholic soggy distrust. This is one unhappy kid, I thought." Leary was also intimidated by Kerouac's celebrity and his overbearing drunken persona. Early on in their trip, Leary withdrew into Ginsberg's bedroom in despair. "Kerouac had propelled me into my first negative trip. Maybe it was the drabness of the slum, so different from our carefully prepared session rooms. Perhaps it was jittery New York itself, never a town for serene philosophers. Or was it Kerouac's French-Catholic gloom? Anyway, I went down."

Much as Leary had rescued Ginsberg during his first

trip at Harvard, now Ginsberg fulfilled his curandero role by pulling Leary out of his downward spiral. Tim rebounded, and the next twelve hours were spent talking, goofing, laughing, and tripping in Ginsberg's apartment. Kerouac still dominated the evening, but he did it in a playful, Zen way that Leary came to appreciate. He would later write to Allen that he had even taken to incorporating some of Kerouac's swagger and antics into his own classroom teaching. More important though, the trip had taught Leary further lessons on the importance of set and setting. Leary wrote to Ginsberg, "Learned a lot from you and the last weekend in NYC with Jack. Have run several agapes recently and it's so clear—when I'm detached and doing it out of duty, trying to [be] conscientious curandero etc then it gets scattered. When I or someone else present is battereied [*sic*] up with huge charges of energy and love and goodfeeling etc then it swings godly. Also a small room with doors closed adds to the good."

As for Kerouac's experience, Allen had reminded him that Leary was gathering reports after each person's trip, and certainly a report from Jack Kerouac was a major score for the Psilocybin Project. Rather than file a traditional report, Kerouac put his reflections into letter form using his "spontaneous prose" approach to sketch out his impressions. In this letter to Leary—whom he addresses as "Coach"—he details both the positives and the negatives of his mushroom experience.

Among the positives Jack notes: "Mainly I felt like a floating Khan on a magic carpet with my interesting lieutenants and gods . . . some ancient feeling about old geheuls [*sic*] in the grass, and temples, exactly also like the sensation I got drunk on pulque floating in the Xochimilco gardens on barges laden with flowers and singers . . . some old Golden Age dream of man, very nice."

Among the negatives: "The bad physical side-effects involved (for me) stiffening of elbow and knee joints, a swelling of the eyelid, shortness of breath or rather anxiety about breathing itself. No heart palpitations like in mescaline, however."

Kerouac also reported positive lingering effects that continued beyond the initial mushroom trip. "In fact I came home and had the first serious long talk with my mother, for 3 days and 3 nights (not consecutive) but we sat talking about everything yet went about the routine of washing, sleeping, eating, cleaning up the yard and house, and returning to long talk chairs at proper time. That was great. I learned I loved her more than I thought."

This positive feeling, which he describes as "mushroomy," continued for a week following his trip, at which point he began his weekend carousing around Northport, where the feeling was kept "alive by drinking Christian Brothers port on the rocks."

Kerouac concludes his letter: "In sum, also, there is temporary addiction but no withdrawal symptoms whatever. The faculty of remembering names and what one has learned, is heightened so fantastically that we could develop the greatest scholars and scientists in the world with this stuff. . . . There's no harm in Sacred Mushrooms if taken in moderation as a rule (not the first time, tho) and much good will come of it. (For instance, I remembered historical details I'd completely forgotten before the mushrooms, and names names millions of names and categories and data)."

In short, Kerouac's trip had been a success for him, as well as for Leary and Ginsberg. However, the elder of the Beat inner circle was a tougher sell.

While Kerouac was the most famous of Allen's friends to participate in the early experiments with Leary, William S. Burroughs was the most drug-savvy. With Burroughs' reach into the international avant-garde, both Ginsberg and Leary knew that it would be a coup to get him involved with their doings. On January 5, 1961, Leary sat down and wrote Burroughs a letter. At that time, Burroughs was living in Paris at what came to be known as the Beat Hotel. The Beat Hotel was a typical cheap European rooming house that at different times housed Gregory Corso, Ginsberg, Peter Orlovsky, and many other poets and artists, including Brion Gysin. Inspired by Gysin's visual experiments, Burroughs was deep into the "cut-up" experiments that would play a role in many of his most famous pieces of writing. If spontaneous prose was Kerouac's abiding creative technique, then cut-ups were Burroughs'. Even before he put that name to the experiments, Burroughs was never one for orderly, linear writing. When Allen Ginsberg arrived to visit Burroughs in Tangier in 1957 he found the middle-aged writer living in a cluttered room surrounded by pages and pages of "routines" (another Burroughsian literary conceit). Burroughs would write his prose while high on kif, morphine, majoun (a candy-like confection of fruits, nuts, honey, spices, and THC), or whatever else was handy, and when he came to the end of a page, he'd simply flip it onto the ground and load another one into the typewriter. Where Kerouac had tackled the single-page limitations of a typewriter by taping his pages together or, eventually, working on long rolls of teletype paper, Burroughs simply disconnected from the necessity of linear narrative. He would not be constrained by the machine or the tedious process of ordering a manuscript. So the pages piled up around him in Tangier. Eventually, it would be up to his visiting friends Jack Kerouac and Allen Ginsberg to shape those pages into Burroughs' acclaimed novel *Naked Lunch*. While going through this editorial process, Kerouac said that working with Burroughs' manuscript gave him terrible nightmares.

Going from scattered pages to intentional cut-ups wasn't a big leap for Burroughs. He believed that words were viruses that infected human "hosts" and that the true intention of language could be read, as it were, between the lines. This cut-up technique was originated and also being used by Brion Gysin. Both were living in Paris at the Beat Hotel and spending long, high hours cutting up and reconfiguring newspapers, magazines, novels, letters, and anything else they came across. In addition to other theoretical and aesthetic interests in the cut-up, Burroughs and Gysin were pushing into its potential for non-drug-induced hallucinogenic experiences. Burroughs wrote to Leary, "Actually I have achieved pure cut up highs without the use of any chemical agent." Gysin, in particular, was also heavily into stroboscopic hallucinations induced by something called a "dream machine." The dream machine consisted of a metal tube with shapes cut out of the sides that revolved on a record player around a naked light bulb. The user's face, with eyes closed, would be placed close to the tube. With the tube revolving at 78 or 45 revolutions per minute, light would emit at roughly 8 to 13 pulses per second. This range was said to mimic alpha waves in the brain while a person is in a relaxed state. The goal was to have the light pulsations stimulate the optic nerves, creating patterns of color and light that lead to a hypnagogic state somewhere between wake and dream.

Dear William Burroughs,

Maybe Allen Ginsberg has told you something about our research project on the new drugs. In any case he asked me to write you—in general about our celestial ambitions and in particular to see if you want some mushrooms.

In hindsight, it seems unlikely that William Burroughs would jell with Timothy Leary. A letter sent on Harvard stationery was probably impressive to many whom Leary first contacted, but Burroughs had already been through the Harvard mill and had turned up his nose at all things Ivy League. His anti-authoritarian streak was as deep as they come and extended to all manner of authority figures, including Harvard professors with an eye on nirvana.

Given Burroughs' attitudes, the first paragraph of Leary's introductory letter was just right. He offered Burroughs free drugs. Beyond that though, it's likely that Leary's approach triggered the standard response of any junkie faced with being dragged out into blinding daylight: retreat. In this letter, and in subsequent letters, Leary extended invitations to join him on the public podium. "Medicine has already preempted LSD. Marijuana is the football for two other powerful groups—bohemia and the narcotics agents. Mescaline and psilocybin are still up for grabs and it is our hope to keep them ungrabbed, uncontrolled, available. . . . When the issue comes up for legislation we hope to have a strong team to fight the non-control game."

One can practically see Burroughs sitting on the edge

of a lumpy, blanket-and-clothes-strewn mattress in Paris, surrounded by the accoutrements of art and smack, and re-reading these words down the long shaft of his nose: Legislation? Team? Non-control?

"The second approach," Leary continued, was "to build the use of these drugs into ongoing and respectable institutions."

Ongoing and respectable institutions?

Leary explained to Burroughs that they (his "team of Allen, Aldous Huxley, Alan Watts, etc.") had identified education as the most likely target for integrating mescaline and psilocybin into mainstream society. Religion was out—too regimented, hierarchal and established to make a dent there. Medicine was also a fixed game. Social clubs were out—"The chance of turning on the Masons or Knights of Columbus seems unlikely." Instead, Leary would use his post at Harvard to insert mescaline and psilocybin into the curriculum. He told Burroughs that he was arranging a symposium for the upcoming American Psychological Association in an attempt to get cultural figures and scientists together to publicly advocate for use of these psychedelics in the educational process.

Leary continued to reassure Burroughs of his establishment credentials. Ginsberg had advised him that these credentials would ingratiate them with larger, polite society, and Leary carried that theory over to Burroughs. "Among the psychology tribes I have a moderately respectable name for doing MEASURABLE kinds of research on unmeasurable, human issues, and this has certain values." He concluded the letter by telling Burroughs of the various artists and intellectuals that they had been turning on in New York and dubbed their work that of "nirvana salesmen," adding,

"Spent an evening with Olsen [*sic*] last week. He talks of you with great respect. I've read Naked Lunch and am still reeling (some months after). Visions endure."

Writing from 9 Rue Git Le Coeur in Paris, Burroughs first responsed favorably. He told Leary that his letter was "most interesting" and that the work he and Allen were doing was "vitally important." He agreed to receive a package of mushrooms from Leary and write a report on the effects. He told Leary that his own writing had "gained MEASUR-ABLE [*sic*] from the use of hallucinogens" and agreed that their use would "better conditions on all levels." Perhaps the breakthroughs could even lead to "mass therapy" whereby "whole areas of neurosis could be mapped and irradicated [*sic*]." Finally, he mentioned that he and Brion Gysin were working with cut-ups and that Gysin was also interested in trying the mushrooms. Perhaps they could even put together an anthology of mushroom drawing and writing.

Leary was encouraged by Burroughs' response. In a letter sent to Ginsberg on February 1, 1961, he brims with optimism: "Then too, when a note came from Burroughs full of great agreements and offers to help, and to contribute to a mushroom anthology which he suggested, well then, too, I felt good about the things that you got going and that I'm now swept up in. . . . Burrough's [*sic*] letter made me feel proud and good. I had sent him air mail some Sacred Ms and will send more when I'm sure those arrived."

For the moment, Burroughs was onboard. Recycling the term he used for the tiny drinking club he formed when he first got to Harvard, the "White Hand Society," Leary told Allen, "And it all goes so well, pieces falling into place, running along with some great nine foot tide that's pushing this white hand."

Leary's "white hand" reference turns up in a letter to another key, early literary advocate for the psychedelic tests, too. One of the men he had referenced in his first letter to William Burroughs: the poet Charles Olson.

Charles Olson came to Newton House in December 1960. He and Allen had crossed paths at various points throughout their literary careers, primarily at large poetry festivals in which they both participated. In addition to being the author of *The Maximus Poems*, Charles Olson was the literary center of the experimental Black Mountain College in North Carolina. Though the school was only in existence for 24 years, such diverse avant-garde luminaries as Buckminster Fuller, John Cage, and Robert Rauschenberg attended and taught on campus. Its most enduring legacy, however, was the literary scene fostered by Olson. In this unlikely rural setting outside of Asheville, North Carolina, a group known as the Black Mountain poets was born, with Robert Creeley at the helm and Charles Olson as its guiding figure. Through the *Black Mountain Review*, edited by Creeley, Olson's Projective Verse philosophies were propagated and like-minded poets were given voice. After leaving Black Mountain's campus and moving to San Francisco, Robert Creeley's astute editorial and networking skills brought the Beat writers into the Black Mountain fold, forever intertwining their legacy with that of Black Mountain College.

By 1960, Olson was a well known and highly regarded avant-garde poet and teacher as well as a groundbreaking Herman Melville scholar. He was also a Harvard dropout, a big drinker, and no stranger to intoxicants in their many forms. In other words, he was a perfect "subject" for Allen to introduce into Leary's circle.

Standing 6'7" and husky, Charles Olson was not just intellectually imposing, but physically enormous. His size gave Ginsberg momentary pause with regards to the psilocybin experiments. After all, what would happen if this grizzly bear of a man got out of control? Who among them could restrain him? However, his worries were put to rest and, as Ginsberg would later recall, Olson took to the drug "like a duck to water." Indeed, perhaps because of his size, Olson astounded them with his ability to ingest massive doses of psilocybin pills, which he referred to as "peanuts." While Ginsberg and Leary watched in awe, Olson began to act like a Mohawk "peace sachem." Olson would recall, "The moment the peanuts affected me I started talking longhouse talk. And created, because I was the responsible person . . . I was the tone, I created the tone for the evening." As with Ginsberg and Leary, the emerging terminology of psychedelics was also floating back and forth between participants—poets and scientist—leading Olson to conclude, "And it was absolutely a pure ceremonial set." Olson went on to write, "The startling & unbelievable first impression of going under the mushroom is that everyone & everything is nothing but itself so that all—everything—is therefore well, and there's no push, there's no fuss, there's nothing at all to worry about, or press at, no sweat of any sort called for, it's all too real and way beyond any attitude or seeking some greater or bigger answer. . . ."

On June 28, 1961, Timothy Leary wrote a letter to Charles Olson not only revealing his affection for the man, but offering a telling snapshot of the lessons he was taking away from his early time among the poets and bohemians:

Well we have been not idle, Charles, with the business of the *white hand.*

F

   i

     r

       s

         t of all, let me say, if I can say it, how great it was to have you here. Well it's hard to say it in roman type but maybe I can say it—that meeting you and knowing you makes me see that

    life can be right
        and
    man can be divine.

I've spent about two hours a day reading Maximus and have it so underlined with pencil slashes that . . .

The business goes well. Allen lined up a "talk" with Robert Lowell last Sunday—after twenty minutes he said "why not now." His bursts of creativity have been connected with crazy American abstractions and there is a good chance that the mushrooms have pulled him off this set of abstractions. In any case he is part of the gang now—which adds to the esteem in which I held him.

The department head and dean here have approved a seminar next year in which theological, humanity and social science graduate students take the mushrooms and then figure them out. Huston Smith (check his book on comparative religion) a prof from MIT starts off the New Year in the right way and may turn his seminars on to the intuitive scene next year.

We continue to be convinced that a great decade is in the making.

I am improving as a lecturer—thanks to the advice of you and Allen. Told a group of psychiatrists at Boston Psycho hosp yesterday that they should act as gods and treat their patients as gods.

Didn't get committed.

Have lots of manuscript stuff to show you. Can I come up to see you next Friday? Drop me a note if you'll be tied up.

Spent last weekend with Allen—we wandered around NYC like
barefoot healing friars—Lowell, Dorothy, Norman, Barney Rosset etc
etc. We actually did accomplish some healing.
    Your great presence still sits with us in this house.
                                                    Love,
                                                    Tim

Without a doubt, Tim was flying high. His network of
interesting and influential subjects had expanded expo-
nentially, and each one was asked to provide feedback that
would support the research necessary to keep the Psilocybin
Project going. Effective July 1, 1961, Tim was given another
one-year appointment to serve as a lecturer in clinical psychology at Harvard. With that goal accomplished and the
spring semester ended, he set off to meet Allen Ginsberg in
Tangier. Allen and Peter Orlovsky were visiting Burroughs
there, and the visit would give Leary a chance to meet and
administer psilocybin to Burroughs directly while experiencing an exotic (and drug-filled) new destination. Timothy
Leary was going on a "working vacation."

Applied Mysticism: From Tangier to Copenhagen

When William S. Burroughs first lived in Tangier in 1954, the city was overseen by the consuls of eight European nations, which basically amounted to no regulation at all. This was post–World War II Tangier, the international zone located on the northwestern tip of Africa. A cluttered mixture of French, Spanish, and Arabic was heard in streets that, at one time, had been occupied by the Berbers, the Phoenicians, the Romans, the Portuguese, the British, Morocco, the French, and the Spanish. Now, this stunning city overlooking both the Mediterranean and the Atlantic Ocean attracted droves of hustlers, thieves, smugglers, pimps, prostitutes, addicts, artists, and any number of fringe escapees from mainstream society. In other words, it was a perfect home for a forty-year-old struggling junkie author who—despite cultivating a nondescript, ethereal presence that had earned him the nickname "El Hombre Invisible"—never lasted long in any one location without drawing attention from the law, the locals, or whoever else crossed paths with his strange, otherworldly vibrations.

Burroughs felt a freedom in Tangier that had eluded him in South America, Mexico, Europe, and certainly in the United States. Boy prostitutes were cheap and plentiful, and there was no stigma attached to homosexuality. Hard drugs were sold over the counter in many stores, and softer drugs like hash and kif were smoked out in the open by men of all ages. Of course, these freedoms did not extend to the female population of Tangier where women moved through the streets veiled, shrouded, and nearly invisible themselves. There was also a strong air of mysticism, magic, and witchcraft hanging over Tangier, with medicine men, sorcerers, and secret brotherhoods concocting potions and casting spells as openly as vendors sold their wares. In Tangier, Burroughs had found a hotbed of debauchery, freedom, and mysteries unlike any other place he had ever lived. His libido, drug appetite, and creativity were in full blush.

Tangier is also the place that Burroughs wrote his most famous book, *Naked Lunch.* By shortening the term "International Zone" to "Interzone," Burroughs imagined a bleak, end-of-the-world setting that was disturbing and fascinating, at once frightfully alien and troublingly human. "Interzone" became the setting for a new set of "routines" in which Bourroughs would exorcise his deepest demons and most hilarious, outlandish hallucinations. While Jack Kerouac was visiting Burroughs in Tangier and helping him assemble the manuscript, Kerouac, who had been suffering nightmares courtesy of Burroughs' writing, asked "Why are all these young boys being hanged in limestone caves?"

Burroughs replied, "Don't ask me. I get these messages from other planets. I'm apparently some kind of agent from another planet but I haven't got my orders clearly decoded yet. I'm shitting out my educated Midwestern background once and for all. It's a matter of catharsis, where I say the most horrible things I can think of. Realize that—the most horrible dirty slimy niggardliest posture possible."

Paul Bowles, a musical composer and author of two novels that Burroughs, always a tough critic, actually admired—*The Sheltering Sky* (set in Fez) and *Let It Come Down* (set in Morocco)—was another American expatriate living in Tangier. He was one of the few people that Burroughs had an interest in tracking down when he got to the city. Bowles' visit to see Burroughs at his apartment while he was writing *Naked Lunch* sheds further light on Burroughs' frenzied artistic process. Burroughs was smoking a lot of pot and hash at the time and also eating large quantities of homemade majoun. His chair and typewriter were surrounded by piles of loose pages. The pages had been stepped on, spilled on, ashed on, and even shit on by mice. When asked how he would possibly assemble this mess of papers into a coherent book, Burroughs replied, "Oh, I figure it'll be legible."

The truth is, without the advocacy of such dedicated friends as Jack Kerouac, Allen Ginsberg, and artist Alan Ansen, it is likely that *Naked Lunch* would have never found its final form. Burroughs had broken free from the more narrative forms of his first published book, *Junkie*, to such an extent that he needed the lifeline of his friends to pull him back down to earth. It was his friends who ultimately helped *Naked Lunch* find its first publication in 1959 with the edgy Parisian publisher Olympia Press.

By the time Timothy Leary arrived in Tangier in July 1961, Burroughs was already a Beat legend. The correspondences between Leary and Burroughs had been consistently upbeat and of mutual interest, and, of course, Ginsberg was greasing the wheels in both directions. In fact, Ginsberg was waiting in Tangier with Peter Orlovsky, Gregory Corso, and Alan Ansen when Leary arrived. After a dinner at Leary's hotel, the men adjourned to Burroughs' room to eat some mushroom pills. Accustomed to enjoying highs in the privacy of his room, Burroughs decided to stay alone there after eating his pills while the rest of the group explored the narrow streets of Tangier through dilated, beshroomed eyes. The men wandered giddily through the streets of Tangier, enjoying the lights, the strange scenes, and the vast array of humanity. In fact, they were enjoying themselves so much that they felt compelled to get Burroughs in on the fun. Together, they made their way back to Burroughs' apartment, where Ginsberg—in his New York style—yelled out Bill's name from the street.

While high on heroin, Burroughs had always been content to stare at the end of his shoe for hours on end: no angst, no conflicts, just staring down at his shoe. However, mushrooms are not a passive drug. They encourage exploration—both physical and mental—and are generally lousy drugs for doing on your own, in your room, with no one to talk to. So it was perhaps predictable that, when Burroughs finally opened his front door, he was ghostly pale, haggard, and covered with sweat. Burroughs was on a bad trip. The men tried in vain to pull him along with them into the Tangier night (which would most likely have improved his circumstances) but Burroughs resisted. Instead, he told them that he would take apomorphine to come down on his own.

Though Burroughs' mushroom trip may not have been what Leary had hoped, he did manage to secure an agreement from Burroughs to visit Harvard and participate in the Psilocybin Project. Before leaving Tangier, Leary also secured an invitation to visit Paul Bowles at his home. While he didn't take mushrooms with Bowles, he did have a powerful majoun experience while listening to tapes of Middle Eastern music that Bowles had field-recorded.

As Leary's experiments with psilocybin progressed, so did his thesis that all human behavior is essentially a "game." After leaving Tangier—eight months after the start of his collaboration with Ginsberg—Leary traveled to Copenhagen in August 1961 to present a paper for the International Congress of Applied Psychology. In that paper, Leary laid out his theory of "game-playing" and also introduced the Eastern influence that would increasingly shape his thinking.

In this presentation, Leary made his first public break with conventional Western psychology and set the tone for the radical proposals to follow. He stated that he had previously thought of himself solely as a behavioral scientist. In that role, he had focused on overt and measurable behavior, which, as he put it, is the basis—and ultimately, the great failing—of American psychology as it was defined fifty years earlier. American psychologists, Leary argued, sought to observe, measure, manipulate, control, and predict their subjects' overt behavior. Thus, they were obligated to focus on observable, quantifiable results. Leary proposed that this approach created a fissure that kept psychologists from dealing with their patients as whole beings. Most important, it ignored the development and state of one's consciousness in favor of fixating on their behavior.

In addressing this split between behavior and consciousness, Leary referenced the work of Professor Huston Smith of the Massachusetts Institute of Technology. Smith had researched differences between Eastern and Western approaches to working with patients and concluded that whereas Western medicine focused on control and quantifiable behaviors, Chinese philosophy emphasized the rules of social encounter, and Indian philosophy emphasized the development and expansion of human consciousness. Leary didn't mention the fact that the highly respected Dr. Smith was also a regular participant in his psilocybin sessions back at Harvard. He continued, "Tonight I speak to you from a point midway between the Western and Eastern hemispheres of the cortex presenting a theory and method which is Chinese in that behavior is seen as an intricate social game; Indian in its recognition of consciousness and the need to develop a more cosmic awareness; and finally Western in its concern to do good measurably well."

In essence, Leary had just begun the more spiritual and mystical proselytizing that would turn him into the famous, notorious Timothy Leary. The last few words of this introduction to this presentation, "do good measurably well," can also be viewed as a reference to, perhaps even a break with, Leary's old mentor Aldous Huxley. Huxley was also at the 1961 Congress of Applied Psychology. He presented a paper there called "Visionary Experience" that emphasized the importance of integrating mystical experiences with an intellectual view of reality. However, Huxley, a scholarly student and devotee of the arcane, had emphasized that Leary should "do good stealthily." If one were so crass as to reduce a great man, a great mind, to a bumper-sticker slogan, this could have been Huxley's. As Leary was taught by Huxley, Gerald Heard, and other philosophers, the unspoken (naturally) law of arcane knowledge had always been "*He who speaks does not know; he who knows speaks privately or not at all.*" So while Huxley often addressed mysticism in his talks and writing, he was not one to publicly advocate for widespread use of hallucinogens.

However, in his Copenhagen presentation, with a poet's concision, those four words "do good measurably well" marked Leary's decision to make public his studies of consciousness-altering drugs, spiritualism, and mystical philosophy. Thus Leary broke away from the discretion that Huxley emphasized, and, as he and Allen Ginsberg had discussed, he also began to attempt to bridge the gap between Western science and Eastern spirituality.

While introducing Eastern thought into psychology may have been new in 1961, the modernist poets, most notably Ezra Pound, had been infusing Western literature with Eastern philosophy for fifty years—and Ginsberg was well aware of these lineages. The school of poetry that Ezra Pound had dubbed "Imagism" and which T.S. Eliot noted as "the starting-point of modern poetry" is closely linked to Chinese and Japanese poetry techniques that emphasize concision, clarity, and precision of language.

Kenneth Rexroth, another poet who influenced the Beats and presided over the famous Six Gallery reading, can be credited for injecting Eastern poetic influences into West Coast poetry. Throughout his life, Rexroth—quite vocally—espoused and studied Buddhism, mystical Catholicism, anarchism, pacifism, Marxism, and ecology, always through the lens of literature. He was also an early supporter of Ginsberg and Kerouac, as well as of Gary Snyder, Robert Duncan, and other mid-century West Coast poets of note.

By the time Allen Ginsberg met Timothy Leary, Allen was already steeped in Eastern philosophy via his poetry and art studies. In fact, it was Allen who first introduced Kerouac to Buddhist texts by suggesting that he read D.T. Suzuki's essays on Buddhism in the spring of 1953. By January 1954, after many travels and a great deal of rejection for his writing, Kerouac began earnestly studying Buddhism while living in the attic of Neal and Carolyn Cassady's house in San Jose. Soon after, Kerouac hit upon his Buddhist-influenced, guiding literary principle of "spontaneous prose" and, through his books and essays, became the unofficial ambassador for Buddhism to American youth.

In Copenhagen, Leary built his case slowly and persuasively, moving toward the final unveiling of his psilocybin experiments. But first he had to lay the groundwork for the "game-playing" philosophy that drove his theories. Always a master communicator, Leary told the crowd that aside from the pure physiological responses of reflex and muscular movement, all behavior is learned. Because behavior is learned, he continued, it must be culturally determined. Finally, because we learn behavior through our culture, we are essentially learning to play "the game" that surrounds us. The game of life. Or life as game. Leary was aware that this conclusion would seem shocking and frivolous to the crowd of scientists; however, he barreled forward. To extend the "game" metaphor: if this was a boxing match, Leary's gloves were off.

Leary proceeded to say that, just like baseball and football, all "learned artifactual sequences which define roles, rules, goals, rituals, and which involve special languages" are games. That list included religion and politics, along with psychology, psychiatry, and all their diagnoses. In fact, he insisted, the "play-games" (e.g., baseball and football) are superior to the "not-called-games" of psychiatry and psychology. Using baseball as his primary model, Leary praised the sport's ability to predict behavior based on quantifiable statistics: RBIs, ERAs, and so forth. Moving from the "behavorial science" of baseball to the "behavior-change" model it represented, Leary praised the way baseball teams understood the "cosmic lesson of percentage: that the greatest players get on the average one hit in three tries," and similarly, no team can dominate every year. He also remarked on the fact that baseball players and coaches understood that they needed to work together in their given environment (the baseball field) and practice constantly to achieve their desired outcomes.

"But only the rare Westerner we call 'mystic,'" Leary continued, "sees clearly that life is a game. And the rest spend their days struggling with roles and rules and goals and concepts of games which are implicit and confusedly not seen as games."

As Leary saw it, the root of Western psychological disorder was that people didn't accept that life was a game. In fact, life was a series of many games. The family game. The race game. The nationality game. The ego game. The religion game. Even "the Timothy Leary game." Each situation called for a different game; learn to accept that you were constantly playing multiple roles in an ever shifting series of games, and life would seem less puzzling and more enjoyable. Thus, Westerners would be less fraught with neuroses. At that point, Leary also leveled the antiestablishment charge that "The men who run the games think that they can't afford to have them seen as a game." This indictment was leveled at psychotherapists (his immediate audience) and, in a much larger sense, the monotheistic "Judaic-Christian tradition" that was "manipulating, predicting, controlling . . . breeding helplessness."

Once the problems were made clear, Leary set out to provide a solution: "applied mysticism." The first step was to get outside the game. Cut yourself off from your daily rituals of geography, language, and comfort. This disengagement was often experienced by people who suffered greatly (e.g., psychiatrist, neurologist, and Holocaust survivor Viktor Frankl) or lived in foreign cultures (e.g., anthropologist Margaret Mead), or even by those who lived in "monastic cells" (here, Leary might have mentioned one of the psychedelic precursors, St. Anthony). However, for most Westerners, Leary continued, the most efficient means for subverting game structures was to take drugs. In case anyone was unclear about what he meant when he referred to "CA drugs," Leary explicitly stated that these drugs were LSD, mescaline, and psilocybin.

The genie had left bottle.

Leary quickly acknowledged that there was not enough "neuro-physiological" data to describe the process and impact of a hallucinogenic experience. However, there were countless metaphors to describe the experience. In other words, literary craft would pick up where science was not yet prepared to tread. Here, Leary referenced a concept Huxley had introduced in his own talk: reducing valves. Reducing valves were mental programs that limited the number of responses one has to stimuli, thus automatically categorizing them in familiar ways. In other words, our previously understood games overruled our capacity to assimilate brave, new games. Consciousness-altering drugs, Leary argued, unplugged those limiting programs and expanded the capacity of one's reducing valves. The most efficient way to cure the anguish of having overconstricting reducing valves that overemphasized the importance of a single game or, worse, made one unable to play any game at all, was, in Leary's words, "drug-induced satori."

The problem was that the West had no ritual for such psychic, visionary expansion. Instead, Westerners fell back on the known and accepted games that prized external authority (law, medicine, even bohemian "back-alley secrecy") over individual seeking. Now, Leary was reaching his conclusion: He and his team were working on theories and processes toward developing a new game. The organizing principle of their mission was equality. Equality in determining the "role, rule, ritual, goal, language, commitment . . . in the explicit contractual definition of the real, the good, the true, the logical. . . . Equality of the right to speak and to have access to relevant information."

He and his team at the Center for Personality Research at Harvard University were busy putting this new egalitarian study into play. The process was twofold. On one end, they would focus on how Americans from various backgrounds integrated, or resisted integrating, psilocybin experiences into their lives. On the other, they would study the potential of psilocybin as a tool for criminal rehabilitation.

Leary proceeded to explain the testing they had undertaken. The number of subjects they had tested on was broken down into categories: male (124), female (43); internationally distinguished intellectuals, scholars, and artists (26), medical doctors (10), professional intellectuals (73), nonprofessional normals (21), drug addicts (27), and inmates in a state prison (10). He reemphasized the principles of equality governing the study as well as the importance of set and setting in maximizing the benefits of the experience. He noted that preliminary findings were too vast to summarize in this particular presentation; however, the first conclusion that they had reached was that "the psilocybin experience is pleasant and educational." Using the categories that were provided subjects on their report forms, Leary stated that 73% of subjects reported the experience as very pleasant or ecstatic; 95% had learned something or had tremendous insights; 91% were eager to take the drug again; and 77% thought that the experience had changed their lives for the better. Additionally, three out of four subjects reported happy and insightful reactions.

At the time of this paper, Leary's Concord Prison Experiment was only five months old; it would continue for another year and a half. Leary had been approached by members of the Department of Legal Medicine who wanted to involve Harvard graduate students in prisoner rehabilitation. Faced with a 70% recidivism rate across the Massachusetts prison system, Concord's warden was willing to try anything that might help. The premise of the study was as simple as the goal was dauntingly high: Could a properly planned and executed psilocybin experience lower recidivism rates among inmates at Concord Prison?

Because mushrooms were a drug, Leary needed approval from the prison psychiatrist before he could begin the study. The psychiatrist, Dr. Madison Presnell, was the first African American psychiatrist that Leary had ever met. Leary had picked up Ginsberg's hipster reverence for all things black, thus in an April 13 letter to Ginsberg, Leary reports, "The psychiatrist, naturally, is a Negro. Christ after what I've learned this last year I've started drinking chocolate milk." Exactly a month after sending that letter, Dr. Presnell and his wife would take psilocybin at Tim's house along with Gunther Weil and Ralph Metzner. Exactly two weeks after that, Leary, Weil, and Metzner walked into Concord Prison equipped with a record player, tape recorder, art books, and enough mushrooms for all three of them and five prisoners. The Concord Experiment had begun.

Because Concord was just getting started, Leary's Copenhagen presentation was not meant to be a comprehensive statement of findings. Rather, it was meant to show the processes that his team was undertaking toward gathering concrete clinical data. And, as with any researcher at the outset of a major project, he was enthusiastic about the potential. Their theories were in place. They were actively testing subjects. So far, the short-term feedback was reaffirming their thesis. Psilocybin had major potential as a drug that would benefit mankind spiritually and mentally. The question they were, as yet, unable to answer was whether a change in consciousness predicated a positive change in behavior. Did it make people happier? More well-adjusted? Less likely to commit crimes or turn into drug addicts?

Leary concluded his talk by saying that their progress was slow, but their work would continue despite opposition from doubters within the medical, prison, and academic establishment. "Next season will reveal how well we have played our game." In the end, however, he wanted to make clear that this game, the psilocybin-testing game, the Concord Prison Experiment game, the Timothy Leary game, was only temporary. Their game was as ephemeral as any other game played from time immemorial. It was a fleeting game, because it was a human game, and the one thing he had learned without a doubt was that "anger and anxiety are irrelevant because you see your small game in the context of the great evolutionary game which no one can win and no one can lose."

Fallout at Harvard

Copenhagen might have been a bold victory for Leary on a personal level, but it was the first major chink in his professional reputation. Another Harvard psychology lecturer named Herbert Kelman was in the audience for Tim's talk. He summed up his response: "The overall reaction I had, and I then checked it with other people, the general reaction that I heard to Tim's talk was that it was a kind of incoherent rambling. Basically a paean to the drug experience. I couldn't find anything of substance there. It was rather shocking. I am not prone to making diagnoses but I remember one Danish psychologist saying it sounded like the talk of someone who had been on drugs for a long time."

Another group of psychologists told Tim that he had "set Danish psychology back twenty years."

Until the Copenhagen speech, Leary's professional/academic transgressions had stayed within the womb of the Harvard campus. He had certainly generated a heady mix of adulation and resentment in his short time there, but the issues remained local, and Leary was given space to experiment based on his academic credentials. However, Leary's intellectual leaps at Harvard were mainly of the non-quantifiable variety; his Concord experiments were an attempt to remedy that, to gather hard scientific data. But, as of Copenhagen, there was no data to present. Instead, Leary fell back on the language he had begun developing to explain the psychedelic experience: a mix of psychology, poetry, Eastern mysticism, and doe-eyed optimism. While that language played well with the poets and artists within his orbit, it didn't hold water with psychologists. In Copenhagen he was surrounded by his professional peers—and to many of them he sounded like a misguided loon. Leary had certainly known that would be the case, but he had also spent the past several months taking psychedelics with the cream of the New York City (and international) avant-garde art scene. The lines were getting blurry, and it was clear that Leary now saw his role as a balance between revolutionary philosopher and scientist. The question remained: What was the balance? How much science and how much revolution?

At Copenhagen, Leary still believed that he could reconcile those two postures. In his terms, he could "play the game" based on whatever role was necessary at a given time. He could be a scientist with the scientists, and a revolutionary with the revolutionaries. Leary was now living out one of the primary theories of his professional career: game-playing. Unfortunately, he was also letting both sides down. In his first major public presentation for the Psilocybin Project, it was clear that the psychologists didn't buy Leary's mystic, unquantifiable drug rap. With that professional validation in jeopardy, Leary's value in helping take these underground ideas into mainstream culture was also going to be limited. Ginsberg was already playing the role of ambassador to the counterculture; Leary was supposed to be the professional front man. Now that balance was shifting and no one could be sure where it would land.

After he left Copenhagen, Tim made a side trip to London before returning to the States. While there, he reconnected with William Burroughs. Burroughs would only stay in London a short time (its society was too similar to the United States for his comfort), but this connection gave Leary another chance to give psilocybin to the author. Burroughs' hallucinogen experience in Tangier had been completely negative. This time, however, Burroughs enjoyed himself. Together, they walked the streets of London while Bill held forth on everything from shady publishers to his favorite authors to his theories about drugs and the word virus. This positive psilocybin experience seemed to bode well for Burroughs' upcoming talk to the American Psychological Association.

The APA conference was held in New York City in September 1961. Leary had taken great pains to secure Burroughs' participation in his symposium on consciousness-altering drugs. Frank Barron and Gerald Heard were also involved. The room was packed and everyone was eager to hear what the outlaw writer and known drug addict would have to say.

To Leary's chagrin, Burroughs never mentioned psilocybin during his talk. Given his obsession with cut-ups, dream machines, and his experiences abroad, it is likely that his talk focused on those topics. But while this omission disappointed Leary, it didn't deter him from wanting to get Burroughs more deeply involved with the Project.

At the beginning of the fall 1961 semester, William Burroughs moved into Timothy Leary's attic in Newton Centre. While there, he kept largely to himself, staying up in the attic surrounded by the accoutrements of his art (cut-up magazines, photos, newspapers, etc.) and riding around in a discarded wheelchair that had been left up there. But Leary's Harvard experiments were not for Burroughs. He left abruptly, shortly after arriving, with barely a goodbye. It was clear that the iconoclastic writer was not on board with Leary's program. The final nail was hammered when Burroughs went back to New York City and published a letter denouncing the Psilocybin Project. In his words, "They steal, bottle, and dole out addictive love in eye-droppers of increased awareness of unpleasant or dangerous symptoms."

Allen Ginsberg summed up the division this way: "Bill had the idea that all this experimentation involved machinery, equipment, stroboscopes, electronic stuff, measurements. Where instead Tim's basic idea was no scientific measurement. So Bill was pissed off that there was no science in the sense of laboratories where you can really experiment with rats or something like that. So he thought that Leary was a horse's ass."

In a 1989 interview in *Pataphysics*, Leary himself summed up the situation by saying, "He thought we were a bunch of dumb bozos running around and trying to save the world with these drugs and he was very uh, rightfully cynical about what we were doing. He's a very scientific person. The only psychedelic he likes is marijuana. He never really liked other psychedelic drugs. Burroughs has forgotten more about drugs in his life than I've learned. . . . He's not the guy that goes around with a grin on his face saying peace and love. He's a very crusty, introverted guy with a very deep sense of humor."

Eventually, the two men would reconcile, and they would become quite close in later life. Burroughs even provided an introduction to a reprint of Leary's autobiography,

Flashbacks. But at this crucial juncture in Leary's emergence into the larger countercultural scene, Burroughs had dealt him a painful blow. Ironically, Burroughs' main argument paralleled those being leveled at Leary from the psychological establishment. He was simply not going about his work in a sufficiently scientific manner.

In February 1962, a series of articles about the Psilocybin Project began appearing in the school newspaper, *The Harvard Crimson*. On February 20, a student named Andrew T. Weil wrote an article titled *Better Than a Damn*. Since his Harvard days, Weil has become a major player in alternative, or integrative, medicine, which combines traditional Western medicine with a more holistic, natural, and preventive approach. His smiling, bearded visage can be seen on the cover of many best-selling books on related topics, and in 1994 he founded the Arizona Center for Integrative Medicine at University of Arizona. Weil's first book, *The Natural Mind*, was published in 1972 and had an emphasis on drugs and altered states of consciousness.

Weil's 1962 *Harvard Crimson* article focused on mescaline and revolved around a discussion of the drug in Aldous Huxley's *The Doors of Perception*. Of course, by that time, it was well known that Huxley was a supporter of Leary's work at Harvard. The article concludes with statements about the use of psilocybin in the Project. "Investigators of psilocybin at Harvard's Center for Research in Personality are unbounded in their enthusiasm for this new drug, reporting that it frequently increases powers of creative thinking in both artistic and scientific areas. A number of authors (Aldous Huxley, William Burroughs, Allen Ginsberg, and others) studied in the Harvard project found that their work benefited enormously from the influence of psilocybin, and preliminary investigations have indicated that the 'mushroom experience' may be of value in the rehabilitation of prisoners."

In the following issue of the *Crimson*, Leary and Richard Alpert felt compelled to immediately counter this article with a jointly written letter to the editor. In the letter, they acknowledged that Weil's article was a "gallant attempt to summarize a most difficult subject matter," but insisted that "clarification seems needed."

Their clarification was presented in three parts. The first part took issue with the idea that "Budda [*sic*] drugs (mescaline, psilocybin, LSD)" were useful for those looking to "escape from society." Rather, they insisted, "Confrontation, intense (and often painful) contact with reality more accurately characterize the experience." Next, they wanted to make clear that psilocybin research was only one facet of the Center for Research in Personality. There were many other studies being carried out that were of equal value. Finally, they stated that they were far from "unbounded in their enthusiasm" for the drugs. "Unbounded concern would be a more accurate diagnosis," they wrote. "Concern for the many problems created by consciousness-expanding drugs. Problems of conceptualization. Problems of measurement. Problems of application and follow-up. Problems of interpretation. Problems of control."

They ended their letter on an optimistic note, "Consciousness-expanding drugs may someday contribute to human welfare," but they had clearly acknowledged the challenges they were facing. Increasingly, those challenges were coming from inside Harvard.

On March 15, an article by Robert E. Smith appeared under the title *Psychologists Disagree on Psilocybin Research*.

The article began unambiguously: "Members of the Center in Personality clashed yesterday in a dramatic meeting over the right of two colleagues to continue studies on the effects of psilocybin, a consciousness-expanding drug, on graduate student subjects. Opponents of the studies claimed that the project was run nonchalantly and irresponsibly and that alleged permanent injury to participants had been ignored or underestimated."

The article went on to describe an internal meeting within the Department of Social Relations in which the Project was severely questioned. Leary and Alpert were present at the meeting and defended their research; however they received little voice in the *Crimson* article. The largest section dedicated to their defense was titled "Take Drugs at Home."

Tellingly, the most vocal denunciation of the research came from social psychology lecturer Herbert C. Kelman, the man who had described Leary's Copenhagen presentation as "incoherent rambling." During the internal meeting, he was quoted by the *Crimson* as saying, "I wish I could treat this as scholarly disagreement, but this work violates the values of the academic community. The program has an anti-intellectual atmosphere. Its emphasis is on pure experience, not on verbalizing findings. It is an attempt to reject most of what the psychologist tries to do." Kelman also charged that the Project was creating an insider-vs.-outsider division within the graduate student community: those who had taken the drugs and participated in the project and those who hadn't. In other words, the hip versus the square.

Kelman responded to the article by clarifying that he was not opposed to the research. Rather, he was concerned about "the effects of the Psilocybin Program on our gradu-ate training." He also lashed out at the *Crimson* for writing an article about a private, interdepartmental meeting. "It is unfortunate that other people, including a representative from the *Crimson*, were present at this internal meeting. This was definitely contrary to the intentions of the orga-nizers of the meeting."

Despite Kelman's protests, the *Crimson* (under the edi-torial direction of Andrew Weil)—and, thus, the entire Har-vard community—was now involved in the debate. A flurry of articles and letters to the editor from both sides of the debate would follow.

On March 19, Norman Zinberg, M.D., a lecturer on so-cial relations, made a measured and rational argument of caution with regard to psilocybin testing. In response to a letter published two days earlier by "Mr. Alpert and Mr. Leary" (no mention of their academic credentials and posi-tions), Zinberg zeroes in on their admission that the psy-chological changes catalyzed by psilocybin can be "positive or negative depending on the individual's response to the experiment." Of even greater concern was the subject's abil-ity to return to these newly opened regions—both positive and, troublingly, negative—after the initial experience.

Dr. Zinberg points out that some people will be more profoundly affected by the drug. Particularly for those in late adolescence "and even early adulthood" (no doubt a reference to their graduate student population), he noted, the ramifications could be farther reaching and more haz-ardous, because their "systems of controls have not yet completely integrated." He also cautioned that this at-risk population was the same one most drawn to participating in such experiments. His greatest concern, he stated, was that adequate screening needed to be done on all subjects. He posed the question, "Are the subjects screened in such a way as to make sure that none of them fits into the category of people whose immediate and later reactions indicate that they may have had psychological experiences by way of the psilocybin which have been psychologically harmful?"

Another March 19 article makes the split within the faculty and graduate student population even clearer. "*The nature of the research:* this is the issue that has virtually split open the staff of the Center for Research in Personality. The most vociferous critics to psilocybin research believe that it is not conducted for scientific purposes, and that the experimenters are interested in experience rather than reporting their results. A major element of the defense of research contends that scientific method and reportable results are the goal of the research. But a second element of the defense claims that experience is a legitimate goal of inquiry, and that psilocybin should be used in order to heighten perception so that the experimenters may gain new insight into personality by perceiving behavior more clearly while under influence of these drugs."

Interestingly, this second argument in favor of research is a return to the psychomimetic qualities of the drug that had initially fascinated Dr. Humphry Osmond, Dr. John Smythies, and the Saskatchewan researchers. Given the fact that they were using graduate students, among other people, as test subjects, this argument could only hurt the Project's case. Surely Harvard wouldn't stand by while their graduate students were administered drugs that gave them, even temporarily, the experience of being schizophrenics or having other mental illnesses. That was a far cry from the rehabilitative or creativity-enhancing models that the Project had gravitated toward.

Around this same time, Leary handwrote a rather frantic letter to Allen Ginsberg with the no-nonsense opening:

Dear Allen—

Business

Accounting

Need questionnaires + reports. Some hostile pressure is developing "analysts reporting at cocktail parties that I'm running homosexual dope parties" !!!!!

So—

We're getting very scientific!

Leary's urgency wasn't an exaggeration. On March 21, the *Crimson* published an article titled "State Will Investigate Research on Psilocybin." "The drugs control section of the Massachusetts Department of Public Health has launched an investigation of research involving psilocybin at Harvard's Center for Research in Personality. Alfred J. Murphy, senior food and drug inspector at the Department, will meet with David C. McClelland, head of the center, and others concerned with the consciousness-expanding drug beginning today. Health officials say they did not know of the use of the drug at the University until reading an article on it in Friday's Boston Herald."

Andrew Weil and the *Crimson* had broken the story of the conflicts within Harvard's Center for Research in Personality. Now the issue had spilled out into the mainstream media and filtered out to the first of many governmental agencies that would dog Timothy Leary the rest of his life.

When there were no major developments in the story to report, the *Crimson* generated a little heat of its own.

On March 23, 1962, under the title "University Has Ignored Work with Psilocybin," some history was brought to the forefront: "Experiments with a similar consciousness-expanding drug, LSD, were conducted by researchers at the University in the early 1950s. At that time, the experiments got out of control, with LSD even being put into punch bowls to test its effects on people at a party. After one such experiment, a University student was almost killed when, under the effects of LSD he walked onto Huntington Ave. at the height of the rush hour 'believing he was God and nothing could touch him.'"

There was a temporary media cease-fire between the two parties once it was deemed by Harvard and the Massachusetts Department of Public Health that "In future experiments, a licensed medical doctor will be required to be in attendance while the consciousness-expanding psilocybin pills are administered." This was necessary because the drug was officially classified as "unknown" (at that time, both peyote and mescaline were deemed "harmful" and were thus illegal), placing it under the provisions of Boston's "harmful drug law."

At this point, the psilocybin, or, as Leary had early deemed it, "the ring of power" was officially taken from his complete control. On April 22, Leary gave a version of his Copenhagen consciousness-expanding talk at Harvard under the auspices of the Harvard Humanists. The talk had nothing to do with the psychomimetic properties of hallucinogens, or their potential for rehabilitating criminals. It had everything to do with the mystical potentialities that were now Leary's main focus. The *Crimson* covered the talk: "Consciousness, [Leary] said, is like a phonograph record on which the conceptual mind takes up only five or six grooves. The other grooves on the record can only be reached by cultivation of 'internal experience. The pantheistic tradition of the East supports such mystical experience,' Leary observed, whereas Western habits of thought were more concerned with external action and manipulation of the environment. 'I am convinced that the monotheistic tradition is dangerous. I am scared that we are moving towards an anthill civilization. Unless the aim of life is experience, we are mere puppets playing out roles in complex games. Life is becoming mechanical.'" This talk also, controversially, introduced sexuality into the debate. Leary likened modern Western sex as "a game in which two rubber dolls sleep with each other." He also introduced his notion of the "fifth Freedom, freedom of consciousness." "The internal philosophy implies a new view of science. Orthodox science focuses on manipulation. There is another approach: coming to love the species we wish to understand. Because such science deals with the non-conceptual, the researcher must often speak in metaphorical terms."

It was apparent that Leary had no intention of backing off. If anything, expanding his arguments to the areas of sexuality and even nutrition ("a game in which robots digest food") were bound to stir up even more controversy. But by this time Leary was becoming more familiar, perhaps even comfortable, with controversy. And as for losing control of the psilocybin pills, Leary had recently begun experimenting with a new drug that blasted open the doors of consciousness even more powerfully: LSD. And there was a new inhabitant in his attic at Newton Centre, an Englishman from outside the Harvard community named Michael Hollingshead, who had enough LSD to keep them supplied for a good, long time.

Allen Abroad

On March 23, 1961, a year before Leary discovered LSD, Allen Ginsberg and Peter Orlovsky left New York City on the *S.S. America* bound for Paris and the Beat Hotel. They assumed they would meet Burroughs there, but—always full of strange surprises—Burroughs had checked out and left no forwarding address. They would eventually connect with Burroughs in Tangier, but a combination of drugs, hangers-on, and his obsession with cut-ups had turned his already confounding personality into something alien, cold, and impenetrable. Peter Orlovsky—the most actively heterosexual and least cultured—took the brunt of Burroughs' wrath. Eventually, Peter was so torn apart by Burroughs that he left for Istanbul alone. Allen was heartbroken, but he had seen the abuse Peter was taking and felt frozen and powerless to help him. Burroughs was not above attacking Allen either. At one point Bill lashed out at him, "If we cut you up, who would we find inside? Lionel Trilling?"

Burroughs was aware that Allen had conflicted feelings about his former Columbia professor Lionel Trilling; a mix of respect for an early mentor mixed with a desire to break away from the conservative poetic line that Trilling represented. But Burroughs was ruthless in his mission of "cutting-up" his friends to see what made them tick—no sensitive spots or soft underbellies were off-limits.

In a strange twist of synchronicity, when Peter left Tangier he passed Leary while going through customs. Tim was headed to see Allen and Bill. Peter was running away from them as fast as possible.

Allen wrote about the situation with Peter in a letter to Lawrence Ferlinghetti: "We had big arguments about future of universe in Tangier. He wanted it to be sex-love, Burroughs wanted it to be unknown Artaud mutation out of bodies. I was undecided, confused. I still am except Burroughs seems to have killed 'Hope' in any known form. The Exterminator is serious. Peter wanted innocence and sex apocalypse. It got very serious. I was vomiting."

Allen and Peter would eventually reconnect on a street corner in Tel Aviv and continue on for an extended stay in India. It would be more than two years before Allen was back on U.S. soil, during which time Leary's psychedelic campaign went from campus experiment to headline-making controversy.

While Allen had been living out the full bohemian poet existence for years (doing drugs, living a rootless existence, disrobing at poetry readings, playing fast and loose with sex), he never particularly looked the part. By 1961, poetry readings were a staple of Beatnik enclaves in cities around the United States, and black clothes, bongos, berets, sandals, and wispy beards were part of the look. Allen Ginsberg and *Howl* were almost single-handedly responsible for loosing this scene and its mores onto America. But, somehow, Allen still looked like a conservative Columbia student. His hair was short, usually parted to one side, and his button-down shirts were squared away with a belt. His glasses gave him a studious air, and his intense gaze betrayed only hints of his free-spirited existence.

Strangely enough, Allen Ginsberg—core member of the Beat writers—never actually looked like a Beatnik. However by the time Allen set foot in San Francisco in August 1963, he had surpassed the Beatnik look completely, moving straight from 1950s buttoned-up fashion to prototype of the 1960s hippie. During his two and a half years abroad, Allen had allowed his dark black hair to grow down to his shoulders, filling out everywhere except the pate, which time and genetics had already stolen as a possibility. He now wore a full black beard too. Before returning to the states, Allen wrote a letter to Gregory Corso saying, "I be there, I guess September? With white silk suit? What'll I do with my long hair and beard." The "white silk suit" was a nod to Corso's penchant for expensive, showy traveling clothes that he could ill afford. As for Allen's "long hair and beard," they would stay. While living in India from 1962 to 1963, Allen had also taken a liking to the loose, flowing garb worn there.

Hair, beard, drugs, hand-woven clothes and all, by 1963, Allen Ginsberg looked like Allen Ginsberg. Which is to say, the Allen Ginsberg image that America would know for the rest of his life. Even after his Buddhist guru, Chögyam Trungpa Rinpoche, challenged Allen to disarm his ego by cutting off his beard and hair and wearing a tie, Allen could never completely shake this "hippie look" that he had pioneered.

Allen's travels abroad in the early '60s would take him to such destinations as Paris, Tangier, Greece, Israel, and

Nairobi. However, his longest stay on this trip was also the most influential on his thinking and writing. Allen Ginsberg's time in India would shape his worldview almost as much as his Spanish Harlem Blakean vision. In fact, Allen often used his audiences with Indian gurus and holy men as attempts to come to terms with the Blake vision. Every chance he got, Allen—reunited and typically side-by-side with Peter Orlovsky—would press spiritual leaders for their interpretations of his vision, as well as their opinions on drugs. Most of them responded the same way: drugs were not the path toward lasting spiritual enlightenment.

The most famous—and Ginsbergian—example of Allen's intense desire to seek counsel on his obsessions during this period took place while Allen and Peter were visiting Gary Snyder and Joanne Kyger in the Himalayas. While there, Allen, Peter, Gary, and Joanne were granted an audience with the Dalai Lama.

Gary Snyder and Ginsberg had become fast friends during the heat of the "San Francisco Poetry Renaissance." Snyder was one of the poets who participated in the famous Six Gallery Reading. He was also famously depicted as Japhy Ryder in Jack Kerouac's novel *The Dharma Bums*. As a result, Snyder had become a nationally known icon of the Beat generation right along with Kerouac and Ginsberg. In many ways, he had taken the mantle of San Francisco poet, intellectual, outdoorsman, and student of Eastern cultures from the long-reigning king of the scene, Kenneth Rexroth. Much like Ginsberg, Gary Snyder had been gone when the main heat of the Beat media frenzy was taking place. He had left San Francisco to study Buddhism in Kyoto and spent long periods of time overseas in Japan. During one trip from Japan back to San Francisco in 1958, Snyder met a young woman named Joanne Kyger who had been studying Zen meditation and poetry. By that time, Gary Snyder was already a legend in both of those circles. Gary and Joanne struck up a romance, and when Gary went back to Kyoto in 1959, Joanne followed shortly thereafter. In a ceremony held at the American consulate in Kobe, they became husband and wife.

As with many people Allen and Peter spent time with on their travels, the couple exasperated Joanne. Gary's longer friendship with the men, his intense focus on his Buddhist studies, and, undoubtedly, the fact that he was a man and thus granted more respect than Joanne, gave him a higher tolerance for their eccentricities. For her part, Joanne recorded some scathing observations of the two men during their time together in India. Among other shortcomings, she noted that Allen gulped down his food and Peter never waited for anyone else before he began eating. Both men were also generally obsessed with finding, using, and discussing drugs.

At the time of their visit, Western culture was as strange and unknown to the Dalai Lama and his followers as Tibetan culture was to Americans. In fact, much of the information they received about the outside world came through the pages of *Reader's Digest* and *Time* magazine. Perhaps due to their still-new mission to spread the teachings of Tibetan Buddhism beyond their homeland, there was very little screening of visitors who arrived for an audience with the Dalai Lama. Apparently, the Dalai Lama had missed the issue of *Time* magazine where Allen Ginsberg was excoriated as a false prophet of the new generation. A photo in the magazine showed him clean-cut and bespectacled with the insinuating caption "Calculated Squalor." "Howl" was described as "an interminable sewer of a poem that sucks in all the fraudulence, malignity and unmeaning slime of modern life and spews them with tremendous momentum into the reader's mind." The Beats were summed up thus: "They prefer to wear beards and blue jeans, avoid soap and water, live in dingy tenements or, weather permitting, take to the road as holy hoboes, pilgrims to nowhere. Most of them adore Negroes, junkies, jazzmen and Zen. The more extreme profess to smoke pot, eat peyote, sniff heroin, practice perversion."

When Allen, Peter, Gary, and Joanne met the Dalai Lama, he was only twenty-seven years old. His Holiness reclined on a velvet couch while he received them. In short order, Allen was pumping the Dalai Lama for his opinions of psychedelic drugs. The Dalai Lama smiled sagely and replied, "If you take LSD, can you see what's in that briefcase?" While they were undoubtedly impressed by this koan-like answer, Allen and Peter were undeterred in their questioning. They raved to the Dalai Lama about their drug experiences, wanting to simultaneously "turn on" the holy man to psychedelics and learn his opinions on their potential for enlightening users. As with most holy men they encountered, the Dalai Lama replied that, if anything, drugs were a distraction from true enlightenment.

The Dalai Lama instructed them that drugs could, at best, provide a temporary respite from one's ego (the source of much suffering); however, it was not ultimately a path to enlightenment. He did seem interested in Allen's rap about how psychedelics corresponded to different meditative states—even going so far as to passively agree to receive psilocybin from Timothy Leary. However, this agreement was most likely based on the force of Allen's personality rather than a sincere interest in psilocybin on the part of the Dalai Lama.

Eventually, Gary felt the need to interrupt Allen's raving. "The inside of your mind is just as boring as everyone else's," chided Snyder, so did Allen really have to keep unloading its contents on everyone, including one of the world's most respected holy men? At that point, Snyder was finally able to turn the conversation away from drugs toward questions regarding meditation posture and breathing techniques.

Once again, Joanne's impression of Allen and Peter's self-centeredness drove her to lash out. In a letter to a friend back in the States, she wrote, "[Allen] wants to get instantly enlightened and can't stand sitting down. He came to India to find a spiritual teacher. But I think he actually believes he knows it all, but just wishes he *Felt* better about it."

Allen's time abroad forced him to confront and question every belief and passion that had obsessed him since his late adolescence. In Tangier, both Timothy Leary and William Burroughs proclaimed that poetry, as Allen knew it, was dead. Burroughs insisted that anyone could make poetry, simply by cutting up pre-written poems and other printed materials and pasting them back together in new configurations. Not only could a person become a poet that way, Burroughs argued, but they could become their favorite poet. Cut and paste Rimbaud, and you could write a new Rimbaud poem that gave more insight into the words and poet than one could ever gain by straightforward reading and study. Even Shakespeare could be disassembled, reconfigured and embodied this way. Timothy Leary also insisted that poetry was done. After all, he had seen uneducated

convicts write wild poems under the influence of psilocybin: what made trained poets any superior?

While in India, Allen's views on the potential of drugs
as a path toward enlightenment were also routinely dismissed by holy men. Many denied his Blakean vision as
mere distraction as well. While staying in Bombay, Allen
and Peter were barraged by writers and journalists trying to find out more about these strange, fascinating, and
now internationally famous Beat poets. Even while Allen
questioned every belief he held dear, he was compelled to
hold forth on the tenets of the "New Vision" that the core
Beats had been working toward since the 1940s. Wherever they went in India, Allen and Peter regularly met
with local poets and writers, unfailingly causing a sensation that furthered the notorious reputation of the Beats.
One of Allen's most poignant experiences while in India
was smoking pot with *sadhus* who oversaw the burning of
corpses. At these *ghats*, corpses would be garlanded with
flowers, laid out on wooden blocks on top of wood chips,
and ceremoniously burned. Allen was taught about a spiritual practice called *smasana sadhanas* in which Tantric
sadhus meditated with skulls and corpses, sometimes
even sitting on them and sleeping with them, to overcome
their fear of death. Allen was fascinated by the practice,
and spent a great deal of time smoking pot, meditating,
and observing the sadhus while corpses were incinerated
in front of him.

In a letter to Gary Snyder he described the scene,
"Humans eyes & lips blackened & crackling in flame,
hair smelling with human fat dripping from neck as skin
turns bright red & burns. . . . Boys poking the corpses with
bamboo poles, a lawyer's shoulders and head seared and

puffed up over the flames, pushed by attendants so it falls into the central red coals. . . . Ten feet away group of sad-dhus & devotees around improvised mandir with flowers & incense and prasad on a cloth, shouting loud Boom Boom Mahadeva! lifting faces to sky eyes closed hands clasped to mouth as if in prayer, except in their hands little red clay pipesful of Ganja—passing around the pipe with great mantras. . . ."

Not all of the spiritual leaders that Allen consulted encouraged him to give up on his Blakean vision though. In fact, in Brindaban, he was encouraged to take William Blake as his saint. Instead of trying to come to terms with and move past his obsession with the Blake vision, Allen was told to embrace it, to pray to Blake, to focus his devo-tion on Blake. After all, Allen was told, the figure he wor-shipped was less important than the process of uncovering the love inherent in feeling such devotion.

But Allen didn't buy that either. At this point, he had spent fifteen years chasing down his Blakean vision to the point of madness. While he would continue chanting Blake, even making passionate recordings of Blake's poems, over the years, India had helped him break the spell the vision had cast over him all these years. He would later comment, "The remarkable thing is that I stupefied myself from 1948 to 1963. A long time—that's fifteen years preoccupied with one single thought."

On May 26, 1963, Allen and Peter separated in Cal-cutta. Despite Peter's protestations, Allen had accepted an offer from Robert Creeley to teach during July and August at a poetry conference at Vancouver University. A rift had grown between Peter and Allen during their time in India. Although both of them did drugs, Peter was unable to keep

his use to a manageable level and had been regularly shoot-
ing morphine and smoking opium to the point of addiction.
As a result, he was incommunicative and had also acquired
a new set of friends that Allen didn't like. It was time, again,
for the two men to go their separate ways.

Allen arrived at the university in Vancouver and immediately began sharing all the insights he had gained in
India. He did his best to turn the poetry conference into a
love fest: preaching about sexual liberation, touching and
hugging everyone, openly weeping with joy, and telling
anyone who would listen about his experiences. In addition
to his hand-woven clothing, Allen brought back an Indian
harmonium, which he used to accompany himself in the
Hare Krishna mantra. He chanted regularly at the conference, giving North America early exposure to another practice that would become indelibly linked with the 1960s.
The chants and harmonium would stay a part of Allen's
poetry reading repertoire for the rest of his life.

Along with such poets as Robert Creeley, Denise
Levertov, Robert Duncan and—at Allen's insistence—Philip
Whalen, Charles Olson taught at the Vancouver conference.
Olson had become another key poet contact in Leary's inner
circle, and now Ginsberg and Olson were reunited in the
name of their first passion: poetry. While they were both
still part of the White Hand Society, Timothy Leary was
now surrounded by dozens of like-minded colleagues and
spiritual, artistic, and underground contacts that he hadn't
had at the start of the decade. For better or worse, these are
the relationships that most influenced Leary's next phase.

Allen had helped introduce Tim to the counterculture with which he would forever be linked, but both men
were driven, intensely social creatures with projects that

demanded all of their attention. For Allen, those projects revolved around poetry and social change. For Tim, they revolved around spreading the gospel of psychedelics and, increasingly, staying one step ahead of the law.

Enter LSD, Exit Harvard

Shortly after William S. Burroughs vacated the attic at Newton House another colorful character moved into the room at Leary's invitation. This man was also eccentric and mysterious, and came from a checkered past. Unlike Burroughs though, this new resident brought with him a mayonnaise jar filled with 4,975 200-milligram doses of Albert Hofmann–synthesized LSD. Until his arrival, Timothy Leary had never tried acid.

Michael Hollingshead had come to New York City while working as an executive secretary for the Institute of British-American Cultural Exchange. While there, he persuaded a physician friend, John Beresford, to write to Sandoz Laboratories to request LSD for, depending on who tells the story, either bone-marrow experiments or a study of how spiders spin webs under the effects of the drug. The reasons given for the request are less important than the fact that the drugs were promptly delivered. At that time, Sandoz was still eager to find applications for Hofmann's puzzling creation. They sent Beresford a gram of pure LSD along with an invoice for $285. Hollingshead and Beresford diluted the LSD with water and confectioner's sugar, and the hallucinogenic paste was put into an empty mayonnaise jar. This jar of paste became Hollingshead's calling card to the Leary camp.

Hollingshead had begun his journey toward Harvard after taking his own mind-melting trip in Greenwich Village. He had eaten waxed paper containing a massive dose, roughly 1,000 milligrams, of the LSD paste and was completely shaken by the trip. He managed to contact Aldous Huxley after the trip in an attempt to make sense of his experiences, and Huxley, in turn, referred Hollingshead to Leary, telling him that Leary was, "a splendid fellow. If there is any one single investigator in America worth seeing, it is Dr. Leary."

With Huxley's recommendation as entrée, Leary agreed to have lunch with Hollingshead at Harvard. At that time, Leary assumed that LSD was the same as psilocybin and found the man's raving off-putting and even suspect. He wasn't sure what Hollingshead was after, but with the increasing resistance he was facing at Harvard, the last thing he needed was a crazed Englishman thrown into the mix. It took a follow-up letter from Hollingshead begging for help—even threatening to kill himself due to his disordered state of mind—to convince Tim to bring the man to Newton Centre. Tim was, after all, a psychologist. And this man seemed to need the particular sort of therapy that he was now claiming as his specialty. By the time Hollingshead arrived at Newton Centre, Leary had contacted a mutual friend who warned him against getting tied up with Hollingshead. In the man's words, Hollingshead was a "no-good, two-bit English con man." But, if anything, this only further encouraged Leary. After all, criminal rehabilitation was also a part of his experiments.

Upon moving into the house, Hollingshead soon became an integral part of the proceedings. He tried Leary's psilocybin, of course, but regarded it as "the child's toy of the Indians." Every chance he got, Hollingshead nudged Leary to try the LSD paste. Much as he had when Litwin initially suggested that he try psilocybin, Leary resisted: "Everything I had heard about the lysergic acid sounded ominous to me. The mushrooms and peyote had been grown naturally in the ground and had been used for thousands of years in wise Indian cultures. LSD, on the other hand, was a laboratory product and had quickly fallen into the hands of doctors and psychiatrists. Then too, I was scared."

But of course, Leary eventually relented. One night, he and George Litwin, along with jazz trumpeter Maynard Ferguson and his wife, a former model named Flo, all sampled the LSD paste together. The experience was just as paradigm-shifting as Leary's first forays into psilocybin had been. If mushrooms were a pistol blast to the consciousness, LSD was a nuclear explosion: "Michael's heaping spoonful had flipped consciousness out beyond life into the whirling dance of pure energy, where nothing existed except whirring vibrations, and each illusory form was simply a different frequency." The morning after his first trip, Leary managed to fulfill his duties by going out to Concord prison to meet with prisoners. But he was clearly a changed man. Before acid Leary had talked about playing "the game"—the psychologist game, the Harvard game, the professor game, the Timothy Leary game—but with the introduction of LSD, those games no longer seemed useful. In fact, they seemed ludicrous.

Why bother playing those games at all? What sort of situation had he gotten himself into? What was the purpose?

In a prophetic vision during his first trip, Leary saw himself as, "the pathetic clown, the shallow, corny, twentieth-century American, the classic buffoon completely caught in a world of his own making." The Timothy Leary game, as he had structured it at Harvard, began to fray at the edges. And everyone around him could sense the change. Many of his close friends and colleagues were aware of the role that Michael Hollingshead was playing in Leary's transformation and regarded him with suspicion or outright disdain. Richard Alpert felt that "Hollingshead was a paranoid nut. Hollingshead was the closest to evil of most of the people I've ever met. I have this distinction between rascal and scoundrel. Timothy always stayed a rascal. Hollingshead was certainly a scoundrel."

Nonetheless, Leary regarded Hollingshead with something close to awe. Leary believed that for some cosmic reason Hollingshead and his magic paste had been delivered to his door. It was his responsibility to figure out why that had happened, to glean as much as he could from this man and this drug. And, to do so, Leary began to ingest copious amounts of LSD.

In April 1962, Tim helped facilitate a famous psychedelic experiment that came to be known as the Good Friday Experiment. The experiment was to be conducted and written up as a final dissertation by Walter Pahnke, a Harvard Ph.D. candidate in Philosophy of Religion. Pahnke was unusual in that he was already an M.D. Unfortunately, this credential didn't help when the group encountered resistance to its experiment from the man who had been put in charge of Leary's psilocybin supply, Dr. Dana Farnsworth. Conceding to administrative pressure, Leary had agreed to allow Farnsworth and the Harvard Medical Service to control their supply of psilocybin pills, and now Farnsworth was balking at being responsible for giving them to a group of students from the Andover Newton Theological Seminary, who were scheduled to take them inside the Marsh Chapel at Boston University. On Good Friday, no less. It was to be a double-blind experiment, with one group receiving psilocybin and the other receiving a placebo laced with nicotinic acid to mimic the onset of a trip. The purpose was to investigate whether psilocybin could induce an authentic religious experience.

Tim argued back and forth with Farnsworth, but the new keeper of the "rings of power" wouldn't budge. Eventually Leary circumvented the situation by recovering some pills he had given to a psychiatrist in Worcester and giving them to Pahnke to use. The experiment proceeded as planned. Thus, on Good Friday in 1962, a group of divinity students spent the day tripping on psilocybin inside a chapel on the campus of Boston University. The three-hour-long sermon that day was delivered by a black minister, Howard Thurman, who was a mentor to Martin Luther King. The group started out in the basement, but the subjcts were eventually led up to the small chapel where they heard it all: sermon, prayers, organ music, hymns. In *High Priest*, Leary describes the scene: "It was easy to tell who had taken the psychedelics. Ten students sat attentively like good worshippers. Facing the altar. Silent. The others were less conventional. Some lay on the benches—one lay on the floor. Some wandered around the chapel murmuring in prayer and wonderment. One chanted a hymn. One wandered to the altar and held his hands aloft. One sat at the organ bench and played weird, exciting chords."

The experiment was regarded by Leary and others as a success, confirming that hallucinogens were indeed a doorway into deeper religious experiences. Walter Pahnke was awarded his Ph.D. despite the fact that Harvard was less than thrilled that the experiment had gone on in defiance of their attempts to block it.

Leary may have been partly deaf, but he wasn't blind. Despite the outward success of the Good Friday Experiment, resistance from the administration and faculty was increasing and was covered closely by the school paper, which was now being monitored by larger mainstream newspapers. Meanwhile, his LSD trips were distancing him further from any sort of academic sense of purpose. It was clear that he now saw his mission as spiritual. The "miracle of Marsh Chapel" only reinforced this belief: "There was proof—scientific, experimental, statistical, objective. The sacred mushrooms, administered in a religious setting to people who were religiously motivated, did produce that rare, deep experience which men have sought for thousands of years through sacraments, through flagellation, prayer, renunciation. Psychedelic drugs were sacraments."

In the summer of 1962, Leary led a sort of psychedelic summer camp in Zihuatanejo, Mexico. He and Richard Alpert had spotted the quiet fishing village during a trip to Mexico in 1960. Along with millionaire Peggy Hitchcock, an ardent supporter who would play a pivotal role in the next phase of Leary's career, Leary and Alpert had scoped it out in the spring, after the Good Friday Experiment. The village was ideal: isolated, scarcely populated, tropical, and breathtakingly beautiful. Plus there was a hotel there, the Hotel Catalina, that was willing to rent them the entire place during July and August. It was perfect for their needs.

That July, a group of graduate students and Leary colleagues, along with Peggy Hitchcock and her brother,

Tommy Hitchcock, took up residence at the Hotel Catalina. Having long ago been stripped of their psilocybin pills, Leary traveled there with Hollingshead's mayonnaise jar, still filled with plenty of LSD paste. In a letter handwritten on Hotel Catalina stationary, mailed to Allen Ginsberg care of the American Express Company in Bombay, India, Leary described his life in Zihuatanejo: "I'm living serenely in this fishing village—listening to the surf and talking to the breeze—lying in the sand, feeling the pull-push of the waves. Very TAOIST. . . . From now on the campaign is over. No effort. Day to day living and sharing with the few close ones. Internal loyalties." In the same letter, Leary muses that, "We may be starting a move to India in the fall."

While he would remain at Harvard for another year, Leary clearly had one eye on the door. Having tasted communal living while in Zihuatanejo, none of the "campers" wanted to give it up just because they were back at school. Instead, Leary and Alpert, along with ten other people, including a male undergrad whom Alpert was pining for (despite the fact that the man's wife also lived with them), moved in together in a large house at 23 Kenwood Avenue in Newton Centre. Once again, Leary reported back to Ginsberg in India about their developments: "Mexico beach ashram tuned directly in to the current. Beautiful to see people growing like jungle flower-trees—radiance shining from faces and from bodies. We have a 10 bedroom . . . ashram in Newton. Meditation room with no doors. Do you get the messages?" Once again, he also floated out the idea of a move to India, "Litwins are back and planning for a group migration to India. We plan to start next summer. Where will you be." But his ambitions were not focused solely on India either: "Our little oasis is growing naturally and our commitment to the spiritual increases steadily. We are all leaving Harvard in the spring and are working towards a chain of home-centers-ashrams. One here, one in Calif, one in Mexico, one in India." Leary also dropped word of a close poet friend of Allen's, Philip Lamantia, who had paid a visit to Harvard: "Phil Lamantia was up for a week. He's going through a death-rebirth sequence. Painful but he's great."

It isn't surprising that Leary was dreaming of other places, away from Harvard, where he and his group could continue their experiments. Their community living arrangement had drawn complaints from residents almost immediately. Neighbors complained about the traffic running up and down the street at all hours, and, considering the amount of LSD being consumed in the house, there is little doubt that the group's presence was, indeed, disruptive to the usually quiet community. By December 1962 there was a suit filed against Richard Alpert by the city of Newton. The stated cause was that Alpert was violating local zoning laws by using the house as a multifamily dwelling. A *Harvard Crimson* article published February 28, 1963, titled "Alpert's 'Home' Draws Ire" noted that "Residents of Kenwood Avenue have voiced numerous complaints about the conduct of Alpert's 'family unit.' One neighbor stated that there are '15 cars coming and going at 2 and 3 a.m.' and 'wild traffic up and down all night.'" The article, of course, pointed out that "Leary and Alpert have received a great deal of publicity recently for their controversial work with psilocybin."

The Leary camp's reaction to this first official brush with the law would set the blueprint for the next phase of the group's evolution. Rather than acquiesce, they attacked the complaint with righteous indignation, turning it into a public cause. Richard Alpert's father, George Alpert, a wealthy lawyer, represented the group. He appealed the suit on the grounds that the term "family unit" was inadequately defined in the zoning code language.

In the *Crimson* article, the group's argument was presented: "Alpert maintained that the 12 live together as one 'housekeeping unit' and therefore do not violate the Newton housing code." Of course, Leary (being Leary) upped the ante a notch, labeling their group "the BIG family" and threatening to take the case all the way to the Supreme Court if necessary. A few turbulent years later, this idea of a communal family would take hold in the larger American consciousness; but in the early '60s, the argument was new enough to the public as to appear unprecedented.

From the "International Sporting House Set" of the 1950s to the "White Hand Society" of his early Harvard days and now "the BIG family," it is telling that Leary repeatedly saw the benefits of naming his social and professional circles. A natural-born marketer, throughout his life he was quick to "brand" his groups as a way of creating a united front. Additionally, his letters and statements show Leary increasingly using the first-person plural pronoun "we" when discussing his activities. Naturally, it was only a matter of time before he would find another label for his group of intrepid psychedelic experimenters. This time it was the International Foundation for Internal Freedom, or IFIF. In this case, however, IFIF would be officially incorporated as a nonprofit organization, complete with a board of directors consisting of Leary, Alpert, Metzner, Litwin, Gunther Weil, Huston Smith, Walter Houston Clark, and, as honorary director, the philosopher Alan Watts. In addition to creating a

formalized entity from which they could fundraise and continue their work, forming the IFIF would serve notice to the
world that Leary and Harvard were parting ways.

While his Harvard situation fell apart, Leary continued
to keep Allen apprised of the situation. Allen's seemingly
carefree life of spiritual seeking, travel, and artistic and
drug pursuits in India made Tim envious, particularly as
the heat was turned up at home.

Dear Allen and Peter—
   Good to get your letter. India is a fine place to be. The atmosphere
makes such a difference. I envy you. The atmosphere here is amazing.
An electronic lunacy. Lovable people trapped by the machinery they
perpetuate.

He goes on to describe the issues they were facing in
greater details and classic Leary terms:

We are in continual external-game trouble. The local community
has been in aroused alarm for 18 months. Newspaper enquiries. State
drug inspectors. Weekly crucifixions. We have, of course, grown into a
classic mystic cult—so many wise and saintly people rallying around.
We have learned so much, so much since that Sunday afternoon we
talked over our kitchen table.
   I guess you knew it all then.

Much as *Howl* had touched-off a legal battle that City
Lights fought without Allen's presence, now Tim was taking their fight to the system while Allen was away exploring
India. However, Allen was busy fighting plenty of struggles
of his own, some of them related to psychedelics. He was
trying to break through to the next stage of his poetic development, and in some ways his psychedelic training with
Leary had given him a glimpse of the future of poetry. He

recorded his thought process in his *Indian Journals*: "Now poetry instead of relying for effect on dreaminess of image or sharpness of visual phanopoeia—instead of conjuring a vision or telling a truth, stops. Because all visions & all truths are no longer considerable as objective & eternal facts, but as plastic projections of the maker & his language. So nobody can seriously go on passionately concerned with *effects* however seeming-real they be, when he knows inside his visions & truths are empty, finally."

This notion of egolessness and ultimate subjectivity is a very Learyian concept. If life was just a process of game-playing in which the player (in this instance, the poet-player) can slough roles, perspectives, even personalities, on and off depending on circumstances, then what was the point of chasing down ultimate truths to convey in one's poems? "Poetry XX Century like all arts and sciences is devolving into examination-experiment on the very material of which its made. . . . So the next step is examination of the cause of these effects, the vehicle of the visions, the conceiver of the truth, which is: words. Language, the prime material itself."

Allen had just stood face-to-face with what would become the next wave of the American poetry avant-garde: Language poetry. Language poetry was not about the poet howling out his or her vision to a passive audience. Instead, it focused on the building blocks of poetry—words themselves—and the poems were nonlinear in a way that disrupted standard narrative structure. Although Allen would never truly follow this poetic line, as early as 1962, under the powerful, dual, ego-destroying influence of William S. Burroughs and Timothy Leary, he was asking himself, "So the next step is, how do you write poetry about poetry (not as objective abstract subject matter a la Robert Duncan or Pound)—but making use of a radical method eliminating subject matter altogether. By means of what kind of arrangements."

In the same journal entry, Allen goes on to list the literary influences that he viewed as essential in this next level of poetry composition:

Radical Means:
Composition in Void: Gertrude Stein
Association: Kerouac & Surrealism
Arrangement of intuitive key words: John Ashbery's *Europe*.
Random juxtaposition: W. S. Burroughs
Boiling down Elements of Image to Abstract Nub: Corso
Arrangement of Sounds: Artaud, Lettrism, Tantric Mantras
Record of Mind-flow: Kerouac

Gertrude Stein, Surrealism, Artaud, Lettrism, Burroughs, John Ashbery. . . . The list of influences Allen sets down here is like a primer in the building blocks of Language poetry. However, Allen had already spent decades in the pursuit of lyric poetry. His discussions with Leary and Burroughs in Tangier about the "death of the poet" had been deeply troubling and were at the core of this new aesthetic struggle. But while he was willing to struggle with the concept and muse on the implications of language-based poetry in his journal writing, the idea of carrying it out into his poems gave him chills. He had experienced this ego loss before under the influence of psychedelics, and it had nearly driven him insane in Mexico. How could he dedicate his life, his poetry, to replicating the experience? "I seem to be delaying a step forward in this field (elimination of subject matter) and hanging on to habitual humanistic series of autobiographical photographs . . . although my own Consciousness has gone beyond the conceptual to non-conceptual episodes of experience, inexpressible by old means of humanistic storytelling.

"As I am anxious or fearful of plunging into the feeling & chaos of disintegration of conceptuality thru further drug experiences, and as my mind development at the year moment seems blocked so also does my 'creative' activity, blocked, revolve around old abstract & tenuous sloppy political-sex diatribes & a few cool imagistic photo descriptions. . . ."

Allen was not fighting side-by-side with Leary, but he was certainly struggling on his own with the issues that their association had dredged up. Many of Leary's letters to Allen from this time carry a tone of pleading for Allen's deeper involvement: "Keep in touch. Your love is vital." It is obvious that Leary wanted Allen more deeply involved with their "mission" on a regular basis, as they had started out doing. But Allen could not offer such daily support anymore. He was traveling, struggling with his muse, trying to grow as an artist and person, and, if anything, Leary's ideas were now viewed as a hindrance. After all, Allen was a poet. That would always be his role and that wouldn't change. What *had* changed was Tim's role: from Harvard psychologist to rebel philosopher, spiritual leader, and, increasingly, outlaw.

Although Leary announced that he would be departing Harvard when his contract was up in June, the *Harvard Crimson* was still busy publishing blow-by-blow arguments about Leary and Alpert's doings. By this point, the arguments were nothing new—the group wasn't scientific enough; the volunteers were most likely maladjusted, thus not good subjects; the experiments created divisive camps within the student body, and so on—but the copy was good, and a variety of voices joined the chorus. Unfortunately, the chorus was almost uniformly united against Leary.

In spring of 1963, roughly halfway through spring semester, Tim went AWOL from Harvard. Brendan Maher, the new chairman for the Center for Research in Personality, eventually tracked him down in Hollywood where he had been doing publicity for the IFIF. Apparently, Leary had instructed his secretary to hand out a reading list and then dismiss his students from class. Tim had no intention of finishing out the semester at Harvard. Instead, he saw a greater publicity benefit in leaking word to the media that he had been fired by Harvard. After all, anyone can finish out their contract and walk quietly into the sunset. Only a rebel philosopher (which is how Leary had come to view himself) gets fired for taking LSD, which was then legal, and which Leary had branded as a spiritually enlightening sacrament. Thus, Leary could publicly frame his firing on moral grounds, whereas the bottom line was actually rather dull. The resolution from the Harvard Corporation reads, "Voted: because Timothy F. Leary, Lecturer in Clinical Psychology, has failed to keep his classroom appointments and has absented himself from Cambridge during term time without permission, to relieve him from further teaching duty and to terminate his salary as of April 30, 1963."

Nevertheless, as far as the world was concerned, Timothy Leary got fired from Harvard for taking and advocating the use of psychedelics. It was exactly the publicity Tim needed to launch the IFIF, and the psychedelic movement, into the world.

Drop Out

"Superheroes wanted for real life movie work."

—Ken Kesey

In September 1937 Orson Welles became the Shadow. The radio show, which started out as the comic book *The Shadow, A Detective Monthly*, originally appeared on CBS radio on July 31, 1930, as part of its *Detective Story Hour*. At that time, James La Curto voiced the lead role of the Shadow. But when Welles took over the role, his rich, dramatic rendering brought the moody character to life, complete with a haunting sinister laugh. The dark, misunderstood character of the Shadow found a ready home inside the mind of young Jack Kerouac. Through the Shadow, this sensitive, intelligent boy not only found escape from the blue-collar world of Lowell, Massachusetts, but discovered that the right dose of imagination could transform that world—any world—into an epic landscape. Within that transformed landscape, the boy could cast himself as misunderstood hero and protector of the innocent. Kerouac's intellect, imagination, sense of right and wrong, and thirst for adventure were all indulged through his passion for the Shadow. This passion would bubble through in his writing most directly in his 1959 novel *Doctor Sax*. While too peculiar and impressionistic for most at the time of its publication (a full seven years after it was written), the book has taken its place in the "Duluoz Legend" (Kerouac's term for the body of his autobiographical novels) as a unique window into Kerouac's boyhood. In *Doctor Sax*, Kerouac's alter ego is named Jackie Duluoz, and the story begins as a dream that Jackie is having about his boyhood in Lowell, Massachusetts. In the dream, Lowell sits atop "Snake Hill." Underneath Snake Hill, the Great World Snake slumbers while a cast of assorted monsters, werewolves, vampires, and other sinister beings plot to awaken the Great World Snake to destroy mankind. Meanwhile, *Doctor Sax*, a shadowy figure with a black cape, slouch hat, and chilling laugh that echoes into the night, labors away in the nearby town of Dracut, working on a potion that will destroy the snake and save the world.

Kerouac wrote *Doctor Sax* while living with William S. Burroughs in Mexico City. He spent hours holed up in Burroughs' bathroom, working on the book, smoking marijuana, and allowing his mind to slip back into the rich fantasy world of his boyhood. Given his location at the time the book was written, and the fact that he was living with anthropology-minded Burroughs, one suspects that the legend of the Mexican feathered serpent deity Quetzalcoatl also worked its way into Kerouac's hallucinatory prose.

While children's imaginations have always been fired by heroes, villains, and their pleasantly clear-cut struggles between good and evil, Kerouac was among the first generation of writers directly influenced by radio dramas. Soon after, a new breed of heroes—superheroes—would emerge courtesy of DC Comics to fire American children's imaginations beyond the limitations of human abilities. Ken Kesey, a writer born in 1935 and directly influenced by Kerouac, would couple the older writer's passion for adventure, travel, and mythological struggles of good versus evil with a passion for superhero characters. But Kesey didn't just want to write about superheroes. He wanted to become one. Unfortunately, as he once noted, "The trouble with superheroes is what to do between phone booths."

Like Kerouac, Ken Kesey was split down the middle: part athlete, part aesthete. Both excelled at sports (predominantly football for Kerouac and wrestling for Kesey), and both were raised in an environment that prized physicality over intellect. Kesey was born in La Junta, Colorado, the first of two sons born to dairy farmers Fred and Geneva Kesey. In 1946 the family moved to Springfield, Oregon. Kesey, a handsome young man, blond, blue-eyed, intelligent, and athletic, also showed an interest in theater, magic, and ventriloquism. In his senior year, he was voted "Most Likely to Succeed." After high school, Kesey attended the University of Oregon, where he majored in speech and communication. He also continued to excel at athletics, going undefeated in wrestling during his senior year and coming in second in the AAU tournament. During his junior year, he married his high school sweetheart, Faye Haxby, with whom he would raise three children. On the night before their wedding, Ken Kesey got drunk for the first time.

In 1958, Kesey was awarded a Woodrow Wilson National Fellowship that allowed him to enroll the following year in the creative writing program at Stanford University. Kesey was admitted to the program on the strength of a football-themed novel he was writing. That novel and a subsequent novel effort were discarded, but not before Kesey had emerged as one of the strongest writers in a program that also included Larry McMurtry and Wendell Berry. While at Stanford, Kesey was known to staunchly and eloquently defend the value of comic books to his witty, erudite friends. "A single Batman comic is more honest than a whole volume of *Time* magazines," Kesey would proclaim. As a boy, he had devoured comic books about Plasticman and Captain Marvel, along with pulp novels and volumes by Zane Gray and Edgar Rice Burroughs. He not only enjoyed the comic books as narratives with complex characters facing epic struggles—he related to them.

While enrolled at Stanford, Ken Kesey also signed up as a volunteer subject at the Menlo Park Veterans Hospital. For twenty dollars per session, he allowed doctors to administer psychotomimetic drugs to him, including psilocybin, LSD, IT-290 (a heavy-duty amphetamine), and a synthetic version of belladonna called Ditran. Of all the drugs he was given, Ditran was the only one that Kesey disliked. Unlike Leary's work at Harvard, the Menlo Park experiments were funded by the CIA as part of its covert MK-Ultra program.

The fact that the CIA turned Ken Kesey on to psychedelics is one of the great ironies of American alternative history. Little did they know that, far from controlling Kesey's mind, the drugs would liberate him in a way that no one could have predicted. During the tests, Kesey was living in a bohemian enclave of Palo Alto called Perry Lane, surrounded by Beatnik types who went to coffee shops, read philosophy and poetry, played folk music, and consumed marijuana. Kesey told this crowd about the strange experiences he was having at Menlo Park. They were, naturally, intrigued, but few were taking part in the experiments themselves. Much the same as Leary, Kesey knew that these drugs were game-changers, but they were difficult to explain and not yet available on the black market. How could he "share the ring of power" as Leary put it, and turn on the rest of Perry Lane to psychedelics?

In midsummer, Kesey took a job working the night shift at Menlo Park. The job gave him plenty of quiet time to work on his writing. But, equally important, it gave him access to the hospital's supply of psychotomimetics. In short order, Kesey was "liberating" the substances and sharing them with his gang back at Perry Lane. Kesey was also liberally dosing himself with the substances, sometimes while on the job at the hospital. The hospital and drugs mixed with Kesey's literary training and newly formed bohemian identity to create his acclaimed first published novel, *One Flew Over the Cuckoo's Nest*. The novel made Kesey a national celebrity at twenty-six years old. It also provided him with enough money to move out of Perry Lane (which was being razed to make room for a more modern development) to a large piece of property fifteen miles away from Palo Alto, in La Honda, California. A group of the Perry Lane gang, along with a healthy supply of hallucinogens, made the move to La Honda along with Kesey. This was to become home base for the legendary psychedelic group known as the Merry Pranksters.

As different as Ken Kesey and Timothy Leary were, they also shared important similarities, most having to do with their maverick leadership styles. Leary understood that reality is shaped by language, thus to name something is to give it substance. As a result, he was quick to name his groups—International Sporting Set, White Hand Society, IFIF, etc.—as a way to unite the members and create a unified front to observers. Leary also saw reality as a series of "games" that were malleable based on the setting, players, and the individual's needs at a given time. Perhaps more important, as a leader, he was able to influence others to join and support whatever version of the "game" he was playing at a given time. Given his maverick nature, those games were usually at odds with societal expectations.

Ken Kesey, a master writer and trained rhetorician, also knew the power of language and naming. Thus, as his Perry Lane group morphed into a more coherent unit, it took on a group name: the Merry Pranksters. However, the Pranksters took naming one step further. Kesey once remarked, "The purpose of psychedelics is to learn the conditioned responses of people and then to prank them. That's the only way to get people to ask questions, and until they ask questions they're going to remain conditioned robots." If the Pranksters were to push beyond the limits of structured thought and society into new frontiers, they would need names fitting this epic new reality. Names that marked them as nothing short of superheroes of the new consciousness. Names that simultaneously matched their personalities and freed them to transcend themselves.

In this spirit, each member of the band of psychedelic superheroes was rechristened with Merry Prankster names: Gretchin Fetchin, Mal-Function, the Cadaverous Cowboy, Intrepid Traveller, Cool Breeze, Mountain Girl, and so forth. As de facto leader, Kesey went under several Prankster names, but the main one, fittingly taken from his breakthrough novel, was also the most appropriate: Chief.

Where Leary saw life as a series of games, Kesey began to see the Merry Prankster mission in terms of a movie. His Prankster motto: "Get them into your movie before they get you into theirs." As a born leader, Kesey was adept at doing just that. Not only did he foster a group name and encourage individual pseudonyms within the group, but the Pranksters even created costumes that marked them as part of the rowdy band. One trademark outfit was a white jumpsuit with American-flag inspired star insignias on the breast. Others were pure superhero outfits, including tight orange-and-blue body leggings with matching blue masks.

Along the way, the Merry Pranksters also picked up an elder statesman of the countercultural scene. This new member provided a key link between Allen Ginsberg, Jack Kerouac, and the Beat movement, and the new countercultural group that would come to be known as hippies.

Neal Cassady, just out of San Quentin after a two-year stint for marijuana possession, would go by the Prankster moniker Speed Limit.

In July, 1964, Ken Kesey and the Merry Pranksters set forth across the country in a 1939 International Harvester bus bound for New York City. Ostensibly, the trip was meant to get Kesey to New York in time for the publication party for his second novel, *Sometimes a Great Notion*. However, if that were the true purpose of the trip, a plane ticket would have been infinitely faster and easier.

Ken Kesey was struggling with the limitations of literature. Psychedelics had broken his "set," and mere words on a page were no longer satisfying his need to create. The Prankster happenings were helping, but artists don't just create, they document. Kesey began eyeing film as the next logical step. Not film in the hokey Hollywood sense, but unscripted, psychedelic Prankster movies. The bus trip to New York would provide the perfect opportunity to create the Great American Movie. As Allen Ginsberg would say, "To me, the real significance of Kesey's bus trip in the summer of 1964 was as a cultural signal that happened just as the nation was on the precipice of enormous awakening and change. It was like a very colorful flag going up a flagpole, signaling the news that something was about to happen, something was about to shake."

Colorful indeed. The Pranksters' bus was slathered with swirling patterns of paint, creating the country's first psychedelic motor vehicle. The bus had already been outfitted with a refrigerator, bunk beds, and other camping amenities. To this the Pranksters added a sound system that allowed them to broadcast inside the bus and, more significantly, outside the bus. On the back of the bus, a sign read: CAUTION: WEIRD LOAD. On the front of the bus was the singular destination: FUURTHER [sic]. Kesey had also invested in film and recording gear to be sure that whatever weirdness happened was captured on film. A container of LSD-spiked orange juice in the refrigerator assured that weirdness would indeed happen. Naturally, Neal Cassady, AKA Speed Limit, was at the wheel.

If the Pranksters' bus trip had taken place a mere three years later, the groups strangeness would have merely reinforced mainstream America's media-fed image of hippies as drug-addled crazies. But in 1964, America had no context in which to consider the Pranksters. They simply didn't fit into any preconceived rubric other than, perhaps, the sideshow. This gave the Pranksters the upper hand. Kesey's motto, "Get them into your movie before they get you into theirs," was played out all across the country, with everyone from senior citizens to cops getting pranked. When confronted with any sort of hassle, a combination of recording equipment, flagrant disregard for social norms, and fast-talking Prankster jive created a pocket of bafflement that allowed the Pranksters to roll off down the road while the straight folks stared in wonder. In *The Electric Kool-Aid Acid Test*, Tom Wolfe describes a typical Prankster-meets-straight encounter while on the road:

> A siren? It's a highway patrolman, which immediately seems like the funniest thing in the history of the world. Smoke is pouring out of the woods and they are all sailing through leaf explosions in the sky, but the cop is bugged about this freaking bus. The cop yanks the bus over to the side and he starts going through a kind of traffic-safety inspection of the big gross bus, while more and more of the smoke is billowing out of the woods. Man, the license plate is on wrong and there's no light over the license plate and this turn signal looks bad and how about the brakes, let's see that hand brake there. Cassady, the driver, is already into a long monologue for the guy, only he is throwing in all kinds of sirs: "Well, yes sir, this is a Hammond bi-valve serrated brake, you understand, sir, had it put on in a truck ro-de-o in Springfield, Oregon, had to back through a slalom course of baby's bottles and yellow nappies, in the existential culmination of Oregon, lots of outhouse freaks up there, you understand, sir, a punctual sort of a state, sir, yes sir, holds to 28,000 pounds, 28,000 pounds, you just look right here, sir, tested by a pure-blooded Shell Station attendant in Springfield, Oregon, winter of '62, his gumball boots never froze, you understand, sir, 28,000 pounds hold, right here—" Whereupon he yanks back on the hand-brake as if it's attached to something, which it isn't, it is just dangling there, and jams his foot on the regular brake, and the bus shudders as if the hand brake has a hell of a bite, but the cop is thoroughly befuddled now, anyway, because Cassady's monologue has confused him, for one thing, and what the hell are these . . . people doing. By this time everybody is off the bus rolling in the brown grass by the shoulder, laughing, giggling, yahooing, zonked to the skies on acid, because,

mon, the woods are burning, the whole world is on fire, and a Cassady monologue on automotive safety is rising up from out of his throat like weenie smoke, as if the great god Speed were frying his innards, and the cop, representative of the people of California in this total freaking situation, is all hung up on a hand brake that doesn't exist in the first place. And the cop, all he can see is a bunch of crazies in screaming orange and green costumes, masks, boys and girls, men and women, twelve or fourteen of them, lying in the grass and making hideously crazy sounds—christ almighty, why the hell does he have to contend with. . . . So he wheels around and says, "What are you, uh—show people?"

Slowly, strangely, the Pranksters made their way across America toward New York. Despite three thousand miles of separation, Leary's group and Kesey's group were well aware of each other. By this point, Leary's name had been splattered all over the papers as a result of his firing from Harvard and Kesey was famous for *One Flew Over the Cuckoo's Nest*. Psychedelic culture was spreading, but it was still relegated to small in-crowds who were well connected within the burgeoning counterculture society. And, of course, Allen Ginsberg and Neal Cassady were the great-uncles connecting the scenes to each other and tying them back to their origins within the Beat generation.

The Pranksters finally reached New York City in mid-July 1964. An old Perry Lane friend, Chloe Scott, had arranged an apartment on Madison Avenue at 90th Street where the Pranksters could stay and party. Neal Cassady had written ahead to organize a meeting between the Pranksters, Allen Ginsberg, and Jack Kerouac. Kesey's writing was already being compared to Kerouac's in reviews, and his recent experiences on the road with Cassady gave him even more of an understanding of the truth of Kerouac's work. Kesey was eager to meet, and impress, the legendary Kerouac. Unfortunately, that would not be the case.

By the time of their meeting, Kerouac was on the backside of the alcoholism that would kill him only five years later. He had dedicated his life to literature and was clearly uninterested in Kesey's program whereby *lights, cameras, action!* supplanted prose styling. His drugs of choice were booze and nicotine, not LSD. In the most telling episode of the night, Kerouac noticed that the Pranksters had draped an American flag over a sofa in the apartment. Had Kerouac retained the lucidity and humor of his early days, he might have recognized that the Pranksters were reclaiming the quintessential symbol of America—the flag—in the name of the country's founding principles: life, liberty, and the pursuit of happiness. The Pranksters regularly festooned themselves with bits and pieces of American flag, visually proclaiming themselves part of the newest American Revolution. Instead of dumping tea into the Boston Harbor, they dumped LSD into vats of Kool-Aid. However, Kerouac's alcohol- and fame-induced paranoia had turned him increasingly conservative and unyielding. He saw no humor, irony, or revolutionary impulse in using an American flag as a sofa covering. Only disrespect. He gathered himself together, picked the flag off the sofa, and carefully folded it in the proper manner: red and white stripes wrapped snugly into blue to represent day turning to night (when military flags are ceremonially lowered), the entire flag folded into the shape of a tri-cornered hat to symbolize the hats worn by colonial soldiers during the Revolutionary War. He set the flag down and asked the Pranksters if they were Communists. Shortly thereafter, Cassady drove him back to his mother's house in Massachusetts. With Kerouac dedicated to booze and Cassady hell-bent on speed, the two might as well have been a continent apart. It was the last time they would see each other.

The next stop on the Pranksters' East Coast tour was Timothy Leary and the International Federation for Internal Freedom's new home base in Millbrook, New York.

Between May and August 1963, Leary and IFIF had been tossed out of Harvard, Mexico, Antigua, and Dominica. Every attempt at establishing a utopian home base where they could carry on their psychedelic sessions was eventually thwarted by the authorities. Each expulsion cost the group more money and threw their ranks into greater disarray. As Leary would say, "We cravenly decided that the authorities were not ready for the 21st century concept: Every Citizen a Scientist. So we fell back to the familiar historical turf upon which most earlier freedom movements had fought the battle—religion."

Indeed, as much as for their drug advocacy, Leary and IFIF had been expelled from Harvard for turning away from science and scholarship toward the esoteric, non-academic pursuit of spiritual enlightenment. After all, Harvard was in the business of turning out intellects, not monks. As with many of the mid-twentieth-century American seekers, the group made the mistake of romanticizing the more "primitive," less industrialized regions (e.g., Latin America, the Middle East, the Far East) as the keys to realizing their own spirituality. However, two-thousand-year-old religious dogma is impervious to American can-do sensibilities.

Wherever Leary and IFIF attempted to set up compounds in South America, they ran afoul of the authorities. Regardless of their spiritual intentions, they were regarded as outsiders and potential troublemakers. Their most successful attempt at setting up a base at the Hotel Catalina in Zihuatanejo, Mexico, ended with the appearance of two policemen. By that time, there were twenty Americans staying at the hotel, participating in IFIF activities, and paying to be there. The policemen informed Leary that the IFIF operation was being shut down because they were "besmirching the name of Mexico" with all the bad publicity and scandal they were generating. To prove the point, they showed Leary the headline from a Mexico City newspaper reading, "Harvard Drug Orgy Blamed for Decomposing Body." Apparently, a corpse had been found in a village 100 miles away from the Hotel Catalina, but the papers were claiming that Leary's "marijuana orgies, hairy women, black magic, venereal disease, and profiteering" were to blame. Additionally, their visas did not allow them to run a business on Mexican soil. IFIF was given five days to leave the country.

Their next attempt at setting up a home base consisted of a brief visit to an experimental commune on the island of Dominica, a Caribbean island between Guadeloupe and Martinique. After barely time to unpack, the group was handed deportation orders from there as well. Apparently, their reputation had preceded them. After only a week of scouting sites on the island, Tim was escorted to the office of the governor of the island and accused of being an international heroin dealer. On the governor's desk was a copy of *Time* magazine expounding on the growing menace of LSD in America. The group was ordered to leave Dominica immediately. To ensure safe passage, Leary and his colleagues, including his thirteen-year-old son Jack, spent the preceding night sewing hits of LSD into teddy bears.

The next stop of Leary's deportation tour was Antigua. One of Tim's West Point classmates owned two small islands near Grenada. He made an agreement that if Tim's group built permanent structures on the island, he would give them half of the property. While the structures were being built, the group would be allowed to stay in a World War II–era Navy club called "The Bucket of Blood." When Dick Alpert arrived in Antigua to join the group, he was appalled at what he found. The party was in full swing, but there was no sign of construction going on anywhere. Alpert had sold nearly all his possessions to fund the group, and they had also received $20,000 from their wealthy patron saint, Peggy Hitchcock. Now the group had been expelled from Harvard, had been ousted from two different countries, and was $50,000 in debt, and they had nothing of substance to show for it. The Antigua dream ended when one of the group, Frank Ferguson, walked into town while flying on acid and requested a lobotomy from a local surgeon. Ironically, this same act—a request for an elective lobotomy—was what got Carl Solomon, Allen Ginsberg's dedicatee for "Howl," committed to Columbia Presbyterian Psychological Institute, where the two men met. In Solomon's case, the act inspired a powerful passage in Ginsberg's landmark poem. In Ferguson's case, it led to the group's immediate expulsion from yet another country.

In August, 1963, the group returned to Cambridge. They were broke, dejected, but not deterred. Once again, their patron saint Peggy Hitchcock came to the rescue. As she explained it, "They kept getting thrown out of everywhere. They clearly needed a place to live and my brothers, Billy and Tommy, had just bought this lovely big property for a tax thing. Because it actually functioned as a cattle ranch, it was also a good investment. Billy told me there was a big house there and I asked if he had anyone living in it and he said no. So Richard Alpert and I went up and looked at it and we thought it was great. The rent was a dollar a year."

The Millbrook estate—which was known by the locals as "Alte House"—consisted of 2,500 acres in a seat of quiet wealth and bucolic upstate New York beauty, two hours from New York City, filled with forests, pastures, streams, and lakes. The mansion grounds contained all of these natural attributes, making it possible to move from distinct environments (forest to meadow to waterfall) all within the course of a single trip. In short, one could tailor one's psychedelic experience to whatever environment was most desirable. This was also the place where Leary met (and soon split up with) his third wife, Nena von Schlebrugge, and his stalwart fourth wife, Rosemary Woodruff Leary. Rosemary, a former model and actress, would stand by Leary through the difficult times ahead and ultimately pay a heavy price for her role in Leary's doings.

The mansion was four stories, containing sixty-four rooms, located at the end of a long, winding driveway, nearly isolated enough to constitute its own township. However, the Millbrook house—no matter how much its occupants wished differently—was far from its own sovereign nation. It was very much subject to the laws of the land.

In November 1963, a CIA memo was circulated at the agency detailing Leary, Alpert, and IFIF's movements. The subjects of the memo were listed as:

> International Federation for Internal Freedom (IFIF)
> ALPERT, Richard, Ph.D.
> LEARY, Timothy F., Ph.D.
> Drugs, Mind Affecting, Agency Policy Regarding

The memo cites several articles that had already appeared as the group moved from Harvard to various misadventures in Latin America and finally to Millbrook. It details Leary and Alpert's firings from Harvard and the establishment of IFIF, stating "Drs. ALPERT and LEARY had set up an organization known as the International Federation for Internal Freedom (IFIF), which obviously was a cover for additional experimental work in the hallucinogenic drugs." In short, the memo gathers information on Leary and IFIF that was readily available through articles and Leary's own interviews and public statements. However, points three through six of the memo reveal the CIA's increasing concern about IFIF's activities.

- SRS/OS has for a number of years been engaged with certain other Agency areas in research and operational work with some hallucinogenic drugs. This work has been under rigid Security and Agency control, and the then Director of Security laid down rigid instructions that these types of drugs were not to be used under any circumstances on Agency personnel. Operational use of the drugs was handled through a special committee under the specific control and only with the consent of Mr. Richard Helms, DDP.

- It should be noted that the aforementioned hallucinogenic drugs are considered by the Office of Security and by the Medical Office as extremely dangerous. Uncontrolled experimentation has in the past resulted in tragic circumstances and for this reason every efforts is made to control any involvement with these drugs.

- SRS has not been able to determine whether any staff employees of the Agency have engaged in unauthorized taking of any of these drugs, but there is information that some non-Agency [illegible] particularly on the West

Coast, have taken these drugs in a type of religious experimentation. While as previously mentioned, there are no staff employees involved, some individuals known to have these drugs have sensitive security clearances and are engaged in classified work.

- Any information concerning the use of this type of drug for experimental or personal reasons should be reported immediately to Chief/SRS/OS with all specific details furnished. In addition, any information on Agency personnel involved with the International Federation for Internal Freedom, or with Drs. ALPERT or LEARY, or with any group engaging in this type of activity should also be reported.

The IFIF, newly rechristened the Castalia Foundation, after a similar-minded group in a Herman Hesse novel, moved into Dutchess County, which was under the jurisdiction of an ambitious young prosecutor named G. Gordon Liddy. Prior to his position as Dutchess County prosecutor, Liddy, at age twenty-nine, had become the youngest bureau supervisor at FBI headquarters in Washington, D.C. He left the FBI to pursue his legal and prosecutorial career in New York, but he was never far from the Washington loop. Liddy could practically smell Leary coming.

The November 1963 CIA memo claims that the organization's hallucinogenic testing had been kept under "rigid Security and Agency control." However, somehow they had managed to leak acid to the leader of the very West Coast faction they were now concerned about: Ken Kesey. It was under such federal scrutiny, in the summer of 1964, that the leading psychedelic outlanders from the West Coast and East Coast would meet on the grounds of the Millbrook estate, directly under the nose of G. Gordon Liddy.

The meeting between the Pranksters and Castalia had all the makings of an epic countercultural moment. Both groups were planting the seeds of a psychedelic subculture and those seeds were about to burst forth. Although Leary had already begun tangling with the law, he had mainly escaped unscathed. Now back in their own country, away from the strictures of Harvard life, the Castalia group felt a new freedom to push their hallucinogenic experiments even further. Interestingly, through their psychedelic experiments, the Pranksters and Castalia had both stumbled into the early stages of an enduring artistic movement: multimedia. For Castalia, video, audio, lights, and various "props" were ways to guide the tripper into specific areas of the mind. The "tower rooms" of the Millbrook estate were outfitted with speakers, and many hours were dedicated to recording music-to-trip-by, including the sort of whispered instructions that would make their way into Leary, Metzner, and Alpert's book, *The Psychedelic Experience*:

> *Oh nobly born, listen carefully:*
> *The life flow is whirling through you.*
> *An endless parade of pure forms and sounds,*
> *Dazzlingly brilliant,*
> *Ever changing.*
> *Do not try to control it.*
> *Flow with it.*
> *Do not try to understand;*
> *There is plenty of time for that later.*
> *Merge with it.*
> *Let it flow through you.*

This time, the poetic feel of the Leary group's book was the result of converting *The Tibetan Book of the Dead* into a tripping manual. The language, structure, and tone of *The Psychedelic Experience* parallels the ancient Tibetan Buddhist manual, which guides the dying through various stages of death and afterlife. Leary saw LSD as an opportunity to experience an "ego death" and rebirth during which previous "games" could be reprogrammed and the tripper could evolve. The book affected John Lennon so profoundly that he wrote "Tomorrow Never Knows," the last song on the Beatle's *Revolver* album, after reading the book and using it a guide for his own LSD trip. Years later, in an interview with *Rolling Stone* founder Jann Wenner, Lennon would complain, "I got a message on acid that you should destroy your ego, and I did, you know. I was reading that stupid book of Leary's and all that shit. We were going through a whole game that everyone went through, and I destroyed myself. . . . I destroyed my ego and I didn't believe I could do anything."

The Pranksters had integrated multimedia aspects into their world right from the start. Even at Kesey's woodsy spread at La Honda, the entire property was wired for sound, and random props and artworks were scattered in places as unexpected as tree trunks and stuck inside bushes. Tom Wolfe described the multimedia sound scene during the first trip the Hell's Angels paid to La Honda: "Sandy Lehmann-Haupt, Lord Byron Styrofoam, had hold of the microphone and his disco-freak-jockey rapping blared out of the redwoods and back across the highway: 'This is Non-Station KLSD, 800 micrograms in your head, the station designed to blow your mind and undo your bind, from up here atop the redwoods of Venus!'"

The difference between the ways the Pranksters and Castalia used multimedia speaks volumes about the differences between the two groups. The Pranksters used it to "blow your mind," while Castalia conveyed the message "When in doubt, relax, turn off your mind, float downstream."

The Pranksters arrived at Millbrook in classic Prankster style. Cassady piloted the rattling day-glo bus up the long, well-manicured driveway at high speed with Pranksters hanging out of windows, hooting like maniacs. American flags fluttered off the bus and rock music blared out of the speakers, filling the peaceful glades of Millbrook with a vibrating cacophonous roar of life. As the bus neared the mansion, Sandy Lehmann-Haupt, a.k.a. Lord Byron Styrofoam, a.k.a. DJ of radio KLSD, started heaving green smoke bombs out of the bus. Soon the air stank with green smoke, and explosions punctuated the driving beat of the rock-n-roll music and the howls of the Pranksters. The Pranksters were making an arrival on par with the historical importance of the meeting. They were writing the book, making the movie as it happened, and as always, particularly with the Pranksters, truth was much stranger—and louder—than fiction. But Castalia was more Zen than rock-n-roll, and, in good koan fashion, the sheer volume of the Pranksters' arrival made the silence of Millbrook that much louder.

The bus rolled to a stop in front of the mansion and the Pranksters piled out, still whooping it up. From this point on, everyone's take on the particulars of the meeting differs. Allen Ginsberg, fresh off the failed attempt to unite Kerouac with the Pranksters, rode the bus up to Millbrook to foster the connection between the Pranksters and Castalia. He tells the story this way: "I remember when we finally went up with Kesey to visit Leary. There was already some kind of rule at Millbrook about not making a big noise. The bus came honking down the driveway like an animate painted rhinoceros with a loudspeaker on it. It was like Kesey was calling attention to himself and at first, people were a little bit hesitant even to come out and look at the bus and greet them for fear they would precipitate a bust. They were being pretty discreet. Eventually, Leary and Kesey met. It wasn't a happy open thing because there had been so much trouble from notoriety that Leary, and particularly his household group, were a little leery—l-e-e-r-y—of such a big show. Kesey and his friends had never been busted, really. They had driven their way across the United States as Pranksters, pranking up the cops, and hadn't had the taste of the iron law, so they couldn't understand why Leary's group was so reticent. Leary wasn't paranoid. He was guarded."

Leary's memory of the meeting is that he was sick with the flu. He had just returned from a business trip and Richard Alpert picked him up at the train station and informed him that the Pranksters had arrived. Leary could tell that Alpert was disturbed by the Pranksters' disruptive presence, but he was functioning through the foggy delirium of a high fever and felt helpless to do anything more than crawl into bed and try to get healthy. Thus it was left to Alpert to play host to the group and, eventually, broker a meeting between Kesey, fellow Prankster Ken Babbs, Leary, and himself. Leary recalls, "Ken Kesey, Ken Babbs, and I did meet, quietly in my room. We looked each other in the eye and promised to stay in touch as allies."

For his part, Alpert felt abandoned to deal with these crazies on his own. His memory of the event seems the most likely and straightforward (from the Castalia perspective). Simply put, his group had been tripping all night and were all burnt out when the Prankster bus arrived. Their

inner resources were simply overwhelmed by the incongru-
ous appearance and outlandish behavior of the Pranksters.
Castalia was on the come-down period of an all-night acid
trip, and the Pranksters were just making their entrance,
flying on speed, LSD, and whatever else. When the bus arrived, Castalia members scattered inside and went to bed
rather than deal with this crazy, discordant new scene. Thus
it was left to Alpert, Peggy Hitchcock, and the Fergusons to
welcome the Pranksters. Frankly, they weren't feeling up to
the task either.

For a long time, *The Electric Kool-Aid Acid Test* was
the definitive statement on this meeting of countercultural
legends. Wolfe was "on the bus" with the Pranksters, thus
his take on the meeting comes securely from their perspective. His chapter on the meeting is a brief handful of pages
titled "The Crypt Trip." He refers to Leary's group as the
League for Spiritual Discovery, which was the name that
Leary gave the group *after* the Castalia Foundation, and
roughly two years after the Pranksters visited Millbrook.
In all fairness, considering the speed with which Leary adopted and dropped monikers, it is unlikely that anyone but
a handful of the inner circle knew the group's name at any
given time. This confusion no doubt extended to donors
who gave money in support of one of Leary's groups, only
to have the name change a year or two later. Impressively,
Leary did always manage to have stationery that matched
the current name of his group.

If one went solely on Wolfe's account, it would appear that Leary never met the Pranksters at all. "Where was
Leary? Everyone was waiting for the great meeting of Leary
and Kesey.

"Well, word came down that Leary was upstairs in the

mansion engaged in a very serious experiment, a three-day trip, and could not be disturbed.

"Kesey wasn't angry, but he was very disappointed, even hurt. It was unbelievable—this was Millbrook, one big piece of uptight constipation, after all this."

While Wolfe's tone is undoubtedly correct, the fact is that Leary did meet with the Pranksters. In fact, there is an iconic photograph of Leary sitting on the Pranksters' bus at Millbrook, laughing along with Neal Cassady.

Wolfe's "The Crypt Trip" title comes from a classic prank that Babbs pulled while being escorted around the bungalow and the mansion. As Peggy showed the Pranksters around, Babbs assimilated the décor, artwork, and photos on the walls into his own rap, quickly turning the tables from tourist to tour guide. Suddenly, each photo— no matter how old—was a photo of a Prankster, or, failing that, the ancestor of a Prankster. Through Babbs' rap, Millbrook was transformed into a museum of Prankster history. Instead of seeing the basement meditation area as a quiet space perfectly arranged for guiding a psychedelic session, as Castalia had intended, Babbs called the area "the crypt trip," arranged for bringing down one's trip.

While the specific details of the meeting may vary based on the affiliation and allegiances, the legacy of the failed summit remains the same. Both physically and intellectually, Castalia and the Pranksters were tackling psychedelic exploration from a continent apart. After asking Castalia for LSD for their return trip—and being turned down—the Pranksters piled into the bus and started back to California.

The King of May

Throughout 1964 and 1965, Allen Ginsberg was deeply involved in the newest countercultural movements in New York City. The mid-Sixties saw an influx of avant-garde filmmakers in New York, with Jonas Mekas and Andy Warhol, among others, generating much of the activity and publicity. Allen was no stranger to avant-garde film, having "starred" in Robert Frank and Alfred Leslie's 1959 short film *Pull My Daisy* which was adapted from Jack Kerouac's play, *Beat Generation*. The film also featured, among others, Peter Orlovsky, Gregory Corso, David Amram, and Larry Rivers, with Jack Kerouac providing spontaneous narration. Over the years, Allen would appear in numerous films, ranging from the avant-garde to straightforward documentaries and low-budget indie films.

Of course, Allen was always a poet first. When the city began cracking down on coffeehouses that hosted poetry readings without a cabaret license, he formed the Committee on Poetry, or COP, to organize efforts to defend the establishments. After numerous appeals from COP and benefit poetry readings to support the establishments, the License Department of New York City agreed to stop issuing the summonses. Perhaps taking a page from Leary

regarding the power of naming to gain power for an organization, Ginsberg continued to use COP to defend everyone
from the Living Theatre and the Pocket Theatre to come-
dian Lenny Bruce. In a classic piece of Ginsberg poetic
protest theater, he cut off his hair and beard and mailed
it to Assistant District Attorney Richard H. Kuh, who was
prosecuting these cases. He wrote to Kuh, "Please accept,
the enclosed offering of my shorn locks as a sort of spiritual
bribe that you look with friendlier kindlier heart on the ear-
nest strivings of the artists of N.Y. to communicate with all
men including myself and yourself. . . . There is a definite
social value I think you are going to be happily surprised
to find. Meanwhile accept and guard this part of my head
which I have cut off in your honor, as a devotional offering
to the God in you."

Along the way, Ginsberg also got to know the circle of
writers, artists, and activists who were using Ed Sanders'
Peace Eye Bookstore as their meeting grounds. Sanders was
a Classics scholar who edited a magazine called *Fuck You,
A Magazine of the Arts*. Eventually, Peace Eye became a
second home for Ginsberg, who was only too happy to support this new wave of irreverent New York literary activity.
Everywhere he looked, Ginsberg saw explosions of artistic
energy rife with roiling undercurrents of political and social activism. These were the children of *Howl*, and Allen
Ginsberg was their presiding spirit.

Allen had been to Cuba once, briefly, in 1953, prior to
Castro's revolution. Following the revolution, the country
had taken on an idealistic glow in the eyes of many U.S.
political activists who saw communism as a solution to
minority oppression and the consuming drive inherent in

capitalism. Among his poet friends, LeRoi Jones was one of the most fervent and outspoken about the positive model the revolution served. Of course, Allen had grown up hearing debates about the pros (his mother, Naomi) and cons (his father, Louis) of socialism and communism. As with many Russian émigrés, Naomi and Louis had both grown up in families that supported variations of socialist and communist dogma. However, after they were married, Naomi joined the local Communist Party cell and eventually espoused Stalinism, while Louis became more democratic and, some would say, Americanized. Regardless, Naomi was never dissuaded from her beliefs, and the differences in their views were aired as part of the daily flow of conversation in the Ginsberg household. As a result, Allen grew up with a precocious grasp of and acute interest in politics. His increasing involvement in defending social and artistic movements against political intrusion had rekindled that passion—it would remain a core of his activities and personality for the rest of his life.

In January 1965 Allen accepted an invitation from the Cuban minister of culture to participate in a writers' conference in Havana. The only catch was that, due to the two countries' poor relations, Allen would have to reenter America by first flying to Prague and then traveling from Prague to the United States. Always game for good travel, Allen was unfazed. In fact, he made plans to extend his trip from Prague to Russia and then back to Prague before returning to the United States. He wanted to see how true socialist and communist societies operated and was eager to report back to LeRoi Jones, as well as to his father and any number of other regular correspondents. Prior to the emergence of underground newspapers, Ginsberg often served as a one-man reporting service for the counterculture through his poems and letters. Once alternative newspapers began appearing in cities across the country, Allen would become a staple in their pages.

It wasn't long after arriving in Cuba before Ginsberg was approached by three teenage poets who had been eagerly awaiting his arrival. The boys had tried unsuccessfully to contact him at his hotel, so it was fortuitous that they spotted him walking through La Rampa, the nightclub area of Havana. They whisked Allen off to a quiet spot, ordered a bottle of rum to share, and began telling him the truth about life in Castro's Cuba. Homosexuals and kids just like the ones Allen had always hung out with (long hair, interest in poetry, outsider views) were regularly rounded up off the streets and arrested. In fact, the kids made clear that they could only tell Allen these things because they were in a private setting and their comments were off the record. As Allen would soon learn though, nothing in Cuba was kept private for long.

The boys' plight struck Allen in his most sympathetic zones: freedom of expression, sexuality, intellectual pursuits. These were the core of Ginsberg's own personality, and he was appalled that Castro's regime was squelching them at every turn. Allen also learned from the boys that the writers who were "succeeding" under Castro were nothing more than lackeys for the government. Ginsberg would report back to Jones and his other friends that, while he still believed in the ideals of the revolution, in this area it was being used as just another tool of oppression.

After this debriefing, Allen continued his itinerary of sightseeing and literary obligations, but he also took every opportunity to draw attention to the issues the boys had raised. Up to this point, he had never experienced the true ramifications of speaking out against a controlling government. Obscenity trials and the banning of artistic creations within a society that allowed for freedom of dissenting opinions and access to legal appeals were nothing compared to the specter of being jailed without recourse for speaking one's mind or exercising one's sexuality. Allen was still functioning under a U.S. mindset. He had previously won battles through candor and appeals for rationality; perhaps, he reasoned, he could effect such change in Cuba as well.

After a couple of weeks in Cuba, Allen received a call from Manuel Ballagas, one of the teenage boys with whom he had been associating. Ballagas had been picked up and questioned all night by the police. He was charged with talking to foreigners. Thankfully, Ballagas had been released into his mother's custody, but he was still wary of meeting Allen for any more conversations outside of official Writers Union events. Soon after, Allen was questioned by a government representative about statements he may or may not have made insinuating that Raúl Castro, Fidel's brother, was gay and that Allen wanted to have sex with him. Reports came in that more of the boys he had been hanging around with were arrested and accused of acting effeminately. Allen's lectures began to be cancelled. He was becoming a danger to his hosts and the boys who had befriended him, and an increasing embarrassment to the government. Despite their mutual understanding that it was best for Allen and the boys not to meet privately, both sides caved in and Allen had sex with Ballagas at another boy's apartment. Two days later, Allen was awakened by an official from the International Cultural Exchange Program (ICEP) and three soldiers. He was ordered to collect his belongings and come with them. Allen was being deported from Cuba for being a liability to the revolution. The plane was waiting on the tarmac when they arrived, and Allen read the destination on the tail of the plane: Czechoslovakia.

After his Cuban experiences, Allen was intent on toning himself down while in Prague. He would play the part of the simple tourist, not the outspoken poet. He was housed by the government in a beautiful nineteenth-century hotel and took in museums, castles—even Franz Kafka's old apartment. He also wrote some new poems and gave readings at coffee shops and at the Univerzita Karlova. The more Allen was able to write and share his poetry, the more relaxed he became. He received a letter from Manuel Ballagas telling him that the official Cuban party line was that Allen had been expelled from the country for smoking pot. While Allen did smoke pot there, this was certainly not the main thrust of his expulsion. Still, the authorities were backing off on Ballagas and Allen was well out of their reach now. He would have to wait until he returned to the United States before he could set the record straight.

After his visit to Prague was over, Allen took a train to Moscow, where he contacted his cousin, Joe Levy. While staying with the Levys, Allen heard stories about his mother's early years and her family's immigration to America. It became apparent that Naomi's mother had also been mentally ill and had struggled to raise her children. The family had all pitched in, especially when Allen's grandfather, Mendel, bribed his way aboard a ship bound for America. It took a year of working and saving money in America before Mendel could afford to have his family, including Naomi, join him there.

Allen also met the Russian poets Andrei Voznesenksy and Alexander Yessenin-Volpin on this trip. While his politics and interests in sex and drugs clashed with Voznesensky's sensibilities (and Voznesensky's ability to speak freely), both men admired each other's poetry and spent hours talking literature. Allen felt a greater affinity for Yessenin-Volpin, who had been committed to an asylum for his political views. Despite the price the poet had paid, he still spoke freely, and passionately, with Allen. Still, Allen remained on his best behavior. He was able to extend his stay in Moscow under the auspices of the Writers Union, and he became more aware than ever of the dualities of communism. He wrote in a letter to LeRoi Jones, "You better think twice before you buy any paradises, or better, take an extended trip thru here and listen to all the story so you can judge. Not that it's so bad here, as a system it works, not that it's so good." Before leaving Russia, Allen was treated to the spectacle of the recently returned cosmonauts being feted in Red Square. On his way home, he spent some time in Poland before returning to Prague for a short stay to say goodbye to friends and take in the May Day celebrations.

Majales (May Day) was a Czechoslovakian festival with a history stretching back to medieval times. The festivities had been suspended after the communists came to power. But now, for the first time in twenty years, May Day was to be celebrated again—and Allen would be there to experience it.

Allen was in his hotel room when he received a strange call from his writer friend, Josef Skvorecky. Apparently Skvorecky had been nominated May King by students at the Engineering School of the Polytechnic, but he was

sick with the flu and could not fulfill his duties. He asked
if Allen would be willing to stand in for him. Allen, still
wary after his Cuban experiences, asked if this would be
a political position. Skvorecky chuckled and assured him
that it was all in good fun—just cheerful students blowing
off steam through the streets of Prague. Nothing to worry
about. Besides, Allen would be just one of the nominees
for the King of May position. What were the odds that he
would be elected?

Allen was met in his hotel by a group of students
decked out in 1890s costumes: top hats, waistcoats, and
canes for the boys; parasols and hoop skirts for the girls.
There were also jesters blowing trumpets. "Mr. Ginsberg,"
they began, "we have the honor to beg your presence in
procession to the crowning of the King of May, and to accept our support for your candidacy of Kral Majales, and
we humbly offer you crown and thrown." Allen accepted.
Not only that, but he packed up his finger cymbals and a
statue of Ganesh to accompany him on this new adventure.
The students placed a cardboard crown on Allen's head
and a scepter in his hands, and placed him on a "throne"
covered with red velvet drapes. They carried him out of the
hotel and placed him on the back of a flatbed truck, where
he proceeded down the street surrounded by students carousing and drinking.

Along the parade route, Allen started drinking beer and
getting into the spirit of the festival. At intervals, a bullhorn
was put to his mouth, and Allen responded with a "Hare
Om Namo Shiva" or hearty "Om Sri Maitreya" mantras.
Other times, he made bold and playful proclamations, "I'll
be the first kind King and bow down before my subjects."
"I'll be the first naked King." When the procession passed

the spot where Kafka had written *The Trial*, Allen spoke up, "On your left, comrades, is the actual house where saintly Kafka lived and cleaned his teeth, and wrote his huge novels which your comrades have not even published!"

Reinstatement of the King of May celebration had marked a turn toward a more liberal climate in Prague. But the officials had woefully underestimated the vigor with which the city responded. A hundred thousand people filled the Park of Culture and Rest at the end of the parade route, and rock music filled the air. Allen was seated onstage in a huge exhibition hall—one of the half-dozen men vying for the position of King of May. Each man was arrayed in some sort of costume and made a flowery, tongue-in-cheek speech in support of his candidacy. When it was Allen's turn to speak, he stood up in his Levis and unwashed shirt and proceeded to chant "Om Sri Maitreya" for five minutes. The crowd exploded with cheers of approval. They had found their Kral Majales—Allen was crowned.

The night went along with the crowd getting drunker and louder and Allen enjoying it all from his perch onstage. During the beauty contest that would result in the election of his queen, he took fifteen minutes to scratch out a poem in silence. The students—and their king—were thoroughly enjoying themselves. However when the Party Secretary for Cultural Affairs learned that Allen Ginsberg—an American poet—had been elected Kral Majales, he was outraged. He ordered the students to depose Allen and put a Czech student in his place. The students had no choice but to concede. Thus, before Allen could fully enjoy the fruits of his position (he would complain in a letter to poet Nicanor Parra, "The May Queen was elected but I didn't get a chance to marry and sleep with her as was tradition for the night. In

fact, I was supposed to have the run of Prague and do anything I wanted and fuck anybody and get drunk everywhere
as King"), he was overthrown.

Allen rallied and enjoyed the night anyway. He continued to drink and talk to students in their dormitory
well into the night. Nevertheless, the scene was turning
into a replay of Cuba. The Allen Ginsberg alarm had been
sounded.

Allen felt invigorated by the King of May festivities.
Despite the fact that he knew he was being followed and recorded by government agents, his true personality emerged.
He granted interviews, participated in the making of a short
film, went to rock concerts, wrote and recited poems, and
generally made himself at home. He also took advantage
of his celebrity by sleeping with Czech boys. In a 1969 interview for *Playboy* magazine, Allen would recall, "When
I was elected the King of May in Prague in 1965, I made
it with all sorts of beautiful Middle European 17-year-old
blond cats. Having a fame identity makes it easy to make it
with young kids who are, like, friendly."

Unfortunately, Allen also recorded all of his escapades
in his journal. One night, Allen was leaving a club when a
man assaulted him on the street, yelling, "*Bouzerant! Bouzerant!*" (Faggot! Faggot!). The man punched Allen and
knocked him to the ground. Within minutes, a police car arrived and arrested the whole group, including the assailant,
who had, no doubt, done the job he was called on by the
authorities to do. Allen was questioned and released, but
the notebook containing all his recent journal entries (including his sexual encounters, masturbation fantasies, and
drug use) was missing. The notebook would provide the
final piece of evidence that Allen was, indeed, a dangerous,

deviant presence in Prague. After another run-in with the police during which his notebook was presented and he was questioned about its contents, Allen was given the final verdict. "Mr. Ginsberg," he was addressed, while seated before a panel of bureaucrats in the upstairs of the police station, "we immigration chiefs have received many complaints from parents, scientists, and educators about your sexual theories having a bad effect on our youth and corrupting the young, so we are terminating your visa."

For I was arrested thrice in Prague, once for singing drunk on
    Narodni street,
once knocked down on the midnight pavement by a mustached agent
    who screamed out BOUZERANT,
once for losing my notebooks of unusual sex politics dream opinions,
and I was sent from Havana by plane by detectives in green uniform,
and I was sent from Prague by plane by detectives in Czechoslovakian
    business suits,
Cardplayers out of Cézanne, the two strange dolls that entered Joseph
    K's room at morn
also entered mine and ate at my table, and examined my scribbles,
and followed me night and morn from the houses of the lovers to the
    cafés of Centrum—
And I am the King of May, which is the power of sexual youth,
and I am the King of May, which is long hair of Adam and Beard of
    my own body
and I am the King of May, which is Kral Majales in the
    Czechoslovakian tongue,
and I am the King of May, which is old Human poesy, and 100,000
    people chose my name,
and I am the King of May, and in a few minutes I will land at
    London Airport,

          — excerpted from "Kral Majales"
          Collected Poems 1947–1997

By the end of the day, Allen was on an airplane bound for London. Like his friend Timothy Leary, he had been deemed a deviant presence and kicked out of two countries on one trip.

Human Be-In

On January 14, 1967, six years after their first discussion around Leary's kitchen table at Harvard, Allen Ginsberg and Timothy Leary shared the stage at the Human Be-In on the polo field in Golden Gate Park, San Francisco. (Ironically, this coming-out party for LSD and precursor to the famous Summer of Love was inspired, in part, by the government's decision to make LSD illegal in California.) The Be-In was not the platonic ideal of the plans Allen and Tim had envisioned during their first meeting, but it was its earthly embodiment: beautiful, spiritual, flawed, and powerful enough to make the world take notice and shake up the power structure of America.

A press release delivered to the media a few days before the event declared, "For ten years, a new nation has grown inside the robot flesh of the old. Before your eyes a new free vital soul is reconnecting the living centers of the American body. . . . Berkeley political activists and the love generation of the Haight-Ashbury will join together . . . to powwow, celebrate, and prophesy the epoch of liberation, love, peace, compassion, and unity of mankind. . . . Hang your fear at the door and join the future. If you do not believe, please wipe your eyes and see."

Even in this optimistic press release, the divide that would drive a wedge into "the movement" is clear. The political activists who sought change through protest were associated with Berkeley, and the hippies who sought change through "dropping out" and creating their own utopian society were associated with Haight-Ashbury. In 1967, this divide was small, but growing rapidly. Among other things, the Be-In was seen as a way to unite the groups before that factionalism grew too large. Even the underground paper of record for the activists, the *Berkeley Barb*, got behind the event with a front page article that promised, "The spiritual revolution will be manifest and proven. In unity we shall shower the country with waves of ecstasy and purification. Fear will be washed away; ignorance will be exposed to sunlight; profits and empire will lie dying on deserted beaches; violence will be submerged and transmuted in rhythm and dancing."

Among the organizers of the Be-In, Allen Ginsberg was the one who could move most easily between all of the related groups. He was the prototypical hippie, but he was also an ardent activist. He spoke out for the legalization of drugs, but just as ardently for the power of chanting and meditation. He was a poet who inspired the world's most famous rock stars. He was sexually liberated in ways that most of the young kids streaming into San Francisco had never conceived. He had long hair, a beard, and flowing Indian garb, but on June 14, 1966, he had worn a Brooks Brothers suit to address a subcommittee of the U.S. Senate Committee on the Judiciary to discuss his drug experiences. (Leary had also testified for Senator Ted Kennedy and the committee a month earlier.) Allen's recent expulsions from Cuba and Prague had only strengthened his already iron-clad countercultural credentials.

On the night before the Be-In, a handful of organizers gathered at poet Michael McClure's apartment to discuss who would speak at the event and how long they would be given at the microphone. While they all knew that the speakers would not be the focus of the event (the focus would be the gathering itself) and no one wanted to get too rigid about the whole thing, they were all experienced enough to realize that some structure would help the event move smoothly. Or perhaps they should forgo speakers entirely?

"Man, I'd just as soon no one says a word tomorrow," said a Haight Street legend who went by the name Buddha, who was to serve as the master of ceremonies at the event. At the meeting, Buddha was advocating for "Just beautiful silence. Just everybody sitting around smiling and digging everybody else."

Some other last-minute ideas were also batted around. Perhaps the event should be moved to the beach? Perhaps everyone should be naked? Perhaps the Be-In should morph into a "groovy naked swim-in" that would "spook the city of San Francisco."

In the end, the Be-In would be held on the polo field at Golden Gate Park, as planned. However, there was one important piece of business to clear up before the organizing party disbanded. Timothy Leary was coming all the way from New York to attend the Be-In. The question was: how much time should be allotted to Leary at the microphone? If he was considered a poet, he would be given seven minutes. If he was considered a prophet, he would be given as much as thirty minutes. None of the organizers gathered in McClure's apartment could agree. They each meditated on the question in their own way: chanting, singing, puffing quietly on pipes, lying on the ground and staring up at the ceiling. Finally Ginsberg spoke up.

"Well, how much time *do* we allow Leary? *I* say he gets the same as the poets."

One of the few women present, Beth Bagby, spoke up: "Is Leary a prima donna?"

"Man, I don't think so," said Buddha, "after all, he's taken acid."

"Leary just needs a little of the responsibility taken off him," said Allen. "Seven minutes, and anyway, if he gets uptight and starts to preach, Lenore Kandel can always belly dance."

By declaring Leary a poet rather than a prophet, Ginsberg may very well have been cutting his old friend some slack. There were many in the Haight who considered Leary a sell-out, out of touch, and too high on his own publicity. The rumor that he had treated the Pranksters shabbily during their visit to Millbrook didn't help his San Francisco reputation either. If he rode into the Be-In and tried to steal the show with too much "speechifying," he could have lost all credibility with the youth movement.

Allen and Gary Snyder arrived at the polo field at 11 AM. They started the day by chanting Buddhist dharanis to ward off any negative energy that might be lurking to ruin the event. They also performed a *pradaksina*, a circumambulation accompanied by prayers meant to sanctify the grounds where a *mehla*, or spiritual gathering, would take place. Allen was wearing blue rubber bathing thong sandals that he picked up at a Japanese stall on his way over to the park, and a loose-fitting white orderly uniform that looked very much like the Indian garb he had grown to appreciate in India. The outfit was capped off with beads, bells, flowers, amulets, and a big flower-patterned tie that someone had just given him.

Gary Snyder kicked off the day's proceedings by blowing into a white-beaded conch shell. More than 25,000 men, women, and children had shown up for the event and were milling around the grounds amazed to see so many like-minded souls. Many in the crowd were arrayed in their finest Haight-Ashbury gear: masks, velvet capes, feathers, body paint, see-through tops, Victorian dandy outfits, stovepipe hats, cowboy outfits, and plenty of beads, bells, tambourines, soap bubbles, and other assorted toys and noisemakers. Seated beside Snyder on the stage were Michael McClure, Lawrence Ferlinghetti, Lenore Kandel, and Allen—a tribute to the Beats' role in helping birth this new era. Throughout the day, speakers and bands alternated stage space. Unfortunately, the sound system wasn't nearly strong enough to reach the whole crowd. To many, the on-stage proceedings might as well have been nonexistent anyway, especially compared to the overwhelming impact of the sheer number of hippies, freaks, mystics, radicals, and gawkers who had turned out en masse to simply *Be*. Still, the speakers spoke, and a roster of San Francisco psychedelic scene bands played on: Moby Grape, The Freudian Slips, The Hedds, Earth Mother and the Final Solution, the Chosen Few, the Jefferson Airplane, Sopwith Camel, Big Brother and the Holding Company, and, of course, the "good ol'" Grateful Dead.

There was a large oriental carpet onstage and Timothy Leary sat on it beside Allen Ginsberg while Gary Snyder blew his conch shell. Tim was high on acid, and, despite his silver hair, his face radiated the youthful energy that, along with his famous smile, had become a Leary trademark. He wore authentic Indian garb and carried a daffodil in one hand. A small array of jonquils was tucked above each ear. Most of the speakers, Leary included, showed impressive restraint when it came their turn at the microphone. Only two months earlier, Ginsberg had caused a major stir when, during a talk at a church in Boston, he urged that every American of good health over the age of fourteen should "try the chemical LSD at least once . . . that, if necessary, we have a mass emotional nervous breakdown in these States once and for all." Between the two of them, Leary and Ginsberg were the media faces of the spiritual psychedelic revolution. Only a half-dozen years after they had sat together plotting this revolution over mugs of warm milk in Leary's kitchen at Harvard, they were now watching its physical manifestation in the form of 25,000 psychedelic voyagers grooving together in a field in San Francisco. It was fitting that they both hold places of honor onstage during the event. Leary, now chidingly nicknamed the Pope of Dope, kept it brief, but just long enough to showcase what would become his most famous slogan. "The only way out, is in. Turn on, tune in, and drop out. Out of high school, junior executive, senior executive. Follow me!" After that, he sat back down and resumed playing pattycake with a little girl, an activity that consumed much of his afternoon.

Allen also kept it brief, tossing out a tidy little poem, "Peace in your heart dear, peace in the park here."

Prior to the Be-In, the legendary Bay Area LSD chemist

Owsley Stanley had made up a batch of acid that he gave to the Diggers to distribute for free. The Diggers performed street theater, gave away free food and clothes, and constantly agitated for the hippie ideal that people should barter for goods and services, not sell them. So this was a sort of test for the group. Since Owlsey's were the only white hits of acid on the street, if they somehow ended up getting sold for money instead of given away, he would have immediately know about it and called the Diggers out as hypocrites. But, true to their word, the Diggers gave away (and personally soaked up) all the acid without any money changing hands. As a reward, Owsley cooked up some more of this powerful White Lightning acid and sent it over to the Diggers along with seventy-five twenty-pound turkeys. The Diggers were to feed and dose the crowd at the Be-In for free, with Owsley an unsung Father Christmas for the day. The Diggers decided to consolidate these tasks by crushing up the LSD and adding it to the bread mix they used for the turkey sandwiches. Thus, thousands of free psychedelic turkey sandwiches were gobbled down at the Be-In courtesy of the Diggers and Owsley Stanley. This sandwich supply was bolstered by other Owsley suppliers who circulated through the crowd wearing robes and distributing free hits of White Lightning out of paper bags. At one point, a parachutist floated down to the field, and rumors circulated that it was Owsley himself, floating down from on high. It was most likely just an instructor from a nearby sky-diving school, but still, the unexpected spectacle only added more mystique to the already mythic event. With the Hells Angels guarding the generators, helping to restore the sound system whenever it cut out, and acting as security for the day, the Be-In had representation from basically every quarter of American counterculture. Overall, it was an event with very few snags, and—as with Woodstock two years later—a shining example of how large-scale unregulated youth-oriented gatherings could be peaceful events without the presence of the police. Allen would eventually call the Be-In "the last idealistic hippie event."

At 5PM, Gary Snyder blew his conch shell again to signal the end of the event. Allen led the crowd in chanting the mantra of the Buddha of the Future, *Om Sri Maitreya*. He also worked along with other volunteers picking up trash, trying to minimize the environmental impact of the enormous gathering. Thousands of people, filled with the Be-In spirit, drifted west, made their way across the Great Highway, and set up camp on the Ocean Beach strand, where they built bonfires and watched the sun go down over the Pacific Ocean. It was an idyllic end to an idyllic day. Unfortunately, the idyll didn't last far beyond sundown. That night, police swept Haight Street, arresting 50 people and making a clear statement that the party was over. The headline of the *San Francisco Chronicle* the following day read, "Hippies Run Wild."

At least one intention of the mass gathering backfired on the organizers. The large turnout showed that there were thousands of people ready to rebel against cloistered mainstream society. However, the dream that the gathering would provide unity between the hippies and the radicals went unfulfilled. If anything, the radicals looked over the crowd and realized the potential of harnessing such a powerful force to protest the war. If the Be-In could draw more than 25,000 people, how many of those could be moved to political action?

Along those lines, Leary's new phrase "turn on, tune in, drop out" impressed many in Berkeley as dangerously irresponsible. Already, many of the hippies considered Leary too messianic and found the whole concept of "leading" a movement dedicated to "dropping out" of society to be hypocritical. Why bring hierarchy into the new world? Even when Leary argued against the need for any hierarchy, the fact that he was covered so closely by the media undercut his protestations.

But the hippie arguments against Leary were minor compared to the radicals' fear that he could undermine their whole movement. As Abbie Hoffman said, "I saw the reverse of Leary's trip: change the world and you'll change your mind. Total absorption with the internal voyage made you easy to exploit and convert." The fear was strong enough that immediately after the Be-In, the *Oracle* organized a summit meeting to debate "the whole problem of whether to drop out or take over." The summit not only marked a clear divide in "the movement" at large, but also laid open a rift between Ginsberg and Leary.

The "Houseboat Summit," as it came to be called, was held on philosopher Alan Watts' boat, the S.S. *Vallejo*, in February 1967. The panelists were Allen Ginsberg, Timothy Leary, and Gary Snyder, with Watts serving as facilitator. The event was recorded and published in issue #7 of the *San Francisco Oracle*. (*A complete transcript can be found at the end of this book.)

Ginsberg was living in San Francisco at that time and was connected to both the Haight-Ashbury hippies and the political activists around Berkeley. The Houseboat Summit began with him and Alan Watts discussing how to strip the violence from the peace movement. Ginsberg talked about "turning on" with Mario Savio, a leader of the Berkeley peace movement, who, according to Ginsberg, "felt one of the things that move large crowds was righteousness, moral outrage, and ANGER . . . righteous anger." Watts contributed that "nothing is more violent than peace movements. You know, when you get a pacifist on the rampage, nobody can be more emotionally bound and intolerant and full of hatred."

For his part, Leary was intent on standing behind his insistence to "drop out" in no uncertain terms: "Mass movements make no sense to me, and I want no part of mass movements. I think this is the error that the leftist activists are making. I see them as young men with menopausal minds. They are repeating the same dreary quarrels and conflicts for power of the thirties and forties, of the trade union movement, of Trotskyism and so forth. I think they should be sanctified, drop out, find their own center, turn on, and above all avoid mass movements, mass leadership, mass followers."

Leary went on to clarify what he saw as the difference between the dropouts and the activists. "I see that there is a great difference—I say completely incompatible difference—between the leftist activist movement and the psychedelic religious movement. In the first place, the psychedelic movement, I think, is much more numerous. But it doesn't express itself as noisily. I think there are different goals. I think that the activists want power. They talk about student power. This shocks me, and alienates my spiritual sensitivities. Of course, there is a great deal of difference in method. The psychedelic movement, the spiritual seeker movement, or whatever you want to call it, expresses itself . . . as the Haight-Ashbury group had done . . . with flowers and chants and pictures and beads and acts of beauty and harmony . . . sweeping the streets. That sort of thing."

It is a testament to the complexities of 1960s America that even individuals as simpatico as Leary and Ginsberg were being divided by the times. Leary's attitude about whether to engage with or retreat from larger society would continue to shift over the years, based on whatever hardships or opportunities he encountered; however, he always maintained his drive to organize people into groups to forward his agenda. At the time of the Houseboat Summit, his focus was on his small group at Millbrook and how they could collectively "drop out" of society. Ginsberg, as always, was interested in making connections between people rather than inflating their divisions. But when it came to the dropouts versus the activists, he was often faced with an unbridgeable gap. He supported the spirit of the dropouts, but he also recognized that active engagement would be necessary to shape the youth movement into a force that could affect public policy. Throughout the Houseboat Summit, this fundamental rift played itself out through the voices of Ginsberg and Leary, and was subsequently recounted in the *Oracle* for the counterculture to read and reflect on. The longer the debate went on, the deeper Leary dug himself into the dropout camp, the more Ginsberg came down on the side of active engagement, until the discussion became a war of wills between two countercultural heavyweights:

LEARY: Yes. . . . I think this point must be made straight away, but because we are both [the dropouts and the activists] looked upon with disfavor by the Establishment, this tendency to group the two together. . . . I think that such confusion can only lead to disillusion and hard feelings on someone's part. So, I'd like to lay this down as a premise right at the beginning.

GINSBERG: Well, of course, that's the same premise they lay down, that there is an irreconcilable split. Only, their stereotype of the psychedelic movement is that it's just sort of the opposite. . . . I think you're presenting a stereotype of them.

LEARY: I think we should get them to drop out, turn on, and tune in.

GINSBERG: Yeah, but they don't know what that means even.

LEARY: I know it. No politician, left or right, young or old, knows what we mean by that.

GINSBERG: Don't be so angry!

LEARY: I'm not angry. . . .

GINSBERG: Yes, you are. Now, wait a minute. . . . Everybody in Berkeley, all week long, has been bugging me . . . and Alpert . . . about what you mean by drop out, tune in, and turn on. Finally, one young kid said, "Drop out, turn on, and tune in." Meaning: get with an activity—a manifest activity—worldly activity—that's harmonious with whatever vision he has. Everybody in Berkeley is all bugged because they think, one: drop-out thing really doesn't mean anything, that what you're gonna cultivate is a lot of freak-out hippies goofing around and throwing bottles through windows when they flip out on LSD. That's their stereotype vision. Obviously stereotype.

LEARY: Sounds like bullshitting.

GINSBERG: No, like it's no different from the newspaper vision, anyway. I mean, they've got the newspaper vision. Then, secondly, they're afraid that there'll be some sort of fascist putsch. Like, it's rumored lately that everyone's gonna be arrested. So that the lack of communicating community among hippies will lead to some concentration camp situation, or lead . . . as it has been in Los Angeles recently . . . to a dispersal of what the beginning of the community began.

LEARY: These are the old, menopausal minds. There was a psychiatrist named Adler in San Francisco whose interpretation of the group Be-In was that this is the basis for a new fascism . . . when a leader comes along. And I sense in the activist movement the cry for a leader . . . the cry for organization. . . .

GINSBERG: But they're just as intelligent as you are on this fact. They know about what happened in Russia. That's the reason they haven't got a big, active organization. It's because they, too, are stumped by: How do you have a community, and a community movement, and cooperation within the community to make life more pleasing for everybody—including the end of the Vietnam War? How do you have such a situation organized, or disorganized, just so long as it's effective—without a fascist leadership? Because they don't want to be that either. See, they are conscious of the fact that they don't want to be messiahs—political messiahs. At least, Savio in particular. Yesterday, he was weeping. Saying he wanted to go out and live in nature.

LEARY: Beautiful.

GINSBERG: So, I mean he's like basically where we are: stoned.

Finally, Ginsberg, with an assist by his old friend Gary Snyder, fed up with the circular nature of the debate, tried to pin Leary down.

GINSBERG: Precisely what do you mean by drop out, then . . . again, for the millionth time?

SNYDER: Drop out throws me a little bit, Tim. Because it's assumed that we're dropping out. The next step is, now what are we doing where we're in something else? We're in a new society. We're in the seeds of a new society.

GINSBERG: For instance, you haven't dropped out, Tim. You dropped out of your job as a psychology teacher in Harvard. Now, what you've dropped into is, one: a highly complicated series of arrangements for lecturing and for putting on the festival. . . .

LEARY: Well, I'm dropped out of that.

GINSBERG: But you're not dropped out of the very highly complicated legal constitutional appeal, which you feel a sentimental regard for, as I do. You haven't dropped out of being the financial provider for Millbrook, and you haven't dropped out of planning and conducting community organization and participating in it. And that community organization is related to the national community, too. Either through the Supreme Court, or through the very existence of the dollar that is exchanged for you to pay your lawyers, or to take money to pay your lawyers in the theatre. So you can't drop out, like DROP OUT, 'cause you haven't.

LEARY: Well, let me explain. . . .

GINSBERG: So they think you mean like, drop out, like go live on Haight-Ashbury Street and do nothing at all. Even if you can do something like build furniture and sell it, or give it away in barter with somebody else.

LEARY: You have to drop out in a group. You drop out in a small tribal group.

SNYDER: Well, you drop out one by one, but. . . . You know, you can join the sub-culture.

GINSBERG: Maybe it's: "Drop out of what?"

The conversation on the boat wound around and around through the major, and often prescient, concerns of the group, including communal living, artisanal commodities, macrobiotic food, yoga, meditation, and the psychedelic implications of the seven-day week. ("There is also some neuro-pharmacological evidence in support of the weekly cycle. That is, you can only have a full-scale LSD session about once a week."—Leary.) At one point, Leary responded to Ginsberg by declaring, "I'm the poet and you're the politician. I've told you that for ten years!" But while Allen and Tim never fully reconciled during the interview, their mutual good humor shone through in almost vaudevillian banter:

LEARY: I want you to be very loving to me for the rest of . . . and the tape will be witness . . . whether Allen is loving or not to me, for the rest of this evening.

GINSBERG: That's all right, I can always use a Big Brother. . . .

Allen and Tim's bond remained solid through the debate, but their paths were diverging. In many ways, the Be-In was the culminating activity to the six years of their psychedelic partnership. Allen would remain a vocal, visible presence in the antiwar movement for the duration of the U.S. engagement in Vietnam and, in fact, for the rest of his life. Tim got involved in politics (including a cheeky run at the governorship of California) when it suited his best interests, especially if it kept him in the spotlight or kept him out of jail. By the time of the Be-In, he had already been arrested multiple times. His first bust, suspiciously well executed at the Mexican border in 1965, had already started him on a collision course with the law that would resonate through the counterculture.

Shoot to Live. Aim for Life.

In "Howl," Allen Ginsberg penned the line, "who got busted in their pubic beards returning through Laredo with a belt of marijuana for New York." The line would turn out to be prophetic for Leary in 1965. Tim had already been expelled from Mexico for setting up an IFIF psychedelic center in Zihuatanejo in 1963. The odds of having the same policeman who expelled him greet him at the border two years later were unfavorable, to say the least. Improbable is a better word. Better yet: a setup.

In December, 1965, Tim, Rosemary, Susan, and Jack drove a station wagon all the way from upstate New York to the border of Mexico. Tim wanted some quiet time to work on a new book and felt the whole family could use time away from Millbrook. When Tim went inside the Mexican Immigration building to clear them for entry into the country, he was greeted by a strangely pleased Mexican policeman. "Where do you think you are going?" the man asked. "Do you remember me? You aren't allowed in Mexico. I know because I am Jorge García who deported you from Mexico in 1963. You are *persona non grata* in Mexico. *Prohibido.*"

Even though they never made it into Mexico proper, Leary and his family (along with another young man who had the unfortunate luck of catching a ride with them) were busted for transporting marijuana back into the United States. Before leaving on the trip, Leary had taken the trouble of securing permission from the Ministry of Gobernación to return to Mexico as a tourist. He presented the documentation to García, who assured them that they would straighten out the situation in the morning. In the meantime, he told Leary to head back to the states for the night. While all this was going on, Tim had instructed sixteen-year-old Jack to dump their small personal stash of marijuana. Jack managed to do this, but just before going over the border, Rosemary remembered another small stash they had hidden. Susan Leary, eighteen years old, tucked that stash into her underwear, but that wasn't good enough. As soon as they reached the border going back into the States, bright lights hit the car and policeman materialized to methodically search the vehicle and each passenger. They were busted. In February, 1966, Susan Leary pleaded guilty to smuggling marijuana, transporting smuggled marijuana, and—most ironically—failure to pay the federal marijuana tax. Tim, accused of the same charges, decided to plead not guilty. His defense was that, as an initiated Hindu and legitimate scientist, he had the right to possess, worship, and experiment with marijuana.

In deciding to fight the marijuana charges, Tim made yet another decision to step into the public spotlight. Each time he did so, he provoked the government more, while simultaneously drawing attention to a topic—U.S. drug policy—that he felt obliged to address. In his opening statements for the Laredo trial, he said, "I am pleading not guilty in this case, because I am an American citizen. As such, I am entitled to the free exercise of my religion. I am entitled to engage in scientific research. I am entitled to live in my home, travel in my car and bring up my children the best I can in accordance with my beliefs and values. My motives before and during the incident of my arrest, are clearly spiritual, interior and not ulterior." Despite the many hours of legal preparation that Tim put into the case, he and Susan were both found guilty by a jury that took little more than twenty minutes to deliberate. Tim was sentenced to twenty years in prison and a $20,000 fine for unlawful transport of marijuana and another ten years and $10,000 for failure to pay the federal tax on marijuana. He was also ordered to be committed to a psychiatric hospital for evaluation. Susan was to be sent to a reformatory for an unspecified amount of time. They were released on bail, and Leary immediately kicked into mouthpiece mode to fight the verdict and draw attention to the case.

After Laredo, Tim's subsequent busts came fast and publicly. In April 1966, Millbrook was raided by armed deputies under the direction of G. Gordon Liddy. Once again, Tim was arrested for a small amount of marijuana. He spent a night in jail and was bailed out to begin fighting these new charges. The *New York Times* headline read, "LSD Psychologist Arrested Again." In December 1967, while Tim was in New York City, Liddy and his posse raided Millbrook once again. This time the raid turned up marijuana and methamphetamine. Tim returned and surrendered to the Dutchess County authorities. He was booked, fingerprinted, and released on $2,500 bond.

Tim was free for the moment, but Liddy had made his point. In addition to the major busts, any car that left Millbrook estate grounds was likely to be searched for drugs, and the group was constantly on guard against police informers who tried to insinuate themselves into their inner circle. In short, there would be no peace for Tim and his cohorts as long as they remained in Dutchess County. The owner of the house, Billy Hitchcock, had also had enough; to facilitate their exit, he made generous donations that would help Leary and some of the others get settled in new locations. The experiment in psychedelic communal living at Millbrook was through. When the group dispersed, Tim decided to head back to the West Coast with Rosemary and the kids.

Then, on December 26, 1968, Tim, Jack, and Rosemary got busted for pot in Laguna Beach, California.

Timothy Leary was going to have to do prison time. No matter where he moved or how many times his lawyers could post bail and get him back onto the street, eventually the authorities were going to send Tim to jail. They were tracking his movements and coordinating information across departments—Timothy Leary was in their sights. Ironically, the more the authorities harassed and hounded Leary and his family, the more publicity they drew to "Turn On, Tune in, Drop out" and Leary's other mantras. In trying to silence him, they were turning him into an underground legend. In compelling him to raise funds to defend himself in court, they pushed him onto the lecture circuit, where he spread the gospel of LSD and railed against the police state that was persecuting him. And, ironically, while Leary was fighting the Millbrook and California busts, the Supreme Court overruled Tim's Laredo bust. Justice John Marshall Harlan handed down the forty-six-page decision, which stated that the Fifth Amendment guarantee against self-incrimination invalidated the charge of not paying the Federal Marijuana Tax. The decision also stated that possession of marijuana did not sufficiently prove that it had been illegally imported. The court ordered that the case be remanded to a lower court for dismissal, retrial, or resentencing. It wasn't an absolute victory, but it was an encouraging one. Tim had forced the Supreme Court to confront the hypocrisy inherent in the drug charges he was facing. A statement had been made.

While waiting for the Supreme Court decision to be handed down, Tim and Rosemary had moved into an eighteen-foot-tall Sioux tepee on a ranch between Hemet and Palm Springs, California. The ranch sat at the base of a rocky ridge along the Pacific Crest Trail, the next closest town being Idyllwild. The ranch was owned by an operation called the Brotherhood of Eternal Love and the Learys were staying as their guests. From the outside, the Brotherhood compound looked like any number of hippie communes cropping up around the country: tepees, cabins, bonfires, long-haired men, women, and children, acoustic guitars, sweat lodges, vegetable gardens, a swimming hole, and shared daily duties. It was set back off the highway by a half-mile-long dirt road and secured by a gate with a combination padlock. However, the Brotherhood was no simple commune. The group had bought the land with profits from drug deals that involved moving kilos of hash, marijuana, and other drugs, often smuggled in from as far away as Afghanistan and frequently across the Mexican border. The group would sometimes be presented in the media as "Timothy Leary's Brotherhood," but that was far from the truth. Closer to reality was its other media nickname "The Hippie Mafia." The group *did* revere Leary, using his book *The Psychedelic Experience* as a bible of sorts, which is why the members allowed him to stay on their land rent-free.

However, Leary had no part in the group's day-to-day smuggling and dealing operations, which brought in hundreds of thousands of dollars and flooded the country with the most infamous batch of LSD ever produced: Orange Sunshine. One day Tim and Rosemary spotted a group of sedans snaking down the long driveway toward their tepee. Naturally, their first assumption was that they were being busted again. But these were not federal agents or police officers. They were television crews from ABC and NBC, who were looking to interview Leary about the Supreme Court's ruling on his Laredo bust. With the cameras rolling, Tim declared that he felt "high and happy for ourselves and the thousands of young people who are imprisoned for psychedelic crimes." And then, riding a euphoric wave, Tim declared his intention to run for governor of California.

Once again, Tim had made a move most likely to piss off the maximum number of people. Many of his longtime followers felt that this move betrayed Tim's spiritual message in favor of a political one. For diehard political activists, this was no time for a joking campaign: tensions in America were too hot, the stakes too high for these types of goofball antics. For her part, Rosemary didn't know that Tim had been planning to run, even if it was only a symbolic campaign. The Brotherhood certainly had no interest in television crews poking around their property and activities in search of a radical gubernatorial candidate. In Leary, the three other candidates running for the Democratic nomination saw only a man who would make a mockery of the process and siphon votes away from their campaigns. Perhaps the incumbent Republican governor, Ronald Reagan, had the most to gain from Leary's stunt. He had made a political name for himself on the national stage by bashing California's counterculture at every turn. Now he got to take down their guru as a legitimate part of his election campaign, while his opponents scrambled and divided up votes amongst themselves. But then again, the media loved to air Leary's proclamations, and Leary loved to heap ridicule on Ronald Reagan.

If there was a single moment that marked Leary's final fall from grace, this impulsive bid for governor of California could be it. No doubt, the ride was fun. During the campaign, posters were made with Leary's face and such slogans as "Luv for Guv." One poster mimicked the familiar packaging found on Zig-Zag rolling papers. In classic Leary style, he quickly named his political party the Free Enterprise, Reward, Virtue and Order Party, otherwise known as FERVOR. None other than John Lennon sang a campaign song for him based on Tim's campaign slogan, "Come Together, Join the Party." While Leary sat beside Lennon and Yoko Ono during their famous Bed-In for world peace at the Queen Elizabeth Hotel in Montreal, Lennon improvised a tune: "Come Together / Right now / Don't come tomorrow, don't come alone / Come together / right now / Over me / All that I can tell you / You gotta be free." The free association rap would soon evolve into the song "Come Together" the lead track on the Beatles' *Abbey Road* album. The campaign was high theater, and Leary soaked up the attention.

Tim would not stay a free man long enough to make it to Election Day. All of his travel, speeches, and politicking would soon come to an end. The Supreme Court had overturned the charge of failure to pay the Federal Marijuana Tax, but the case had been sent to a lower court, and Tim was now put on trial at the state level in Houston, Texas.

With only ten minutes of deliberation in this Houston trial, he was found guilty of transporting less than a half ounce of marijuana across the International Bridge in Laredo. Then, while awaiting sentencing on that charge, he was flown to Orange County to serve trial for the Laguna Beach bust. The judge for this trial, Superior Court Judge Byron McMillan, had been appointed by Governor Ronald Reagan. Leary pleaded not guilty to possession in the Laguna Beach bust, but Judge McMillan quickly denied him bail. A number of press clippings, including an article Leary had written for *Playboy* magazine, were used as evidence that, if allowed to go free on bail, Leary would continue to advocate drug use.

After years of running and fighting, Tim was finally caught. The Laredo case netted him ten years and a $10,000 fine. The Laguna Beach sentence was one to ten years, to run consecutively with the Laredo time. In all, Leary was sentenced to serve a minimum of four and half years in prison before he could be paroled. On March 18, 1970, Timothy Leary was issued a new identity, one not of his choosing: California prisoner number B26358.

Tim was initially incarcerated in Orange County jail and then transferred to the state prison in Chino. Once in Chino, prisoners were separated into minimum, medium, or maximum security sections. The decision on where prisoners were assigned depended on the length of their sentence, the nature of their crimes, and a psychological test administered to each inmate. On his third day at Chino, Tim was administered this psychological test. In a turn of astounding irony, the personality assessment he was given was based on his own research and the tests that he had developed. Tim manipulated his results in order to achieve the highest intelligence score he could while still showing that he was better suited for outdoor work like gardening and forestry than for clerical work. He also rigged it so that his personality profile would show him to be, in his own words, "normal, non-impulsive, docile, conforming." Tim was angling for assignment in the west wing of the California Men's Colony in San Luis Obispo. This was considered to be the country club of the penal system, with the least violent inmates, the most privileges, a golf course, a swimming pool, and plenty of time outdoors. In contrast, Black Panther leader Huey Newton was being held in the medium security part of the prison under heavy surveillance by armed guards.

Tim succeeded in being assigned to the minimum security area of the prison. Early on in his incarceration, he held on to the hope that his legal appeals would meet with success. But as the days wore on, those chances seemed dimmer. Vocal support and fundraisers featuring such youth culture celebrities as John Lennon, Yoko Ono, Wavy Gravy, Abbie Hoffman, Jerry Rubin, Alan Watts, and, of course, Allen Ginsberg, were used to help Rosemary Leary raise money for his defense. They also assured that Leary's fight was kept public and that he was presented as a political prisoner of conscience. However, when Tim was returned to court in Orange County for one last appeal to be released on bail, the district attorney made a strong case that, once freed, Leary would continue to spread his "messianic ideas about psychedelic drugs to young people." The steady stream of hippies who came to stand outside the gates at Chino as a show of support for Leary did nothing to detract from the idea that Leary was a charismatic leader who needed to be kept under wraps. Bail was denied and Leary was sent back to Chino. With supporters unable to free him and bail denied, Leary finally whispered to Rosemary during one of her visits that he wanted to escape. From that moment on, Rosemary's efforts were no longer focused on freeing Tim by legal channels. Instead, she would work to secure funds and hatch plans to help her husband escape from prison.

Leary's trip from the California penal system to exile in Algeria and, ultimately, to life on the run throughout Europe is the stuff of underground legend. It involved a coordinated effort between four of the most notorious countercultural groups of the Sixties to free one its most controversial spokesmen. While the breakout itself was planned by Tim and another prisoner, the larger operation involved the efforts of the Brotherhood of Eternal Love, the Weather Underground, the Yippies, and the Black Panthers. Rosemary Leary served as the project coordinator, raising money and assuring that all the pieces were in place and ready for Tim's escape.

Leary was incarcerated a total of 204 days before his escape. During that time, his fame served him well among the prison population. The famous Dr. Leary—the "Pope of Dope"—was often given small but important tokens such as free tobacco, reading material, and special bits of food and drink. He was also approached by prisoners asking questions about drugs or more pressing psychological issues they were facing. Leary had traveled a lifetime away from his Concord Prison Experiment, but his current situation certainly echoed those days loudly. He was still accorded privileges and respect as a noted, cutting-edge psychologist, but now, instead of coming and going at his leisure, he was serving time right along with the rest of the prisoners.

Tim also took the opportunity to work on his handball game—becoming one of the better players in the prison, while also building up the physical strength he would need to make his escape. In *Prison Notes*, a book about these first prison days that carried an introduction by Allen Ginsberg in which he called Leary "a hero of American consciousness," Tim talks about the Zen of Handball he discovered in prison: "Handball. Zen ball. Now and then ball kundalin man ball. Whirl and shuffle Sufi trance, high intoxication, drumming rhythm. Partner left, slide right. Weaving lines embroider opponent's loom. The game shifts from muscular competition to magic."

In typical Leary fashion, while recounting some of the brutal and tedious realities of prison life, *Prison Notes* casts Tim as a strong lead character, providing peace, understanding, and leadership to cons, many of whom he regarded as fellow victims of America's draconian drug laws. "He was 23 in prison since age 16 seething energy, completely at war with system, resigned life time brutal confinement. . . . He gazed on me his culture hero. Oh man wait til I tell my sister I met you. You're her idol. How old is she? Fifteen."

Despite the projection of a relatively smooth transition to prison life, Tim, of course, wanted out. Unlike most other prisoners, he had the contacts, financial means, and chutzpah to make it happen. Getting himself assigned to the west wing of the California Men's Colony in San Luis Obispo was the first major step toward freedom.

The principal organizers for the Brotherhood of Eternal Love were now scattered, literally, across the world. They still supported Leary, but they were too far away and too hunted themselves to provide anything more than financial support. Working on the outside, Rosemary Leary got money from the Brotherhood and offered it to the Weather Underground to pay for the expenses of breaking Tim out of prison. Weatherman founder Jeff Jones described their interest in helping Tim escape: "We were well aware that he had been arrested and jailed and given a rather lengthy sentence for possession of one or two joints. And we thought that was outrageous. I certainly remember the Brotherhood. I never actually met any of them. They gave the money to someone who gave it to us. It wasn't our idea to get Tim out of jail. We never helped break him out of prison. He broke himself out. . . . It was a real poke in the eye to California and the drug laws. It was a big fuck-you."

Enlisting the help of an experienced inmate who knew the prison, Tim developed his plan. Near cell block 324 there was a telephone wire strung across the yard and above the wire fence. The wire was higher than the lights, so once he was on it Tim would be hard to spot. He would make his break on a Saturday night, because everyone would either be watching a movie or in the TV rooms, thus he'd have fewer eyes on him and longer to get away before being noticed. To ensure the least visibility, Tim changed his white sneaker laces to brown ones, covered the white strip on his sneakers with black paint, and blackened the handball gloves he'd need to protect his hands as he inched across the wire. He left a farewell note in his prison locker saying, in part:

> IN THE NAME OF THE FATHER . . . AND OF THE SON . . .
> AND OF THE HOLY GHOST . . . AVE MARIA. PRISON
>   GUARDS
> LISTEN TO CAGE A LIVING CREATURE IS . . .
> A SIN AGAINST GOD
> LISTEN GUARDS . . . TO THE ANCIENT TRUTH . . .

HE WHO ENSLAVES . . . IS HIMSELF ENSLAVED . . .
THE FUTURE BELONGS TO THE BLACKS AND THE
  BROWNS
AND THE YOUNG AND THE WILD AND THE FREE

As planned, on the Saturday night of Tim's escape, most of the prison was tucked away watching TV or a movie. Tim made it through the prison and across the illuminated prison yard just before 9PM. He climbed up a tree and dropped onto a rooftop. He took off his sneakers and socks to step as quietly as possible as he made his way across the roofs to building 324. Once there, he slipped his shoes and socks back on and pulled his hands into his blackened handball gloves. The gloves had served him well on the prison courts. Now they would be used one last time as he pulled himself across the wire to freedom. This would prove to be the most challenging part of the breakout.

The telephone wire swayed and bounced with every move. Tim's arms and legs, wrapped around the wire as he hung below, were cramped and exhausted within minutes. He made his way, literally inch by inch, across the length of the prison yard. He was high enough above it that at one point a patrol car drove beneath Tim but didn't notice him dangling in the night air. Tim could look down and see the officer stub out his cigarette in the ashtray as he drove past. The anxiety rush of this near detection gave Tim the jolt of energy he needed to make it the rest of the way across the wire. He got to the pole outside the perimeter fence and slid down the rough wood, dropping his eyeglasses in the process. Tim scrambled around to find his glasses, then made for the railroad tracks that ran parallel to Highway 1. He hid in the tall grass of a ravine near the tracks and watched for a car with its right blinker flashing. This was the signal that his rescuers—the Weather Underground—had arrived.

Once he was picked up by the Weathermen, Tim was given a change of clothes and a new set of identification. For the moment, Tim was to be known as William McNellis, born November 14, 1929. Tim's prison clothes were transferred to another car to be driven south and then dumped in a gas station restroom. Meanwhile, Tim headed north. His hair was dyed. He was given a fake mustache. He was stashed in a duplex in North Oakland, where he bathed and got some much needed sleep. Then it was back on the road, heading north, where he would meet up with the leadership of the Weathermen—Mark Rudd, Jeff Jones, Bernardine Dohrn, and Bill Ayers—to discuss his next move. Tim offered to stay in the United States and help the underground revolution, but he was far too high-profile and hunted to be of use to anyone. They needed to get Tim out of the country. But to do that, they needed a new plan and better fake IDs. For now, they would have to move him around the Northwest just ahead of the manhunt that had begun. When J. Edgar Hoover was asked about Tim's escape, he replied, "We'll have him in ten days."

With headlines across the country screaming the news of Leary's prison escape, Tim sent out a formal statement through the Weathermen. The violence of the missive shows just how fearful Leary was—and how he had adapted his peaceful "drop out" philosophies since the Be-In and the Barge Summit on Alan Watts' houseboat. It seemed Leary was abandoning the anti-political peace and love movement and was now throwing in his lot with the armed revolutionaries. His words further divided the already splintering counterculture as they closely echoed the Weatherman party line. "There is a time for peace and a time for war. There is the day of laughing Krishna and the day of Grim Shiva. Brothers and sisters, at this time, let us have no more talk of peace. . . . Brothers and sisters, this is a war for survival. Ask Huey and Angela. They dig it. Ask the wild free animals. They know it. . . . There are no non-combatants at Buchenwald, My Lai or Soledad. . . . Remember the Sioux and the German Jews and the black slaves. . . . Remember the buffalo and the Iroquois! Remember Kennedy, King, Malcolm, Lenny!" Leary built to a frenzy, pushing every oppression-button that would resonate with his supporters. Then he unleashed the violence, "To shoot a genocidal robot policeman in the defense of life is a sacred act. . . . Listen, the hour is late. Total war is upon us. Fight to live or you'll die. Freedom is life. Freedom will live." Tim concluded with the most ominous part of his statement: "**WARNING**: I am armed and should be considered dangerous to anyone who threatens my life or my freedom."

The truth was that Leary was never armed, and aside from his ideas, he was far from dangerous. He was scared, and he was taking on the voice of those who had helped free him from prison. Still, he had put the word, put the vibrations of violence, out into the world. In so doing, he burned up much of the goodwill he had gained by "sticking it to the man" with his prison escape.

After the meeting in northern California, Tim was taken to a safe house in Seattle, where he was finally reunited with Rosemary. Without her help, this plan would never have materialized, and they were not about to be separated again. Traveling in disguise as William McNellis and Mary Margaret McCreedy, Tim and Rosemary boarded a plane to

Chicago. There, the Weathermen helped them secure the passports they would need to travel abroad. From Chicago, it was on to Paris. Tim had made it off of U.S. soil, but he needed to get to a country that had no extradition agreement with the United States. As it turned out, Eldridge Cleaver, Minister of Information for the Black Panthers, was living in such a country: Algeria. Algeria had allowed the Panthers to set up their own embassy in a big white house behind a wrought-iron gate. From this compound, the Panthers reached out to leaders in North Korea, China, Lebanon, and Palestine, among other places, while they carried on the work of creating a revolution back in the States. Tim traveled to Algeria and met with Cleaver, and Cleaver agreed to let Tim and Rosemary stay there under the auspices of the Panthers. Tim, ever the optimist, called Rosemary back in Paris telling her, "It's great here. You've got to some over right away. It's wonderful!" The couple had, at long last, found temporary asylum in exile with the Black Panthers. Although they had found respite, it was clear from the start that this was Eldridge Cleaver's turf. Tim and Rosemary were only visitors to the Panther's revolution.

On October 10, 1970, Tim sent a letter to Allen Ginsberg. The letter was mailed from Algeria.

> Beloved Brother,
> How we have thought of you with love.
> It was all a miracle! Incredible luck . . . high adventure . . . weathermen are the most beautiful brave, wise people. Young gods & goddesses. We are so proud to be part of them!
> Panthers are the hope of the world. How perfect that we were received & protected here by young Blacks.
> Algeria is perfect. Great political Satori . . . socialism works here . . . young people smiling . . . no irritation . . . no money hustle, spir-

it of youth & growth. We've been given papers as political refugees—we are no longer americans!!

greatest thing is our love . . . we have just started our honey-moon . . . olympian bliss . . . Finally escaped the heavy heavy weight of the repression which has been a dead weight. We are like teen-agers just discovering love & free life. Delicious freedom. Rosemary is so beautiful—no man ever had a more loyal loving wife—she put her life & freedom on the line time after time. She followed me on the plane (under eyes of 6 Federal pigs!) & we flew together (she has 28 years over her head).

Eldridge is genial genius. Brilliant! Turned on too!

Well, I guess that last incarnation was Irish Revolutionary Poet. We have to fight them. they aren't fooling. they are impersonal, lethal robots. I spent 7 months looking into their gun barrel eyes for signs of human life. I just can't see the point of martyrdom to a machine. We are totally with the Panthers & the third world—Algeria, N. Vietnam, N. Korea, China. We hope to go to Hanoi. So much to talk about dear Brother. Please come over soon. We long to see you & hug you. Thanks for your love. It kept us going. Come soon. Love. Love. Freedom!

T + R

Despite Leary's optimistic tone, the statement he'd de-livered through the Weathermen was weighing heavily on other leaders of the counterculture back in the States. The groups that Leary dealt with at this time were a roll call of America's resistance to war, capitalism, and racism, and each saw a way to benefit from his plight. But despite all of the political posturing, it would be the intellectuals—artists, musicians, philosophers, and writers—who would fight for his freedom. In the end, it was a small handful of such in-dividuals—typified by his old friend Allen Ginsberg—who would continue to defend Leary through his years of exile and recapture.

Ken Kesey was among the first to respond publicly to Leary's post–prison break statement. He wrote an open letter that was widely reprinted in the burgeoning underground newspapers across the country. "Dear Good Doctor Timothy. Congratulations! The only positive memories I have from all my legal experiences was getting away. A good escape almost makes up for the fucking bust." But Kesey quickly got to the crux of the issue: "In this battle, Timothy, we need every mind and every soul, but oh my doctor we don't need one more nut with a gun. I know what jail makes you feel but don't let them get you into their cowboys-and-Indians script. . . . What we need, doctor, is inspiration, enlightenment, creation, not more headlines. Put down that gun, clear that understandable ire from your Irish heart and pray for the vision wherein lies our only true hope. . . . I do not mean to scold someone so much my senior in so many ways; I just don't want to lose you. What I really mean is stay cool and alive and high and out of cages. . . . And keep in mind what somebody, some Harvard holy man I think it was, used to tell us years ago: 'The revolution is over and we have won.' "

Playing out the "cowboys-and-Indians script" that Kesey was talking about, Leary told a reporter from *Rolling Stone* who interviewed them in Algeria that he thought the letter was written by the FBI, who had "ripped off his [Kesey's] energy." Since the FBI was, indeed, infiltrating the Black Panther party using such means, Leary was no doubt being coached on evading such tactics. In the same interview, Leary reinforced his armed-revolutionary stance. When asked if he approved of using guns, Leary replied, "It's inevitable. Their [America's] system is based on guns. The Weathermen and I have rapped this through on acid and agree totally. Arms is one of their weapons . . . and one of ours. . . . Anyone who's been through the LSD experience with us is an acid revolutionary now. Dynamite is just the white light, the external manifestation of the inner white light of the Buddha."

Tim also wrote "An Open Letter to Allen Ginsberg on the Seventh Liberation," which restated that he had thrown in with the armed revolution. "Turn on, tune in, drop out" had been replaced. Tim's new slogan was, "Shoot to Live / Aim for Life."

Allen handwrote a letter to Tim—a closed letter, not for public consumption, mailed from Stuyvesant Station in New York City directly to Tim in Algeria—in response to the flurry of missives from his old friend. While chiding Leary at times, the letter also showed remarkable restraint and support. It also illustrates Allen's attempt to model calm for Tim by reminding him of the effects of meditation and breathing on the body. Allen was trying to pacify Tim from thousands of miles away.

Dear Tim,

Thanks for your fresh card and letter—glad you're out & hope things stay secure there—desert culture could be absorbing study if visas unavailable for other societies—odd effect of your Weatherman letter on me was, in sum, I now sit steadily an hour meditation every morning rain or shiney business, Guru om mantra in heart area silently repeated, slow breath back straight eyes closed, & get a little body high (not unlike a bit of junk)—given the busyness of my chatter & all the tickertape going thru my head, it's like going into a dark closet for privacy for a sweet long peaceful hour. . . . I don't know what good "armed & considered dangerous" mantra will do but for that matter not certain on large scale what "unarmed & not considered dangerous" mantra does except in close quarters does keep some peace along with rigorous mass oming from solar plexus sigh. . . . Opinions mixed on your turn, some folk elated, some (white) (& some black) holding steady to old charms. Do you need anything from here I can send you? Regards to Cleaver whom I met in Nashville '67. I'll try to visit in spring or summer.

Allen also informed Tim about a fact that he was just learning from the Panthers and Yippies, a fact that poked a gaping hole into his vision of Algeria as a free zone for his libertarian views on drug use.

Arab countries as well as socialist countries as well as west white all very puritanical about grass, & Black Panther Phila Temple U. convention note reorganizing psychedelics as revolutionary substances may not be exportable or welcome in mysterious East. I could try to sound out India for you via Indira Ghandi if you think it's possible—tho I had a little visa/police trouble there after a year. I would say next up if you both can—trouble is that revolution involving unconditional consciousness may not actually be welcome anywhere—my first thought when I hear you were out, was, Where could he go??

The letter was signed:

Love, as ever, Allen.

"America I've given you all and now I'm nothing."
—Allen Ginsberg

As world traveler Allen Ginsberg had anticipated, there would be no safe place for Timothy Leary to hide. Although the Black Panthers and Yippies tried to present him as a political revolutionary, Leary's vocal advocacy for drug use caught up to him wherever he went. He was simply not a political revolutionary. He was a philosopher whose outspoken opinions about attaining higher consciousness through psychedelic drugs put him at odds with essentially every governing body, secular or religious, across the world. And even in places where he might have found acceptance, the reach of the U.S. authorities was long—they wanted Leary, and other countries wanted to maintain good relationships with the United States. To abet Leary was to defy the United States.

Eventually, Leary's high profile drew too much heat to the Panther compound. Leary had tried, unsuccessfully, to get Cleaver onto a more peaceful wavelength by taking LSD with him. But although Cleaver was a regular pot and hash smoker and had no problem with Panthers using psychedelics on their own time, he wasn't about to turn the Panthers into some mellow Haight Street head scene. Cleaver was juggling too many razor-edged balls of his own: power struggles within the Panther party, strained relations with Algerian officials, constant CIA and FBI surveillance, not to mention a wife and a mistress he had to manage to keep apart on a small patch of land. All of this along with the constant presence of guns and the fear of being tossed back onto U.S. soil at any moment made for what Leary might have described as the ultimate poor "set and setting."

As the situation with the Panthers disintegrated, Leary and Rosemary started planning their next move. In addition to their previous obstacles, Cleaver had now confiscated their passports in an attempt to tamp down their interactions and run-ins with Algerian officials. Tim had also promised Cleaver $2,000 of the $7,500 advance he was expecting from Random House for a book about his prison escape. Unfortunately, Random House had killed the book. There was no money forthcoming, but Leary was still using the promise of the funds as the last card in his deck to keep Cleaver on his side. Without the promise of that money, Cleaver had no further use for Leary.

While it did not reveal the situation with the Panthers, there is a thick waft of desperation, the need for money, in a letter Tim sent to Allen during this period. "As you must know, Allen, our situation is changed. As exile-outlaws our logical business status in USA is unconventional. . . . Personally, we do need funds and would appreciate any monies you could send. Mike Standard has indicated that you told him you would do so. . . . After we receive funds our phone will be re-connected and we can be in closer touch." Then, Leary gets closer to the truth—that he needs the money to appease Cleaver—while also hitting Allen's soft spot for supporting worthy groups in need:

Politically too, there is need for funds. Any funds from USA to Algeria will be used to support our colony here and the important work that is being done and planned here. The US government knows this and tries to keep our funds in USA. We expect that our comrades and friends will also recognize that all funds earned by our energy (our means Eldridge etc) and transmitted too out of USA to us is doubly blessed. Any funds due us and not sent to us is doubly hurtful to our colony here. It has amazed us Allen (and this is an aside) that ninety percent of the people who come to visit us here come empty handed expecting to be entertained, supported here by us and be given stories, pictures etc to take back to USA to contribute to USA. It would be nice if comrades saw the importance of an exile revolutionary center and voluntarily contributed to its expansion.

Leary was desperate and he knew that Allen, in kind terms, was a supporter. In less kind terms, Allen was a soft touch. Throughout Leary's most difficult struggles, Allen helped with fundraisers and often gave money out of his own pocket. He was also quick to head up letter-writing campaigns in support of Leary's cause. Tim wasn't alone in receiving this type of support from Allen. In fact, support for various causes was a hallmark of Allen's behavior his entire life, starting from the time he was a fifteen-year-old boy writing letters to the editors of the *New York Times* chastising the U.S. for not joining the League of Nations. ("I am normally a more or less passive individual. However, I think I am growing cynical. I chuckle and feel a bit of grim humor when I read of our growing regret for the world's biggest blunder, our refusal to join the League.")

Ironically, Tim and Rosemary eventually had to escape from the Black Panthers. The relationship with Cleaver had deteriorated so dramatically that, at one point, Leary and Rosemary were taken out of their living quarters at knife-point and held captive in a room guarded by armed Panthers. And now, on top of it, Leary knew that he would never get the money from Random House.

Once again calling on his friends in the Brotherhood of Eternal Love (whose pockets were undoubtedly deeper than Ginsberg's), Leary received a secret stash of money to fly him and Rosemary out of Algeria. He told Cleaver that the Random House money had arrived, but that he needed their passports to access their joint bank account. Then Tim secured the passports and they boarded a plane bound for Copenhagen with stopovers in Geneva and Zurich. When they landed in Geneva, the couple found a message waiting for them from a French psychiatrist friend of Leary's. The man told them that the authorities were waiting for them in Zurich. To help them out, he had made arrangements for Tim and Rosemary to be picked up and taken care of by a wealthy friend in Geneva named Michel Hauchard.

In the short run, the Leary's were indeed taken care of by Hauchard. They were housed, feted, and treated like visiting royalty, all the while being told by this wealthy international con man and arms dealer that it was his duty to help out philosophers in distress. The truth is that by the end of their relationship Hauchard had secured the rights to all the proceeds from Tim's writing for the next twelve years. Not only that, but when it was clear to Hauchard that Tim wasn't working hard enough on the book, he pulled strings to have him locked up—along with plenty of good food, drink, and, of course, a typewriter—in a Swiss prison.

Not realizing the depth of Hauchard's deception, Tim and Rosemary feared that this imprisonment in Switzerland meant that the jig was up: Tim would be extradited back to the United States and the great escape would be over. Fearing the worst, Rosemary sent a harried letter to Allen Ginsberg. "Tim in Swiss prison . . . locked in solitary as 'most dangerous etc.' Friends worked miracle and I am still out and will see him for 15 minutes today. Wednesday will know if government here will . . . allow extradition. Some karmic mistake—having to regret last year all over again. Handicapped by long range difficulties and vast amount of money needed. New friends here extraordinary but need help from the states united. What to do? Love, R"

Allen responded by spearheading the "Declaration of Independence for Dr. Timothy Leary (July 4, 1971)." The letter was presented as a document written by the "San Francisco Bay Area Prose Poets' Phalanx" and signed by a distinguished—albeit often notorious—group of "Poets, Essayists, and Novelists" including Ken Kesey, Lawrence Ferlinghetti, Anais Nin, Laura Huxley, Ted Berrigan, Don Allen, and, of course, Allen Ginsberg. In addition to being the initial draft of a letter that was delivered to the Swiss Consulate in San Francisco as well as the State Department and Department of Justice in Washington, D.C., it also called on the International PEN Club to intercede on Leary's behalf by declaring him a "literary refugee persecuted by Government for his thoughts and writings."

In the letter, Allen declares:

Whatever one's opinions, or natural or national preferences amongst intoxicants, Letters, religions, and political or ecological theory, the Bay Area Prose Poets' Phalanx hereby affirms that Dr. Leary must certainly have the right to publish his own theories; that at stake in this case, once and for all, is Dr. Leary's freedom to manifest his thoughts in the form of poems, psychological commentaries, dialogues, and essays of literary nature before a public whose younger generations, by themselves credibly experienced with the machines, politics and drugs that are the subject of Dr. Leary's writings, include a large minority (perhaps a majority in his native land) who wish Dr. Leary well, and pray for his security, peace and protection from persecution by Government Police Bureaucracies everywhere.

The letter was picked up in New York by playwright Arthur Miller, who sent a cable to the head of the Federal Department of Justice and Police in Bern, Switzerland, on behalf of all one hundred members of the International PEN Club. PEN urged, "It would seem that Dr. Leary has been sentenced, if not convicted, for his views on drug use; he, therefore, qualifies as an intellectual refugee and we ask the Swiss government to grant him asylum as it has hundreds of other writers, artists, and political figures who have sought refuge in Switzerland after having been forced to flee from other countries."

The intervention of PEN International via Allen Ginsberg no doubt helped secure Leary's release from the Swiss prison. However, it also appears that the group's efforts were secondary to Hauchard's scheming. Even after Leary's old friend Walter Houston Clark mortgaged his home to raise $20,000, which he sent to cover bail, Leary was only released after he signed over the proceeds from all his literary work to Michel Hauchard. Leary was free again, if only for the moment. He would remain free for roughly two years: staying with wealthy patrons, soaking up his notoriety as an international bad-boy celebrity, learning to ski, careening around the mountains in a new Porsche, and taking copious amounts of LSD along with cocaine, Quaaludes, heroin, and any number of other drugs. Pushed apart by the constant stress of life on the run, Rosemary and Tim split-up shortly after his release from the Swiss prison. In short order, Tim hooked up with an erratic, aristocratic twenty-six-year old Swiss woman named Joanna Harcourt-Smith. Joanna would ride with Timothy Leary on his last hurrah in Switzerland and on to his final bust in Kabul, Afghanistan.

In late 1972, under the mistaken impression that they would be welcomed and protected in Kabul as friends of the Brotherhood of Eternal Love, Tim and Joanna boarded a plane bound for Afghanistan. The Brotherhood had made some people in Kabul very rich by acting as their drug distributors, and now Tim and Joanna were assured that they would be taken care of by those same people. As Tim and Joanna were sitting on a bench waiting to go through customs, still high from the acid they had dropped on the plane ride, an official stalked up to them and asked, "Are you Timothy Leary?" Without waiting for a response, the man grabbed Tim's passport and hustled away. Tim made a scene, yelling and screaming that the man had just stolen his passport, but they all knew what was happening. Tim turned to Joanna and the other man they were traveling with—Dennis Martino, the brother of Susan Leary's husband, the Brotherhood connection who had urged them to fly to Kabul—and said, "I'm going back to America." The authorities knew that Tim was coming; he had been snitched on. But the worst deception was still unknown to Tim: it was his own son-in-law, David Martino, who had tipped off the feds about Tim's travel plans. David had been busted for a small amount of marijuana in California and had given up his famous father-in-law in return for freedom.

Tim was returned to the United States and landed back in the same prison he had broken out of three years earlier, the California Men's Colony in San Luis Obispo. But this time, he wouldn't be allowed to stay in the relatively cushy west wing. Tim was placed in solitary confinement and stripped of any creature comforts beyond the starkest prison basics. On April 23, 1973, he was sentenced to six months to five years for his prison escape—that sentence was in addition to the fifteen-year state sentence for his pot bust in Laguna and ten-year federal sentence for his bust at Laredo.

Upon sentencing, Tim was transferred to Folsom Prison. There he was locked in the bottom tier of the prison, a 138-cell "jail within a jail" called the adjustment center. In a matter of months, he had gone from swishing down ski slopes in Switzerland to sitting alone in the dankest section of one of the most foreboding prisons in America, staring down the barrel of accumulated sentences that could keep him imprisoned well into his seventies. Tim was out of luck; the countercultural organizations that had helped him out in the past had either been squashed by the Feds or torn apart by internal squabbling, and his main tie to the outside world, Joanna Leary (although they were not married, she legally changed her name to assist in his defense), was under increasing pressure to get Tim to turn informant. To make matters worse, Tim's old allies were suspicious of Joanna—some going so far as to accuse her of helping get Tim busted. Allen Ginsberg told Tim that, at the very least, rather than helping his cause, Joanna was "blowing precious money and turning off a lot of otherwise sympathetic people."

With Joanna alienated from Tim's old counterculture allies, the people she communicated with most were bracing her for the reality that unless he cooperated, Tim would be in prison for a long, long time. Joanna was desperate. Tim was out of options.

In November 1973 Tim was transferred to the medium-security California Medical Facility at Vacaville, where he was allowed to work as a trusty in the psychiatric facility. The facility was certainly an improvement over Folsom, but freedom was still well out of reach. According to Joanna, during one visit to Vacaville, Tim asked her to send a telegram to the FBI and the DEA telling them that he was ready to cooperate. He wanted out of prison, and if that meant playing the informant game, then Timothy Leary would become an informant.

Om Ah Hum

On September 18, 1974, a new group calling itself PILL staged a press conference before an audience of nearly two hundred press and public in the regal Georgian Room of the St. Francis Hotel in San Francisco. PILL was an acronym for the damning full title: People Investigating Leary's Lies. At the height of the Sixties, a group with such a mission would surely have consisted of outraged parents, gubernatorial hopefuls, and over-the-hill celebrities chasing down the spotlight while bemoaning the corruption of the country's youth. But this group was made up of those who'd been Tim's allies all along. Now, however, instead of chanting, "Free Tim Leary!" his former supporters were denouncing him as a turncoat.

PILL was organized after it was learned that Tim and Joanna Leary had set up their lawyer and friend George Chula to get busted. Chula was known for his legal defense of counterculture figures, including Leary, and the feds wanted him. On September 4, 1974, Joanna—who had worked with the DEA to record Chula giving her drugs—testified against him before an Orange County grand jury. When asked why she was testifying, Joanna, visibly coked up and high during the trial, claimed, "Because the first year I spent in this country, I met a lot of people who were part of the drug culture. . . . I found ninety-nine percent of them to be dishonest, lying people." Tim backed up Joanna's testimony by saying that Chula had smuggled hash to him in prison. The next day, Chula's office was raided by narcotics agents and he was arrested.

The day after Chula was busted an interview with Tim appeared in the *Los Angeles Times*. The interview spotlighted the new stance Tim had taken. It was his public justification for working as an informant: "Secrecy and cover-up are destructive and dangerous and I wanted to become part of the process of reconciliation and openness that is the spirit of the times." Further, Tim said that the Sixties was a "time when the public forum was captured by the crazies of the left and the crazies of the right. I never felt I was a criminal, and I never dealt drugs. I am still a scientist, I feel, and I want to make a contribution." The headline of the article read, "Leary, 'Former King of LSD,' Tells Radicals: 'War is Over.'"

Abbie Hoffman, among many other Sixties compatriots, saw Tim's turn in a different light. In a letter written during this time, Hoffman wrote, "I'm digesting the news of Herr Doktor Leary, the swine. . . . It's obvious to me he's talked his fucking demented head off to the Gestapo. . . . God, Leary is disgusting. It's not just a question of being a squealer but a question of squealing on people who *helped* you. . . . The curses crowd my mouth . . . Timothy Leary is a name worse than Benedict Arnold."

It was in this spirit that the PILL press conference was organized. Journalist and *Berkeley Barb* editor Ken Kelley introduced the group as "a loosely devised network of concerned individuals and investigators banded together in the last two weeks. We are simply fed up with being victimized by the government's conspiracy mongering and its attempts to shatter the cohesiveness of the left." Kelley continued, "By setting up Timothy Leary as a government agent, the Justice Department is using the same old divide-and-conquer, red-baiting ploys it has used in the Palmer Raids, the McCarthy Hearings, the Rosenberg case, and the Watergate Plumbers."

Supporting Kelley's opening statements was a petition signed by more than a hundred high-profile members of the counterculture, stating, "We condemn the terrible pressures brought to bear by the government on people in the prisons in this country. . . . We also denounce Timothy Leary for turning state's evidence and marking innocent people for jail in order to get out of jail himself."

Seated alongside Kelley were Yippie founder Jerry Rubin, Dick Alpert, Allen Ginsberg, and Leary's own son, Jack. One after another, the panelists denounced Leary's cooperation with the feds and condemned the government for its relentless pursuit of Sixties figures. Rubin said of Leary, "I know from personal experience with him over the past ten years that he never had a firm grasp of where truth ended and fantasy began. He used words and sentences for their effect, not for their internal truth." He also emphasized, "In breaking him in prison and turning him into an agent, the government is consciously trying to spread fear, cynicism, and despair among young people. 'See what kind of person your guru Tim Leary is,' they are saying. 'You cannot trust him.' I deeply regret that Tim Leary is allowing himself to be used."

Tim's former Harvard colleague and staunch supporter, Richard Alpert, now renamed Ram Dass by his Indian guru, denounced Leary as a "scoundrel." However, most damning was the testimony from Tim's son, Jack Leary. The only panelist not accustomed to public speaking, Jack spoke slowly, haltingly, noting that "I have always gone out of my way in the past to avoid publicity. But I feel compelled to come forward now because Timothy is engaged in a very dangerous action which can destroy the lives of many of his former friends and associates."

Like Rubin, Jack noted that this turn was not uncharacteristic for Tim. In fact, Jack's only surprise was that "he didn't do this two or three years ago." He corroborated that Tim "lies when he thinks it will benefit him. He finds lies easier to control than the truth." Reflecting the concern for their own freedom that many of Tim's former allies felt, Jack said, "It would not surprise me if he would testify about my sister or myself if he could. He has already implicated my sister in his escape. Knowing this, I have avoided visiting him in prison, in order to have as little to do with him as possible." Jack concluded by stating, "I do not believe by this statement that I am in any way betraying Timothy's trust. Rather, Timothy Leary, by his deceit, is betraying the very meaning of the word trust."

True to form, of all those speaking up about the situation, Allen Ginsberg gave the most measured statement. And the most poetic. Rather than give a formal statement, Allen wrote and recited, "Om Ah Hum: 44 Temporary Questions on Dr. Leary." While not letting Leary off the hook completely, the poem raised more questions than it answered and made it clear that Allen had not written Tim off yet. In fact, no matter how often Tim might have disappointed—or even publicly insulted—him, Allen would never completely abandon Tim.

Om Ah Hum: 44 Temporary Questions on Dr. Leary

1. Trust. (Should we stop trusting our friends like in a Hotel room in Moscow?)
2. Is he a Russian-model prisoner brought into courtroom news conferences blinking in daylight after years in jails and months incommunicado in solitary cells with nobody to talk to but thought-control police interrogators?
3. Is his head upside down?
4. Will we indulge in cannibalism, eating his mind?
5. Isn't it common sense to turn the other cheek to his forced confessions?
6. What advice give young on L.S.D. (Try it with healthy mind body and speech!)
7. No L.S.D. Cactus mushroom teachers needed now in Cities, isn't Lady Psychedelia big enough to teach by herself with all her Granny-Wisdom?
8. Is it déjà-vu, Leary's forced confession so outrageous—are all my serious prefaces to his books and imperious anti-thought-control declarations reduced to rubbish?
9. "Flow along with the Natural errors of things." Old Chinese wisdom and sense of humor. Will this be harder for those caught in Leary's new truthfulness & new lying?
10. Isn't his new truthfulness a lie to please the police to let him go?
11. Is he like Zabbathi Zvi the False Messiah, accepted by millions of Jews centuries ago, who left Europe for the Holy Land, was captured by the Turks on his way, told he'd have his head cut off unless he converted to Islam, and so accepted Allah? Didn't his followers split into sects some claiming it was a wise decision?
12. Isn't there an element of humor in Leary's new twist?
13. Doesn't he recently hear of voices from outer space, does he want to leave earth like a used-up eggshell? Has he given up on the planet?
14. Is he finally manifesting an Alchemical Transformation of consciousness?

15. Is there more police space henceforth, no opposition allowed?
16. Are not the police, especially drug police, corrupt and scandal-ridden, Watergate person like Liddy & Mardian connected with his long persecution,/ urban narcs sealing and peddling heroin?
17. Is Leary on his way to outer space in Space Ship Terra II still?
18. What of the rumors and messages heard last spring that brain conditioner experiment drugs were to be administered to Leary in Vacaville prison, where such experiments were common?
19. Isn't it clear that no friend has spoken with Leary personally recently, he's been shifted prison to prison, his lawyers can't reach him, he's been incommunicado sequestered for "confessions" surrounded by government agents & informers no one else hears from him?
20. Is Joanna Harcourt-Smith his one contact spokes-agent a sex spy, agent provocateuse, double-agent, CIA hysteric, jealous tigress, or what?
21. What was Joanna's role, isolating him from decade-old supporters and friends, using up all his crucial legal defense money? Remember when I suggested to Leary that she might be some sort of police agent he turned to her asking, "What do you say?" She looked at him and answered "He hates women." Folsom Prison Spring 1973?
22. Shouldn't police give up their case as preposterous and remember that 410,000 other Americans were busted for pot in 1973?
23. Wasn't Leary trusted by many people who contributed to his legal defense funds, wrote declarations, lectured and sang moneyraising in defense of his professional & constitutional rights as a psychologist experimenting new research field?
25. Didn't he turn in his own Lawyer for bringing him pot in jail, is that a light matter like 50-dollar fine, or jail & disbarment?
26. Is Leary exaggerating and lying to build such confused cases

and conspiracies that the authorities will lose all the trials
he witnesses, & he'll be let go in the confusion?

27. Where has Leary's humor gone? Did he ever claim to be
priest except to escape obnoxious law? Is he messianic? Can
his word be trusted in court? Can President Ford's? Or the
entire Government's?

28. Will it end that all the victims of his song are his lawyers?

29. Will there be more political trials like those of Spock,
Berrigan, Chicago 7, Ellsberg, collapsible conspiracy
entrapments of bohemian left by right-wing government
fanatics left over from Watergate conspiracy? More domestic
police violence against non-alcoholic teaheads? Government
prosecutors who have Leary by the balls for smoking pot,
like Guy Goodwin, do they drink cocktails?

30. Does Leary see himself spiritual president like Nixon, & is
he trying to clean the Karma blackboard by creating a hippie
Watergate? Will he be pardoned by the next guru?

31. Is the Government-announced change on Leary's part
rational, objective, free and calm—or angry fearful suffering
jail too long?

32. Will Leary's documentary confession film be seen by friends
in theater or courtroom?

33. Speaking of Acid Capitalism, Leary was too broke to
fund his very solid legal appeals, thousands of people
including myself contributed too little to see it to successful
conclusion, so who makes money on acid and grass, men in
jail, or their jailers and prosecutors? How many millions $
have the police spent entrapping Leary?

34. Prosecutors like Goodwin to whom Leary sings, have
conducted witch-hunts with False Witnesses before, is it
not?

35. Did anybody ever hear of the need to hide Leary
incommunicado to protect him from his old friends who
might harm him, except from police mouths? Is it not police
mind naiveté that imagines "contracts" on his body?

36. Would the Government agree to public symposium (such as
this) & Leary free to present his new thoughts to old friends

in press conference in calm manysided discussion, to clear
the air of false & forced confession? Must his changes be
announced by remote control from secret rooms through
selected media contacts, or via videotape screens behind
which no friend can look?

37. Wasn't it amazing to begin with, prophetic mix of Liddy
    & Leary at Millbrook in mid sixties, and Liddy's dozens of
    illegal raids!?
38. Are there any police here at the press conference?
39. America, must I examine my conscience?
40. In the gaspetroleum ballgames are the police winning a
    metaphysical victory?
41. Will more citizens be arrested and taken to jail as was Leary?
42. What will Kissinger say? Will he also be arrested for
    conspiring "more than 8 million $" Chile subversion lying &
    Allende killed?
43. Will citizens be arrested indicted taken to jail for Leary's
    freedom?
44. Doesn't the old cry "Free Tim Leary!" apply now urgent as
    ever?

Allen Ginsberg, 18 March 1974

From the time of Tim's original imprisonment until his
final release in April 21, 1976, Allen continued to write
letters to Tim, worked to keep his case visible, and fought
for his release. In January 1975, Allen submitted a sworn
affidavit stating that, since Tim had been out of touch with
basically all of his previous friends and supporters, except
for Joanna, he had "strong suspicions that Dr. Leary is being
held *incommunicado* at least to some extent against his free
will, and I am convinced that the only way to determine
whether or not this is true, and whether or not Dr. Leary
really needs and wants assistance, legal or otherwise, is to
arrange an opportunity for him to confer with counsel, and/
or friends, free from interference from or eavesdropping by

authorities of the government, in order that Dr. Leary might feel free to indicate whether he needs and wants assistance, and whether or not his rights have been and are being violated." Allen concluded the affidavit by stating, "I am prepared to be one of those persons who should be authorized to visit with Dr. Leary."

During Tim's final incarceration, Allen had, in fact, been one of the few old compatriots who had actually seen and spoken to him. In 1973, Allen and Lawrence Ferlinghetti visited Tim in Folsom Prison. They drove there from San Francisco in a two-tone VW bus. At the time, Tim had just been moved from "the adjustment center," where he was housed between Geronimo Pratt, the Black Panther who spent twenty-seven years in jail for a murder conviction that was eventually overturned, and Charles Manson. Although they had polar opposite views of the world—one dark and cynical, the other optimistic and hopeful—Tim and Charles Manson held long conversations through the wall while jailed next to each other at Folsom. Wesley Hiler, a prison psychologist who knew them both, said, "They liked each other very much. But they were both on big power trips. They were both megalomaniacs and both felt they were, sort of, supermen. They exaggerated their uniqueness; they believed in their powers. Yet they were quite different. Leary was not at all psychotic."

When Allen and Lawrence showed up at Folsom, Tim had just been moved out of solitary confinement and onto the main line. Prison officials made sure that Tim looked horrible when they met. They had crudely shaved his head so that his skull was covered with nicks and blood, and, unlike the setup for Tim's visits with Joanna, which were conducted across a table, they kept Tim in a glass cage during the meeting. They clearly wanted to show that Tim was now in their control. Lawrence Ferlinghetti recalled, "What I remember most clearly is Tim saying he was going to escape from Folsom by ascending straight up via LSD. He had a spaced-out enraptured look as he said it, as if he had already swallowed some acid." Allen immediately began reciting the Heart Sutra to Tim through the glass. He and Tim had gone through a lifetime together; the rise and the fallout of the Sixties had sifted through their fingers like billions of tiny universes and reshaped the country, and their lives. Allen would do the best he could to help his old partner, but ultimately it would be Tim's betrayal of his counterculture ideals and friends that bought him his freedom.

On April 21, 1976, Timothy Leary was released from prison. Although he was free, his reputation in the countercultural community and, certainly, the academic community had been destroyed. He was seen as having sold out the values and betrayed the trust of every group that had supported him. Immediately upon leaving prison, he began receiving death threats. Federal marshals flew him and Joanna to a secluded A-frame house in the Pecos Wilderness area of the Santa Fe National Forest in New Mexico. They were issued false names (James and Nora Joyce, after Leary's enigmatic, beloved Irish author) and given $700 a month through the Witness Protection Program. However they soon grew restless, bored, and stifled by the isolation. They moved to San Diego only two months after landing in New Mexico.

Three months after his release from prison, Tim sat down at a typewriter in San Diego and wrote a letter to Allen. From his optimistic tone ("I've signed up for a college-lecture tour in the fall—and the response is most encouraging.") to his references to the plights of fellow countercultural figures ("So we are in pretty good shape, our little band of dissenters—Solz is okay in Zurich, Sakharov is still free, Amarik has left for Israel . . . only Patty and Eldridge are left") it sounded much like the old Timothy Leary. In a June 1976 interview with the *Berkeley Barb*, Tim emphatically denied testifying against the Brotherhood of Eternal Love, the Weathermen, or any of his old allies: "I did not testify against friends. I didn't testify against what the press called 'the vast drug conspiracy known as the Brotherhood of Eternal Love' since that was a myth that never existed. I didn't testify in any manner that would lead to indictments against the Weatherpeople. . . . The fact is that nobody has been arrested because of me and nobody ever will be." In true Leary mode, he was refashioning the whole boondoggle of busts, imprisonment, federal cooperation, and the accompanying deluge of public evisceration, as if it had been nothing more than a game. In Leary's mind, he had simply worked the system—providing the feds with useless information—to get himself free. If anything, he insisted, "When the full details of my actual testimony are known, the Weather Underground might even be grateful to me."

Throughout his life, Timothy Leary had proved as malleable as Allen Ginsberg was steadfast. But to his credit, Leary couldn't deny the support, comfort, and aid that Ginsberg had afforded him through his darkest struggles. He wrote to Allen: "Anyway, now that I have a typewriter and a desk I hasten to thank you Allen for your concern and help in getting me out of prison. . . . Thanks for your help. All goes well. May be in New York in the next few weeks—so I'll phone you. Looking forward to seeing you. Long time. Timothy."

Allen Ginsberg, Timothy Leary and John C. Lilly.
Polaroid photograph taken on Easter Sunday
1991, at the home of Dr. Oscar Janiger.
© *Philip Hansen Bailey*

Final Trips

While never closely associated after the 1970s, Allen Ginsberg and Timothy Leary both remained iconic figures for the rest of their lives. By the 1980s, Leary was making his living as a "stand-up philosopher" touring college campuses and even nightclubs, sharing his unique blend of Irish blarney, good humor, and progressive ideas. Ten years after his release, most of the people who had held a grudge against him were either dead, incarcerated, or living outside the country, or had constructed mainstream lives that could only suffer from rehashing their outlaw pasts; Leary had survived and stayed in the public eye long enough to benefit from the aura of his past without being weighed down by its baggage. His most famous—and classically Learyian—events were dual speaking engagements with his old nemesis G. Gordon Liddy.

After running Leary out of Millbrook, Liddy had gained notoriety as a chief operative in the White House Plumbers unit that broke into the Democratic National Committee headquarters in 1972. The break-in led to Richard Nixon's resignation and Liddy's imprisonment for four and a half years. In the end, Leary and Liddy had both ended up in the same place: prison. And after prison, they both ended up "singing for their supper" on the lecture circuit: Liddy as an arch-conservative; Leary, increasingly, as a proponent of then-emerging computer technology as well as space exploration.

Much as in their past incarnations, Liddy and Leary were perfect foils for each other, right down to their physical appearance: Liddy fit, ramrod straight, with a tidy little mustache; Leary with a puckish twinkle in his eye and the rumpled demeanor of a pleasantly stoned Classics professor. While he continued to use drugs in his private life, Leary disavowed the cultural wars of the 1960s. Even as the "drug wars" of the 1980s heated up under the presidency of his other old nemesis, Ronald Reagan, he remained intent on avoiding drug rhetoric in favor of looking ahead into the future, a future built on the twin pillars of technology and space exploration. Still fond of naming his movements, Leary created an acronym for the activities that supported his new belief in technology and space travel: SMI^{2}LE. The "SM" stood for "Space Migration" the "I^2" stood for "Intelligence Increase" and the "LE" stood for "Life Extension." While SMI^{2}LE would never have the mass influence of his most famous phrases or groups, Leary remained committed to these subjects for the rest of his life, and even after death.

Ten months after he died from prostate cancer in 1996, Tim made headlines one last time. He had contracted with a company called Celestis Inc to have his ashes launched into space, and on April 21, 1997, Leary's ashes, along with those of Star Trek creator Gene Roddenberry and twenty-two other people, were enclosed in small canisters engraved with their names and bolted to a motor aboard Spain's first satellite. Once in space, Leary's ashes would orbit the earth for two to ten years, until they reentered the atmosphere and disintegrated in a ball of flame.

In a 1987 interview with Allen Ginsberg, journalist Steve Silberman probed the sexagenarian poet's feelings about drugs and America's policies toward them. Ginsberg responded, "All scientific research on LSD has been stopped, except for very few projects done under the military, and that's a major catastrophe for human mind engineering and scientific advancement and psychology. The heroin problem stands as it always was: a conspiracy by heroin police, narcotics bureaus, their bureaucracies and budgets—with their working relation with Cosa Nostra and organized crime in maintaining a black market and high prices and sales under the desk—as well as regular organized crime dope laundry money, and that whole network extends from the White House to the Vatican. Contras—White House—Vatican. So the whole public approach by Reagan is just complete hypocrisy."

With regard to LSD specifically, Ginsberg said, "I've changed my mind about the relationship between acid and neurosis—it seems to me that acid can lead to some kind of breakdowns maybe. So that people should be prepared with meditation, before they take acid. There should be an educational program to cultivate meditative practice and techniques, so that when people get high on acid and get into bum trips they can switch their minds, easily—and there are ways of doing it, very simple. But nobody is doing mass training in that, and it might be interesting for high school kids. It's like—give junkies needles, give kids condoms if they're gonna screw so they don't get AIDS. If they're gonna try acid—which is probably good for an intelligent kid—they should also be prepared with some techniques in meditation, so that they can switch their attention from bum trips back to their breath, and to the current space around them. So I think in the Sixties I wasn't prepared to deal with acid casualties from the point of view of a reliable technique for avoiding those casualties."

Older, wiser, a dedicated Buddhist, and a college professor, Allen Ginsberg—like Timothy Leary—had tempered his views on drug use, but never compromised his core dedication to speaking the truth as he saw it, even when his ideas (e.g., acid is "probably a good idea for an intelligent kid") were far outside the mainstream. Perhaps especially when they *were* far outside the mainstream. Despite his often controversial views, Ginsberg remained a high-demand visiting poet on college campuses and—whether it was the CIA's role in heroin smuggling, gay rights, environmentalism, or any number of other issues—he wove his concerns into his poetry readings, making each one an authentic encounter with an evolving countercultural hero. In the early 1970s Ginsberg's Tibetan Buddhist teacher, Chögyam Trungpa, challenged him to cut his hair and wear a coat and tie in order to separate himself from his famous Allen Ginsberg image and ego. From that time forward, the classic picture of Ginsberg—fuzzy beard, glasses, spray of dark, curling locks—was offset by sport coats and ties, which the poet would pick up in secondhand stores. In 1974, Ginsberg won the National Book Award for his poetry collection *The Fall of America*. In 1979 he was awarded a National Arts Club gold medal and was inducted into the American Academy and Institute of Arts and Letters. In 1995, two years before he died, Ginsberg won a Pulitzer Prize for his book *Cosmopolitan Greetings: Poems 1986–1995*.

While he may have been lauded by the august institutions of American letters in his later years, Ginsberg was far from defanged. He had simply learned less confrontational ways to forward his agendas. But, more significantly, many of Ginsberg's early views about homosexuality, spiritualism, and the environment had taken hold so securely in America they now seemed almost mainstream. In the same 1987 interview with Steve Silberman he said, "The culture has changed sufficiently that it will take me more or less on my own terms. Although some of my edges are smoothed down now. I don't insult people inadvertently or advertently—I try and treat them with a kind of Buddhist gentility, gentleness, even if I feel that they're neurotic or incompetent I try not to pin them wriggling to the wall, but try and help 'em get out of that space, or make their situation workable rather than challenging them. Trying to enrich them rather than challenge them."

Allen died of liver cancer in 1997. During his last days, he continued to put the finishing touches on a final long poem titled "Death & Fame." In that poem, Allen declares that he doesn't care what happens to his body, as long as there is a "big funeral" attended by everyone whose life he touched and those who touched his. Allen's list in "Death & Fame" is long, but nowhere near comprehensive. That would have been impossible.

NOTES

Specific information on each source can be found in the bibliography.

SECTION ONE—TURN ON

Chapter One—Blakean Vision in Harlem
All Allen Ginsberg quotes related to the Blake vision are taken from his *Paris Review* (Spring 1966) interview as reprinted in *Spontaneous Mind*. Details of Ginsberg's life, relationships, and insights are gathered primarily from *I Celebrate Myself, The Letters of Allen Ginsberg, The Book of Martyrdom + Avarice, Ginsberg: A Biography, Spontaneous Mind,* and Ginsberg's poetry.

Chapter Two—A New Game
The quote from Marianne Leary's suicide note is from *I Have America Surrounded*. Mary Della Cioppa's quote "When we were married . . ." is taken from *Timothy Leary: A Biography*. Quotes about the apartment in Spain ("tunneled into rock . . .") and Leary's breakdown ("There the break-through-break-down . . .") are from *High Priest*. Aldous Huxley's letter to Dr. Humphry Osmond is from *The Letters of Aldous Huxley*. General details of Leary's life are primarily from *I Have America Surrounded, Timothy Leary: A Biography, Flashbacks,* and *High Priest*.

Chapter Three—The Father, Son, and the Holy Ghost
Aldous Huxley quote ("That humanity at large . . .) is from *Heaven and Hell*. Deathbed quote from Aldous Huxley ("Be gentle with them . . .) from *Timothy Leary: A Biography*. Deathbed description of Laura Huxley and quotes ("You are going forward and up . . .") are from "Laura Huxley's Letter on Aldous' Passing" from the Stolaroff Collection. Details of Dr. Albert Hofmann's life are taken from a variety of sources including, but not limited to, *Acid Dreams, Utopiates, Hallucinogens: A Reader,* and *Storming Heaven*. Hofman's quotes about "Bicycle Day" ("I had to leave work . . .) are from *LSD: My Problem Child*. Quotes from the 1996 interview with Hofmann ("This is a very, very deep problem . . .") are from Dr. Charles S. Grob's interview as printed in *Hallucinogens: A Reader*. "Set and setting" quotes from Myron J. Stolaroff's

essay "Using Psychedelics Wisely" are taken from *Hallucinogens: A Reader* and Leary's own writing.

Chapter Four—Immoveable If Not Immortal
Lawrence Ferlinghetti quote ("The first thing . . .") is from *Ferlinghetti: The Artist in His Time*. Details of Ginsberg's troubles at Columbia, the Six Gallery reading, marriage ceremony to Peter Orlovsky, and publication of *Howl* are retold in numerous biographies, articles, and documentaries as well as in Ginsberg's own writing. My descriptions should be considered an amalgamation of all available sources. Quote from Ginsberg's January 21, 1947, journal entry ("Having spent a wild weekend . . .") from *The Book of Martyrdom + Artifice*. Ginsberg's letters written from USNS *Sgt. Jack J. Pendleton* to Louis Ginsberg ("I've been thinking . . .") and Lawrence Ferlinghetti ("I wonder . . .") from *The Letters of Allen Ginsberg*. Leary's quote about Frank Barron ("At this point . . .") from *Timothy Leary: A Biography*. Quotes from Leary's professional paper ("After three orienting . . .") and letter to Ginsberg ("Big deal at the prison . . .") from papers and letters in the Allen Ginsberg Papers archive at Stanford University. George Litwin's quote ("They just sent us back . . .") from *Timothy Leary: A Biography*. Other details of Timothy Leary's life are retold in numerous biographies, articles, and documentaries as well as in Ginsberg's own writing. My descriptions should be considered an amalgamation of all available sources.

Chapter Five—The Road to November
Information about the research of Dr. Humphry Osmond and Dr. John Smythies is from *Storming Heaven*. The quote from Aldous Huxley's essay "Downward Transcendence" ("In Vedic mythology . . .") is from *Moksha*. Osmond's quote about Huxley ("I did not relish . . .") is from *Acid Dreams*. Descriptions of the relationship between Osmond, Smythies, and Huxley are primarily based on *Storming Heaven* and *Acid Dreams*. Leary's initial letter to Ginsberg ("Dear Mr. Ginsberg . . .") is from the Allen Ginsberg Papers archive at Stanford University. Information on the psychological treatment of women in the 1950s is primarily from *Communicating Gender* with additional insights from *Myself and I*. Ginsberg's initial reaction to Leary's house ("Leary had this big beautiful house . . .") is from *Timothy Leary: A Biography*. Dr. Ralph Metzner's quotes about the true identity of "O'Donell" in *High Priest* are from an

email from Dr. Metzner. Details of Leary's bad-trip incident with "O'Donell" and "Charlie" are from *High Priest*.

Chapter Six—Ambassador of Psilocybin
Leary's quote on Ginsberg ("Allen Ginsberg came to Harvard . . .") from *High Priest*. Details of William S. Burroughs' life are well-documented in numerous biographies, articles, interviews, and documentaries as well as in Burroughs' own writing. My descriptions should be considered an amalgamation of all available sources. Richard Spruce's quotes ("Both of these plants . . .") are from *Where the Gods Reign*. Details of the work of Spruce and Richard Evans Schultes, as well as quotes by Burroughs ("In two minutes . . .") and Ginsberg ("the whole fucking Cosmos . . .") are from *The Yage Letters Redux*. Quotes and impressions from Ginsberg's first psilocybin experience with Leary are recounted in various sources, most usefully *High Priest, Timothy Leary: A Biography, Ginsberg: A Biography*, and, *Spontaneous Mind*. Ginsberg's quotes on psychedelics and homosexuality are from a *Playboy* magazine article (April 1969) ("Well, I get those feelings . . .") as reprinted in *Spontaneous Mind*. The Octavio Paz quotes ("We are now in a position . . .") are from *Alternating Currents*. All Leary quotes about Ginsberg ("And so Allen . . .") are from *High Priest*.

SECTION TWO—TUNE IN

Chapter Seven—Dear Mr. Monk
All Leary letters ("Dear Mr. Monk . . .") are from the Allen Ginsberg Papers archive at Stanford University. Details of Jack Kerouac's life are well documented in numerous biographies, articles, interviews, and documentaries as well as in Kerouac's own writing. My descriptions should be considered an amalgamation of all available sources. Leary's quotes on his session with Kerouac ("Jack Kerouac was scary . . ." from *Timothy Leary: A Biography*. Leary's letter to Ginsberg ("Learned a lot from you . . .") and Burroughs ("Dear William Burroughs . . ."), as well as Kerouac's letter to Leary ("Dear Tim (coach) . . .") and Burroughs' letter to Leary ("most interesting . . .") are from the Allen Ginsberg Papers archive at Stanford University. Details of Burroughs' life at the Beat Hotel in Paris are well documented in numerous books, interviews, articles, and documentaries; most useful among these were *The Beat Hotel*,

Literary Outlaw, and *A Portrait of William Burroughs*. *Charles Ol-son: The Allegory of a Poet's Life* provided much of the background on Olson's life. Leary's letter to Olson ("Well we have been . . .") is from the Charles Olson Research Collection at the Thomas J. Dodd Research Center at University of Connecticut.

Chapter Eight—Applied Mysticism: From Tangier to Copenhagen
Details of William S. Burroughs' life and times in Tangier are well documented in numerous biographies, articles, interviews, and documentaries as well as in Burroughs' own writing. My descriptions should be considered an amalgamation of all available sources. Most useful among these were *Literary Outlaw* and *A Portrait of William Burroughs*. Burroughs quotes on *Naked Lunch* ("Don't ask me . . .") are from *Literary Outlaw*. Leary's "How to Change Behavior: Paper prepared for International Congress of Applied Psychology, Copenhagen, August, 1961" is from the Allen Ginsberg Papers archive at Stanford University. All quotes from his Copenhagen presentation are taken from that paper. Kenneth Rexroth's quote ("Mr. Kerouac's Buddhism . . .") is from the *New York Times Book Review* (November 29, 1959). Sections of Ginsberg and Jack Kerouac's discoveries of Buddhism are from *Kerouac: A Biography*. Information and statistics on the Concord Prison experiments from Leary's papers located in the Allen Ginsberg Papers archive at Stanford University, as well as through *Timothy Leary: A Biography*, *I Have America Surrounded*, *Flashbacks*, and *High Priest*. Letter from Leary to Ginsberg ("The psychiatrist, naturally . . .") is from the Allen Ginsberg Papers archive at Stanford University.

Chapter Nine—Fallout at Harvard
Herbert Kelman quote ("The overall reaction . . .") and other psychologists' reaction to Leary's Copenhagen presentation ("set Danish psychology . . .") are from *Timothy Leary: A Biography*. Quotes from Burroughs about Harvard experiments ("They steal, bottle . . .") and Ginsberg on Burroughs ("Bill had the idea . . .") from *Timothy Leary: A Biography*. Leary on Burroughs ("He thought we were . . .") from *Pataphysics*. All *Harvard Crimson* quotes are directly from *Harvard Crimson* back issues available online at www.thecrimson.com. Leary letter to Ginsberg ("Dear Allen—Business . . .") from Allen Ginsberg Papers archive at Stanford University.

Chapter Ten—Allen Abroad
William Burroughs to Ginsberg ("If we cut . . .") and Ginsberg to
Lawrence Ferlighetti ("We had big . . .") from *Ginsberg: A Biogra-*
phy. Ginsberg letter to Corso from *The Letters of Allen Ginsberg.*
Details of Ginsberg in India, including his time with Joanne Kyger
and Gary Snyder ("The inside of your . . .") and meeting with the
Dalai Lama ("If you take LSD . . .") largely from *A Blue Hand.*
Ginsberg letter to Gary Snyder ("Human eyes . . .") from *Indian*
Journals. Ginsberg on Blake vision ("The remarkable . . .") and
details of ending India trip from *Ginsberg: A Biography.* *Indian*
Journals and *A Blue Hand* provided particularly valuable insights
into this period.

Chapter Eleven—Enter LSD, Exit Harvard
Details and quotes related to Michael Hollingshead's arrival at
Harvard, including Aldous Huxley ("a splendid fellow . . .") and
Leary on Hollingshead and LSD ("Everything I had heard . . .")
from *Timothy Leary: A Biography.* Details of the Good Friday Experiment appear in a number of books, interviews, and articles
and appear here as an amalgamation of those resources. Leary
quotes on the experiment ("It was easy to tell . . .") are from *High*
Priest. Leary's letters to Ginsberg ("I'm living serenely . . .") are
from the Allen Ginsberg Papers archive at Stanford University.
Harvard Crimson quotes ("15 cars coming . . .") from online back
issues of *Harvard Crimson.* Ginsberg quotes on his poetics ("Now
poetry instead . . .") from *Indian Journals.*

SECTION THREE—DROP OUT

Chapter Twelve—"Superheroes wanted for real life movie work"
Details of Jack Kerouac and The Shadow appear in numerous
publications and biographies, most usefully in *Kerouac: The De-*
finitive Biography. Details of Ken Kesey's life appear in numerous
biographies, articles, and documentaries as well as in Kesey's own
writing. My descriptions should be considered an amalgamation
of all available sources; most useful among them for this chapter
were *The Electric Kool-Aid Acid Test* and *Storming Heaven: LSD*
and the American Dream. Kesey quote ("The trouble . . .") found
in numerous online Web sites. Kesey quotes ("The purpose of
psychedelics . . .") and ("Get them into . . .") from *Acid Dreams.*
Ginsberg on Prankster bus trip ("To me, the real . . .") from *Can't*

Find My Way Home. Prankster encounter with the police ("A si-ren? . . .") and Tom Wolfe on religion ("In all these . . .") from *The Electric Kool-Aid Acid Tests*. Details and quotes from Mexico and international deportation trip, including newspaper quotes, from *Timothy Leary: A Biography*. CIA memo from Allen Ginsberg Papers archive at Stanford University. "On nobly born . . ." from *The Psychedelic Experience*. Details and quotes "Sandy-Lehmann Haupt . . .") regarding the Prankster compound in La Honda pri-marily from *The Electric Kool-Aid Acid Tests*. Ginsberg on Prank-ster trip to Millbrook ("I remember when . . .") from *Timothy Leary: A Biography*. Leary on meeting with Ken Kesey and Ken Babbs ("Ken Kesey, Ken Babbs, and I . . .") from *Flashbacks*.

Chapter Thirteen—The King of May
Details of Ginsberg's early life and mid-Sixties activities are retold in numerous biographies, articles, and documentaries as well as in Ginsberg's own writing. My descriptions should be considered an amalgamation of all available sources. *Ginsberg: A Biography* was particularly invaluable in providing names, dates, and select-ed quotes from Ginsberg's Cuba-Prague-Russia trip. Ginsberg's let-ter to Richard H. Kuh from *The Letters of Allen Ginsberg*. Ginsberg on Prague ("When I was elected . . .") from *Playboy* (April 1969) interview as reprinted in *Spontaneous Mind*. Poem excerpt from "Kral Majales" from *Allen Ginsberg Collected Poems*.

Chapter Fourteen—Human Be-In
Details of the Human Be-In have been recorded in numerous books and articles. My descriptions should be considered an amalgama-tion of all available resources including, but not limited to, *Hippie*, *The Haight Ashbury, Acid Dreams, Storming Heaven*, and *Allen Ginsberg in America*. "The spiritual revolution . . ." from *Hippie*. Quotes from the planning meeting prior to the Be-In ("Man, I'd just as soon . . .") from *Allen Ginsberg in America*. "The House-boat Summit" appeared in issue #7 of *The Oracle* and is available online at www.vallejo.to/articles/summit_pt1.htm.

Chapter Fifteen—"Shoot to Live. Aim for Life."
Mexican policeman quote to Leary ("Where do you think . . .") from *Timothy Leary: A Biography*. Details of Leary's Mexico bust and legal problems have been recorded in numerous books and articles. My descriptions should be considered an amalgamation of all available resources including, but not limited to, *Timothy*

Leary: A Biography, I Have America Surrounded, Prison Notes, and *Flashbacks.* Among these, *Timothy Leary: A Biography* was the most detailed and valuable. Details about the Brotherhood of Eternal Love's compound and operations from *Orange Sunshine.* Leary letter to Ginsberg ("Beloved Brother . . .") from Allen Ginsberg Papers archive at Stanford University. Leary quote ("He was 23 . . .") from *Prison Notes.* Jeff Jones quote on Leary ("we were well aware . . ."), prison note excerpt, Leary press statement ("There is a time . . ."), Kesey on Leary ("Dear Good Doctor . . .") from *Timothy Leary: A Biography.* Ginsberg's letter to Leary ("Dear Tim, Thanks for your . . .") from the Allen Ginsberg Papers archive at Stanford University.

Chapter Sixteen—"America I've given you all and now I'm nothing."
Details of Leary's time hiding underground have been recorded in numerous books, articles, and interviews. My descriptions should be considered an amalgamation of all available resources including, but not limited to, *Timothy Leary: A Biography, I Have America Surrounded, Prison* Notes, and *Flashbacks.* Leary's letter to Ginsberg ("As you must know . . .") from the Allen Ginsberg Papers archive at Stanford University. Ginsberg's letter to the *New York Times* ("I am normally . . .") from *The Letters of Allen Ginsberg.* Rosemary Leary's letter to Ginsberg ("Tim in Swiss prison . . .") and quotes from Ginsberg's "Declaration of Independence for Dr. Timothy Leary" from the Allen Ginsberg Papers archive at Stanford University. PEN club statement ("It would seem . . .") from *Timothy Leary: A Biography.* Details of Leary's final bust and related quotes ("Are you Timothy Leary . . ."), as well as revelation about David Martino and details of his sequence from Kabul arrest to turning informant are from *Timothy Leary: A Biography.*

Chapter Seventeen—Om Ah Hum
Ginsberg's poem/statement "Om Ah Hum" and individual quotes from the PILL press conference from the Allen Ginsberg Papers archive at Stanford University. Joanna Leary's testimony ("Because the first year . . ."), Leary's public statements ("secrecy and cover-up . . ."), Abbie Hoffman's quote ("I'm digesting the news . . ."), Wesley Hiler's quote ("They liked each other . . ."), and invaluable details regarding Leary's incarceration and activities at this time

are from *Timothy Leary: A Biography*. Ginsberg's letters in support of Leary's release ("strong suspicions that Dr. Leary . . .") from the Allen Ginsberg Papers archive at Stanford University. Lawrence Ferlinghetti quote on Folsom Prison visit ("What I remember . . .") from December 11, 2009, email to the author from Lawrence Ferlinghetti. Leary letter to Ginsberg from the Allen Ginsberg Papers archive at Stanford University. Leary's quotes from *Berkeley Barb* article from *Timothy Leary: A Biography*.

Postscript—Final Trips
Steve Silberman interview with Ginsberg originally published in the *Whole Earth Review*, courtesy of Steve Silberman.

THE HOUSEBOAT SUMMIT

This "Houseboat Summit," as it came to be called, was held on philosopher Alan Watts' boat, the S.S. *Vallejo* in February 1967. The panelists were Allen Ginsberg, Timothy Leary, and Gary Snyder, with Watts serving as a facilitator. The event was recorded and the transcript published in issue #7 of the *San Francisco Oracle*.

PART ONE: Changes

WATTS: . . . Look the, we're going to discuss where it's going . . . the whole problem of whether to drop out or take over.

LEARY: Or anything in between?

WATTS: Or anything in between, sure.

LEARY: Cop out . . . drop in. . . .

SNYDER: I see it as the problem about whether or not to throw all you energies to the subculture or try to maintain some communication network within the main culture.

WATTS: Yes. All right. Now look. . . . I would like to make a preliminary announcement so that it has a certain coherence. This is Alan Watts speaking, and I'm this evening, on my ferry boat, the host to a fascinating party sponsored by the San Francisco Oracle, which is our new underground paper, far-outer than any far-out that has yet been seen. And we have here, members of the staff of the Oracle. We have Allen Ginsberg, poet, and rabbinic saddhu. We have Timothy Leary, about whom nothing needs to be said. (laughs) And Gary Snyder, also poet, Zen monk, and old friend of many years.

GINSBERG: This swami wants you to introduce him in Berkeley. He's going to have a Kirtan to sanctify the peace movement. So what I said is, he ought to invite Jerry Rubin and Mario Savio, and his cohorts. And he said: "Great, great, great!" So I said, "Why don't you invite the Hell's Angels, too?" He said: "Great, great, great! When are we gonna get hold of them? So I think that's one next feature. . . .

WATTS: You know, what is being said here, isn't it: To sanctify the peace movement is to take the violence out of it.

GINSBERG: Well, to point attention to its root nature, which is desire for peace, which is equivalent to the goals of all the wisdom schools and all the Saddhanas.

A PACIFIST ON THE RAMPAGE

WATTS: Yes, but it isn't so until sanctified. That is to say, I have found in practice that nothing is more violent than peace movements. You know, when you get a pacifist on the rampage, nobody can be more emotionally bound and intolerant and full of hatred. And I think this is the thing that many of us understand in common, that we are trying to take moral violence out of all those efforts that are being made to bring human beings into a harmonious relationship.

GINSBERG: Now, how much of that did the peace movement people in Berkeley realize?

WATTS: I don't think they realize it at all. I think they're still working on the basis of moral violence, just as Gandhi was.

GINSBERG: Yeah . . . I went last night and turned on with Mario Savio. Two nights ago. . . . After I finished and I was talking with him, and he doesn't turn on very much. . . . This was maybe the third or fourth time. But he was describing his efforts in terms of the motive power for large mass movements. He felt one of the things that move large crowds was righteousness, moral outrage, and ANGER. . . . Righteous anger.

MENOPAUSAL MINDS

LEARY: Well, let's stop right here. The implication of that statement is: we want a mass movement. Mass movements make no sense to me, and I want no part of mass movements. I think this is the error that the leftist activists are making. I see them as young men with menopausal minds. They are repeating the same dreary quarrels and conflicts for power of the thirties and forties, of the trade union movement, of Trotskyism and so forth. I think they should be sanctified, drop out, find their own center, turn on, and above all avoid mass movements, mass leadership, mass followers. I see that there is a great difference—I say completely incompatible difference—between the leftist activist movement and the psychedelic religious movement. In the first place, the psychedelic movement, I think, is much more numerous. But it doesn't express itself as noisily. I think there are different goals. I think that the activists want power. They talk about student power. This shocks me, and alienates my spiritual sensitivities. Of course, there is a great deal of difference in method. The psychedelic movement, the spiritual seeker movement, or whatever you want to call it, expresses itself . . . as the Haight-Ashbury group had done . . . with flowers and chants and pictures and beads and acts of beauty and harmony . . . sweeping the streets. That sort of thing.

WATTS: And giving away free food.

LEARY: Yes . . . I think this point must be made straight away, but because we are both looked upon with disfavor by the Establishment, this tendency to group the two together. . . . I think that such confusion can only lead to disillusion and hard feelings on someone's part. So, I'd like to lay this down as a premise right at the beginning.

GINSBERG: Well, of course, that's the same premise they lay down, that there is an irreconcilable split. Only, their stereotype of the psychedelic movement is that it's just sort of the opposite. . . . I think you're presenting a stereotype of them.

SNYDER: I think that you have to look at this historically, and there's no doubt that the historical roots of the revolutionary movements and the historical roots of this spiritual movement are identical. This is something that has been going on since the Neolithic as a strain in human history, and one which has been consistently, on one level or another, opposed to the collectivism of civilization toward the rigidities of the city states and city temples. Christian utopianism is behind Marxism.

LEARY: They're outs and they want in.

UTOPIAN, RELIGIOUS DRIVE
SNYDER: . . . but historically it arrives from a utopian and essentially religious drive. The early revolutionary political movements in Europe have this utopian strain to them. Then Marxism finally becomes a separate, non-religious movement, but only very late.

That utopian strain runs right through it all along. So that we do share this. . . .

GINSBERG: What are the early utopian texts? What are the early mystical utopian political texts?

SNYDER: Political?

GINSBERG: Yeah. Are you running your mind back through Bakunin or something?

SNYDER: I'm running it back to earlier people. To Fourier, and stuff. . . .

WATTS: Well, it goes back to the seventeenth century and the movements in Flemish and German mysticism, which started up the whole idea of democracy in England in the seventeenth century. You have the Anabaptists, the Levellers, the Brothers of the Free Spirit. . . .

SNYDER: The Diggers!

SECULAR MYSTICISM
WATTS: THE DIGGERS, and all those people, and then eventually the Quakers. This was the source. It was, in a way, the secularization of mysticism. In other words, the mystical doctrine that all men are equal in the sight of God, for the simple reason that they ARE God. They're all God's incarnations. When that doctrine is secularized, it becomes a parody . . . that all men are equally inferior. And therefore may be evil-treated by the bureaucrats and the police, with no manners. The whole tendency of this equalization of man in the nineteenth century is a result, in a way, of the work of Freud. But the absolute recipe for writing a best seller biography was to take some person who was renowned for his virtue and probity, and to show, after all, that everything was scurrilous and low down. You see? This became the parody. Because the point that I am making—this may seem to be a little bit of a diversion, but the actual point is this; Whenever the insights one derives from mystical vision become politically active they always create their own opposite. They create a parody. Wouldn't you agree with that, Tim? I mean, this is the point I think you're saying: that when we try to force a vision upon the world, and say that everybody ought to have this, and it's GOOD for you, then a parody of it

is set up. As it was historically when this vision was forced upon the West, that all men are equal in the sight of God ans[*sic*] so on and so forth . . . it became bureaucratic democracy, which is that all people are equally inferior.

SNYDER: Well, my answer to what Tim was saying there is that, it seems to me at least, in left-wing politics there are certain elements, and there are always going to be certain people who are motivated by the same thing that I'm motivated by. And I don't want to reject the history, or sacrifices of the people in that movement . . . if they can be brought around to what I would consider a more profound vision of themselves, and a more profound vision of themselves and society. . . .

LEARY: I think we should get them to drop out, turn on, and tune in.

GINSBERG: Yeah, but they don't know what that means even.

LEARY: I know it. No politician, left or right, young or old, knows what we mean by that.

GINSBERG: Don't be so angry!

LEARY: I'm not angry. . . .

GINSBERG: Yes, you are. Now, wait a minute. . . . Everybody in Berkeley, all week long, has been bugging me . . . and Alpert . . . about what you mean by drop out, tune in, and turn on. Finally, one young kid said, "Drop out, turn on, and tune in." Meaning: get with an activity—a manifest activity—worldly activity—that's harmonious with whatever vision he has. Everybody in Berkeley is all bugged because they think, one: drop-out thing really doesn't mean anything, that what you're gonna cultivate is a lot of freak-out hippies goofing around and throwing bottles through windows when they flip out on LSD. That's their stereotype vision. Obviously stereotype.

LEARY: Sounds like bullshitting. . . .

THE NEWSPAPER VISION
GINSBERG: No, like it's no different from the newspaper vision, anyway. I mean, they've got the newspaper vision. Then, secondly, they're afraid that there'll be some sort of fascist putsch. Like,

it's rumored lately that everyone's gonna be arrested. So that the lack of communicating community among hippies will lead to some concentration camp situation, or lead . . . as it has been in Los Angeles recently . . . to a dispersal of what the beginning of the community began.

LEARY: These are the old, menopausal minds. There was a psychiatrist named Adler in San Francisco whose interpretation of the group Be-In was that this is the basis for a new fascism . . . when a leader comes along. And I sense in the activist movement the cry for a leader . . . the cry for organization. . . .

GINSBERG: But they're just as intelligent as you are on this fact. They know about what happened in Russia. That's the reason they haven't got a big, active organization. It's because they, too, are stumped by: How do you have a community, and a community movement, and cooperation within the community to make life more pleasing for everybody—including the end of the Vietnam War? How do you have such a situation organized, or disorganized, just so long as it's effective—without a fascist leadership? Because they don't want to be that either. See, they are conscious of the fact that they don't want to be messiahs—political messiahs. At least, Savio in particular. Yesterday, he was weeping. Saying he wanted to go out and live in nature.

LEARY: Beautiful.

GINSBERG: So, I mean he's like basically where we are: stoned.

GENIUS OF NON-LEADERSHIP
WATTS: Well, I think that thus far, the genius of this kind of underground that we're talking about is that it has no leadership.

LEARY: Exactly!

WATTS: That everybody recognizes everybody else.

GINSBERG: Right, except that that's not really entirely so.

WATTS: Isn't it so? But it is to a great extent now. . . .

GINSBERG: There's an organized leadership, say, at such a thing as a Be-In. There is organization; there is community. There are community groups which cooperate, and those community groups are sparked by active people who don't necessarily parade their names in public, but who are capable people . . . who are capable of ordering sound trucks and distributing thousands of cubes of LSD and getting signs posted.

WATTS: Oh yes, that's perfectly true. There are people who can organize things. But they don't assume the figurehead role.

LEARY: I would prefer to call them FOCI of energy. There's no question. You start the poetry, chanting thing. . . .

WATTS: Yes.

LEARY: And I come along with a celebration. Like Allen and Gary at the Be-In.

NATURE AND BOSSISM
WATTS: And there is nobody in charge as a ruler, and this is the absolutely vital thing. That the Western world has labored for many, many centuries under a monarchical conception of the universe where God is the boss, and political systems and all kinds of law have been based on this model of the universe . . . that nature is run by a boss. Whereas, if you take the Chinese view of the world, which is organic. They would say, for example, that the human body is an organization in which there is no boss. It is a situation of order resulting from mutual interrelationship of all the parts. And what we need to realize is that there can be, shall we say, a movement . . . a stirring among people . . . which can be ORGANICALLY designed instead of POLITICALLY designed. It has no boss. Yet all parts recognize each other in the same way as the cells of the body all cooperate together.

SNYDER: Yes, it's a new social structure. It's a new social structure which follows certain kinds of historically known tribal models.

LEARY: Exactly, yeah! My historical reading of the situation is that these great, monolithic empires that developed in history: Rome, Turkey and so forth . . . always break down when enough people (and it's always the young, the creative, and the minority groups) drop out and go back to a tribal form. I agree with what I've heard you say in the past, Gary, that the basic unit is tribal. What I envision is thousands of small groups throughout the United States and Western Europe, and eventually the world, as dropping out. What happened when Jerusalem fell? Little groups went off together. . . .

GINSBERG: Precisely what do you mean by drop out, then . . . again, for the millionth time?

SNYDER: Drop out throws me a little bit, Tim. Because it's assumed that we're dropping out. The next step is, now what are we doing where we're in something else? We're in a new society. We're in the seeds of a new society.

GINSBERG: For instance, you haven't dropped out, Tim. You dropped out of your job as a psychology teacher in Harvard. Now, what you've dropped into is, one: a highly complicated series of arrangements for lecturing and for putting on the festival. . . .

LEARY: Well, I'm dropped out of that.

GINSBERG: But you're not dropped out of the very highly complicated legal constitutional appeal, which you feel a sentimental regard for, as I do. You haven't dropped out of being the financial provider for Millbrook, and you haven't dropped out of planning and conducting community organization and participating in it. And that community organization is related to the national community, too. Either through the Supreme Court, or through the very existence of the dollar that is exchanged for you to pay your lawyers, or to take money to pay your lawyers in the theatre. So you can't drop out, like DROP OUT, 'cause you haven't.

LEARY: Well, let me explain. . . .

GINSBERG: So they think you mean like, drop out, like go live on Haight-Ashbury Street and do nothing at all. Even if you can do something like build furniture and sell it, or give it away in barter with somebody else.

LEARY: You have to drop out in a group. You drop out in a small tribal group.

SNYDER: Well, you drop out one by one, but. . . . You know, you can join the sub-culture.

GINSBERG: Maybe it's: "Drop out of what?"

WATTS: Gary, I think you have something to say here. Because you, to me, are one of the most fantastically capable drop-out people I have ever met. I think, at this point, you should say a word or two about your own experience of how to live on nothing. How to get by in life economically. This is the nitty-gritty. This is where it really comes down to in many people's minds. Where's the bread going to come from if everybody drops out? Now, you know expertly where it's gonna come from—living a life of integrity and not being involved in a commute-necktie-strangle scene.

SNYDER: Well, this isn't news to anybody, but ten or fifteen years ago when we dropped out, there wasn't a community. There wasn't anybody who was going to take care of you at all. You were completely on your own. What it meant was, cutting down on your desires and cutting down on your needs to an absolute minimum; and it also meant, don't be a bit fussy about how you work or what you do for a living. That meant doing any kind of work. Strawberry picking, carpenter, laborer, longshore. . . . Well, longshore is hard to get into. It paid very well. Shipping out . . . that also pays very well. But at least in my time, it meant being willing to do any goddam kind of labor that came your way, and not being fuzzy about it. And it meant cultivating the virtue of patience—the patience of sticking with a shitty job long enough to win the bread that you needed to have some more leisure, which meant more freedom to do more things that you wanted to do. And mastering all kinds of techniques of living really cheap. . . . Like getting free rice off the docks, because the loading trucks sometimes fork the rice sacks, and spill little piles of rice on the docks which are usually thrown away. But I had it worked out with some of the guards down on the docks that they would gather 15 or 25 pounds of rice for me, and also tea. . . . I'd pick it up once a week off the docks, and then I'd take it around and give it to friends. This was rice that was going to be thrown away, otherwise. Techniques like that.

WATTS: Second day vegetables from the supermarket. . . .

SNYDER: Yeah, we used to go around at one or two in the morning, around the Safeways and Piggly Wigglies in Berkeley, with a shopping bag, and hit the garbage can out in back. We'd get Chinese cabbage, lots of broccoli and artichokes that were thrown out because they didn't look sellable any more. So, I never bought any vegetables for the three years I was a graduate student at Berkeley. When I ate meat, it was usually horse meat from the pet store, because they don't have a law that permits them to sell horsemeat for human consumption in California like they do in Oregon.

GINSBERG: You make a delicious horse meat sukiyaki. (laughter)

A SWEET, CLEAN PAD
WATTS: Well, I want to add to this, Gary, that during the time you were living this way, I visited you on occasion, and you had a little hut way up on the hillside of Homestead Valley in Mill Valley and I want to say, for the record, that this was one of the most beautiful pads I ever saw. It was sweet and clean, and it had a very, very good smell to the whole thing. You were living what I consider to be a very noble life. Now, then, the question that next arises, if this is the way of being a successful drop-out, which I think is true. . . . Can you have a wife and child under such circumstances?

SNYDER: Yeah, I think you can, sure.

WATTS: What about when the state forces you to send the child to school?

SNYDER: You send it to school.

LEARY: Oh no, c'mon, I don't see this as drop-out at all.

SNYDER: I want to finish what I was going to say. That's [the] way it was ten years ago. Today, there is a huge community. When any kid drops out today, he's got a subculture to go fall into. He's got a place to go where there'll be friends, and people that will feed him—at least for a while—and keep feeding him indefinitely, if he moves around from pad to pad.

A WAY STATION: A LAUNCHING PAD
LEARY: That's just stage one. The value of the Lower East Side, or of the district in Seattle or the Haight-Ashbury, is that it provides a first launching pad. Everyone that's caught inside a television set of props, and made of actors. . . . The first thing that you have to do is completely detach yourself from anything inside the plastic, robot Establishment. The next step—for many people—could well be a place like Haight-Ashbury. There they will find spiritual teachers, there they will find friends, lovers, wives. . . . But that must be seen clearly as a way station. I don't think the Haight-Ashbury district—any city, for that matter—is a place where the new tribal is going to live. So, I mean DROP OUT! I don't want to be misinterpreted. I'm dropping out . . . step by step.

SNYDER: I agree with you. Not in the city.

LEARY: Millbrook, by the way, is a tribal community. We're getting closer and closer to the landing. . . . We're working out our way of import and export with the planet. We consider ourselves a tribe of mutants. Just like all the little tribes of Indians were. We happen to have our little area there, and we have come to terms with the white men around us.

WHAT ARE YOU BUILDING?

SNYDER: Now look. . . . Your drop-out line is fine for all those other people out there, you know, that's what you've got to say to them. But, I want to hear what you're building. What are you making?

LEARY: What are we building?

SNYDER: Yeah, what are you building? I want to hear your views on that. Now, it's agreed we're dropping out, and there are techniques to do it. Now, what next! Where are we going now? What kind of society are we going toe in?

LEARY: I'm making the prediction that thousands of groups will just look around at the fake-prop-television-set American society, and just open one of those doors. When you open the doors, they don't lead you in, they lead you OUT into the garden of Eden . . . which is the planet. Then you find yourself a little tribe wandering around. As soon as enough people do this—young people do this—it'll bring about an incredible change in the consciousness of this country, and of the Western world.

GINSBERG: Well, that is happening actually. . . .

LEARY: Yeah, but. . . .

SNYDER: But that garden of Eden is full of old rubber truck tires and tin cans, right now, you know.

LEARY: Parts of it are. . . . Each group that drops out has got to use its two billion years of cellular equipment to answer those questions: Hey, how we gonna eat? Oh, there's no paycheck, there's no more fellowship from the university! How we gonna keep warm? How we gonna defend ourselves? Those are exactly the questions that cellular animals and tribal groups have been asking for thousands of years. Each group is going to have to depend upon its turned on, psychedelic creativity and each group of. . . . I can envision ten M.I.T. scientists, with their families, they've taken LSD. . . . They've wondered about the insane-robot-television show of M.I.T. They drop out. They may get a little farm out in Lexington, near Boston. They may use their creativity to make some new kinds of machines that will turn people on instead of bomb them. Every little group has to do what every little group has done throughout history.

CEREBRAL "FREAK OUTS"

SNYDER: No, they can't do what they've done through history. What is very important here is, besides taking acid, is that people learn the techniques which have been forgotten. That they learn new structures, and new techniques. Like, you just can't go out and grow vegetables, man. You've got to learn HOW to do it. Like we've gotta learn to do a lot of things we've forgotten to do.

LEARY: I agree.

WATTS: That is very true, Gary. Our educational system, in its entirety, does nothing to give us any kind of material competence. In other words, we don't learn how to cook, how to make clothes, how to build houses, how to make love, or to do any of the absolutely fundamental things of life. The whole education that we get for our children in school is entirely in terms of abstractions. It trains you to be an insurance salesman or a bureaucrat, or some kind of cerebral character.

LEARY: Yes . . . it's exactly there that, I think, a clear-cut statement is needed. The American educational system is a narcotic, addictive process. . . .

WATTS: Right!

NEW STRUCTURES; NEW TECHNIQUES

LEARY: . . . and we must have NOTHING to do with it. Drop out of school, drop out of college, don't be an activist. . . .

WATTS: But we've got to do something else.

LEARY: Drop OUT of school. . . .

GINSBERG: Where are you gonna learn engineering? What about astronomy . . . like calculation of star [ratios] . . . things like that?

LEARY: The way men have always learned the important things

in life. Face to face with a teacher, with a guru. Because very little. . . . If any drop-out wants to do that, he can do it. . . . I can tell him how to do it.

SNYDER: I would suspect that within the next ten years—-within the next five years probably—a modest beginning will be made in sub-culture institutions of higher learning that will informally begin to exist around the country, and will provide this kind of education without being left to the Establishment, to Big Industry, to government.

WATTS: Well, it's already happening. . . .

SNYDER: I think that there will be a big extension of that, employing a lot of potentially beautiful teachers who are unemployed at the moment . . . like there are gurus who are just waiting to be put to use; and also drawing people, who are working in the universities with a bad conscience, off to join that. . . .

LEARY: Exactly. . . .

SNYDER: There's a whole new order of technology that is required for this. A whole new science, actually. A whole new physical science is going to emerge from this. Because the boundaries of the old physical science are within the boundaries of the Judaeo-Christian and Western imperialist boss sense of the universe that Alan was talking about. In other words, our scientific condition is caught within the limits of that father figure, Jehovah, or Roman emperor . . . which limits our scientific objectivity and actually holds us back from exploring areas of science which can be explored.

LEARY: Exactly, Gary. Exactly. . . .

WATTS: It's like the guy in Los Angeles who had a bad trip on LSD and turned himself in to the police, and wrote: "Please help me. Signed, Jehovah." (laughter)

LEARY: Beautiful! (more laughter) It's about time he caught on, huh? (more laughter)

WATTS: Yes-ss (laughing) But, here though, is this thing, you see. We are really talking about all this, which is really a rather small movement of people, involved in the midst of a FANTAS-

TIC MULTITUDE of people who can only continue to survive if automated industry feeds them, clothes them, houses them and transports them. By means of the creation of IMMENSE quantities of ersatz material: Fake bread, fake homes, fake clothes and fake autos. In other words, this thing is going on . . . you know, HUGE, FANTASTIC numbers of people. . . . INCREASING, INCREASING, INCREASING . . . people think the population explosion is something that's going to happen five years from NOW. They don't realize it's right on us NOW! People are coming out to the WALLS!

SNYDER: And they're gobbling up everything on the planet to feed it.

WATTS: Right.

SNYDER: Well, the ecological conscience is something that has to emerge there, and that's part of what we hope for . . . hopefully in the subculture.

VOICE FROM AUDIENCE: Gary, doesn't Japan clearly indicate that we can go up in an order of magnitude in population and still. . . .

SNYDER: Well, who wants to? It can be very well argued by some people who have not been thinking very clearly about it, that we could support a larger number of people on this planet infinitely. But that's irresponsible and sacrilegious. It's sacrilegious for the simple reason it wipes out too many other animal species which we have no right to wipe out.

LEARY: Absolutely.

SNYDER: We have no moral right to upset the ecological balance.

WATTS: No, that's true. We've got to admit that we belong to the mutual eating society.

SNYDER: Furthermore, it simply isn't pleasant to be crowded that way. Human beings lose respect for human beings when they're crowded.

LEARY: Out of my LSD experiences I have evolved a vision which makes sense to my cells . . . that we are already putting to work at Millbrook. And that is, that life on this planet depends upon about twelve inches of topsoil and the incredible balance of species that Gary was just talking about. On the other hand, man and his technological, Aristotelian zeal has developed these methods of laying down miles of concrete on topsoil, polluting the waters and doing the damage that Gary was just talking about. Now, we cannot say to this society, "Go back to a simple, tribal, pastoral existence." That's romantic.

FORWARD

SNYDER: You can say "Go FORWARD to a simple, pastoral existence."

LEARY: Yeah. I have come to a very simple solution: All the technology has to go underground. Because metal belongs underground. You take a hatchet out in the forest and let it go. It goes exactly where God and the Divine Process wants it to be: underground. Now the city of New York—the megalopolis is going to exist from Seattle to San Diego in a few years—could just as well be underground. If it goes underground it's there, where it belongs, with fire and metal and steel. I foresee that these tribal groups that drop out—and I mean absolutely drop out—will be helping to get back in harmony with the land, and we've got to start immediately putting technology underground. I can think of different ways we can do this symbolically. The Solstice, last April 21st [March 21st—*Oracle*] a group of us went out in front of the house in Millbrook and we took a sledgehammer and we spent about an hour breaking through the road. And we had this incredible piece of asphalt and rock—about four inches—and then we said: "Hey! Underneath this planet somewhere there's dirt!" It was really magical. And once you get a little piece taken out—it took about an hour to get one little piece—then you just go underneath it and it begins to crumble. So I think we should start a movement to—one hour a day or one hour a week—take a little chisel and a little hammer and just see some earth come up, and put a little seed there. And then put a little ring—mandalic ring—of something around it.

THE GENTLE, NAKED SKIN

LEARY: I can see the highways and I can see the subways and I can see the patios and so forth. . . . Suddenly the highway department comes along, and: "There's a rose growing in the middle of Highway 101!" And then . . . then . . . the robot power group will have to send a group of the highway department to kill the rose and put the asphalt down on the gentle, naked skin of the soil. Now when they do that, we're getting to them. There'll be pictures in the paper. And consciousness is going to change. Because we've got to get to people's consciousness. We've got to let people realize what they're doing to the earth.

GINSBERG: That's the area of poetry you're dealing with there.

LEARY: Here we go. I'm the poet and you're the politician. I've told you that for ten years!

GINSBERG: "There are no ideas but in things," said William Carlos Williams. How does this work out now?

SNYDER: Technologically?

VOICE FROM AUDIENCE: I wouldn't want to work underground.

LEARY: Of course not. The only people that would want to work underground are people that would want to work with metal and steel. But if they're hung up that way, and they want to play with those kinds of symbols, fine. We'll have the greatest, air-conditioned, smooth, airport, tile gardens for them with all sorts of metal toys to play with.

VOICE FROM AUDIENCE: Can I ask you for a clarification on one thing about drop out? You said that in another ten years the young men in the colleges are going to have degrees and the doctors, psychologists and so on, will all be turned-on people. But if they drop out from college now they won't have degrees and these people won't gain control of the apparatus—I mean, I know someone now at State who studies psychology and who doesn't know whether to drop out or not, and who's pulled in two directions. I think there are many people like this.

PART TWO: To Drop Out or Not

LEARY: Yes, I think he should drop out. And I want to be absolutely clear on that. NOBODY wants to listen to that simple, two-syllable phrase. It gets jargled and jumbled, and I mean it. . . . Now, everyone has to decide how he drops out and when, and he has to time it gracefully, but that's the goal.

SNYDER: We understand that. . . .

LEARY: Well, Allen didn't. And Allen, I want to tell you the people in Berkeley that ask you what I mean, I mean ABSOLUTELY have nothing to do with the university, and start planning step by step how you can defect. . . .

GINSBERG: OF course, that's where the big argument is, over the NON-STUDENTS. The guys that dropped out are not involved, and their problem is what kind of communities they organize.

LEARY: Now, I can foresee that you might work for Sears & Roebuck for six months to get enough money to go to India. But that's part of your drop out. And what I'm doing today, Allen, is part of my drop out. I've got responsibilities, contracts . . . and I don't think that anyone should violate contracts with people that they love. . . . Contract with the university—ha! Fine—quit tomorrow. Therefore, I have to detach myself slowly. When I was in India two years ago. . . .

GINSBERG: India . . . but look . . . you know the university is personal relationships also. They're in contact with persons. They can't reflect those persons, necessarily. . . . There might be a Bodhisattva among those persons.

SNYDER: . . . As Tim says, you can gracefully drop out . . .

LEARY: Aesthetically. . . .

SNYDER: . . . at one time or another, which I take to mean. . . .

GINSBERG: I was teaching at Berkeley last week—what do you mean "drop out?" (laughs)

LEARY: You've got to do your yoga as a college professor . . . it's part of the thing you're gonna have to go through, and after you do that then (laughs) you shudder, and run to the door.

SAGES IN THE MOUNTAINS

WATTS: Surely the fact of the matter is that you can do this on a small scale, as an individual, where just a few people are doing this . . . as they always have done. There have always been a kind of elite minority who dropped out—who were the sages in the mountains. But now we are in a position where the conversations that you and I have go to millions, and people are asking this sort of question. Let's suppose that everybody in San Francisco decided to take the six o'clock train from the Third Street Station to Palo Alto. . . . See? We know there's no chance of their doing so. And therefore this catastrophe doesn't happen.

LEARY: That's exactly what I say to people who say, "Well, suppose everybody dropped out?" Ridiculous!

WATTS: Yeah, supposing everyone dropped out. . . . Of course they're not going to.

LEARY: Suppose everyone took LSD tonight (laughs) —Great!

THE LEISURE SOCIETY: PUZZLES AND PARADOXES
WATTS: The thing is this: what we are facing, what's going to happen is this . . . if we do not encounter the final political catastrophe of atomic war, biological warfare and wipe the whole thing out, we're going to have a huge leisure society—where they're going to reverse taxation and PAY people for the work that the machines do for them. Because there's no other solution to it. In other words, if the manufacturer is going to be able to sell his products, the people gotta have money to pay for the products. All those people have been put out of work by the machines the manufacturer is using. Therefore, the people have got to be paid by the government—CREDIT of some kind, so they can buy what the machines produce—then the thing will go on. So this means that thousands and thousands of people are going to be loafing around, with nothing at all to do. A few people who are maniacs for work will go on. . . .

LEARY: I think what you're defining, Alan, is. . . .

WATTS: But that's the kind of situation we're moving into. IF we survive at all.

LEARY: Well, there's another possibility. And, I think you're defining two possible new species. Let's face it, the evolution of mankind is not over.

WATTS: No!

LEARY: Just as there are many kinds of primates: baboons and chimpanzees and so forth. In a few thousand years we'll look back and see that from—what we call man—there may be two or more species developing. There's no question that one species, which could and probably will develop, is this anthill. It's run like a beehive with queens—or kings—(laughs) and it'll all be television and now, of course, in that, sexuality will become very promiscuous and almost impersonal. Because, in an anthill, it always turns out that way. BUT you're gonna have another species who will inevitably survive, and that will be the tribal people, who don't have to worry about leisure because when you drop out then the real playwork begins. Because then you have to, as Gary says, learn how to take care of yourself and your loved ones on this. . . .

SNYDER: I don't think that you're right about that anthill thing at all though. That's a very negative view of human nature. I don't think it's accurate.

LEARY: It's no longer even human nature. We won't call them human anymore. These people. . . .

HUMAN BEINGS WANT REALITY
SNYDER: C'mon, Tim, they're humans and they're gonna be here. You're talking a drama here. You're talking about—you know—anthropological realities. The anthropological reality is that human beings, in their nature, want to be in touch with what is real in themselves and in the universe. For example, the longshoremen with their automation contract in San Francisco . . . a certain number of them have been laid off for the rest of their lives with full pay, and some of them have been laid off already for five years—with full pay—by their contract. Now, my brother-in-law is a longshoreman, and he's been telling me about what's happening to these guys. Most of them are pretty illiterate, a large portion of them are Negroes. The first thing they all did was get boats and drive around San Francisco Bay . . . because they have all this leisure. Then a lot of them got tired driving around boats that were just like cars, and they started sailing. Then a few of them started making their own sailboats. They move into and respond to the possibility of challenge. Things become simpler and more complex and more challenging for them. The same is true of hunting. Some guy says."I want to go hunting and fishing all the time, when I have my leisure . . . but God!" So he goes hunting all the time. Then he says, "I want to do this in a more interesting way." So he takes up bow hunting. . . . Then the next step is—and this has happened—he says, "I want to try making my own arrowheads." And he learns how to flake his own arrowheads out. Now, human beings want reality. That's, I think, part of human nature.

And television and drinking beer is what the working man laid off does for the first two weeks. But then in the third week he begins to get bored, and in the fourth week he wants to do something with his body and his mind and his senses.

LEARY: But if he's still being paid by the Establishment, then you have someone who's going back to childhood. Like, he's making arrows that he really doesn't need. . . .

SNYDER: May I speak my vision about this?

LEARY: I object to this very much. I want him out there really fighting—not fighting, but working—for his family, not chipping.

SNYDER: Well, this is a transitional thing, too. . . . It's too transitional.

GINSBERG: This leads to violence because it divides everybody up into separate. . . .

SNYDER: Oh, he was talking poetry.

LEARY: No, I'm not! I want to be clear about this. Nobody wants to listen to this. We are doing this already. . . .

SNYDER: No, but the difference is, the children of the ants are all going to be tribal people. That's the way it's going to work. We're going to get the kids, and it's going to take about three generations.

THE CHANGE
SNYDER: And in the meantime, the family system will change, and when the family system changes the economy will change . . . and in the meantime, a number of spiritual insights are going to change the minds of the technologists and the scientists themselves, and technology will change. There will be a diffused and decentralized technology . . . as I see it. . . .

WATTS: Well, go on. . . . Are you saying now what you said was your vision?

SNYDER: Now, what I was going to say was very simply this. I think that automation in the affluent society, plus psychedelics, plus—for the same curious reason—a whole catalytic, spiritual change or bend of mind that seems to be taking place in the west, today especially, is going to result—can result ultimately—in a vast leisure society in which people will voluntarily reduce their number, and because human beings want to do that which is real . . . simplify their lives. The whole problem of consumption and marketing is radically altered if a large number of people voluntarily choose to consume less. And people will voluntarily choose to consume less if their interests are turned in any other direction. If what is exciting to them is no longer things but states of mind.

LEARY: That's true.

STATES OF MIND

SNYDER: Now what is something else. . . . People are not becoming interested in states of mind, and things are not going to substitute for states of mind. So what I visualize is a very complex and sophisticated cybernetic technology surrounded by thick hedges of trees. . . . Somewhere, say around Chicago. And the rest of the nation a buffalo pasture. . . .

LEARY: That's very close to what I think.

SNYDER: . . . with a large number of people going around making their own arrowheads because it's fun, but they know better. . . . (laughter) They know they don't have to make them. (more laughter)

LEARY: Now, this seems like our utopian visions are coming closer together. I say that the industry should be underground, and you say it should be in Chicago. This interests me.

WATTS: Well, it's the same idea.

SNYDER: Well, those who want to be technological engineers will be respected. . . . And the other thing is that you can go out and live close to nature, or you can go back and. . . .

LEARY: But you won't be allowed to drive a car outside this technological. . . .

SNYDER: You won't want to! That's the difference, baby. It's not that you won't be allowed to, it's that you won't want to. That's where it's got to be at.

CIVILIZED "PAP"

WATTS: Because, it's the same thing when we get down to, say, the fundamental question of food. More and more one realizes that the mass produced food is not worth eating, and therefore, in order to delight in things to eat, you go back to the most primitive processes of raising and preparing food. Because that has taste. And I see that it will be a sort of flip, that as all the possibilities of technology and automation make it possible for everybody to be assured of having the basic necessities of life . . . they will then say: "Oh, yes, we have all that, but now in the meantime while we don't have to work, let's go back to making arrowheads and to raising the most AMAZING PLANTS."

SNYDER: Yeah. . . . It would be so funny; the thing is that they would all get so good at it that the technology center of Chicago would rust away. (laughter)

WATTS: Right! Right! (laughter)

LEARY: That's exactly what's going to happen. The psychedelic drop-outs are going to be having so much fun. They're going to be so much obviously healthier.

WATTS: But Tim, do you see any indication among people who at present are really turned on, that they are cultivating this kind of material competence? Now, I haven't seen too much of it yet. . . .

SNYDER: Some of those kids at Big Sur have got it.

WATTS: Yeah, maybe you're right.

SNYDER: They're learning. A few years ago they used to go down to Big Sur and they didn't know how to camp or dig latrines.

TECHNOLOGICAL HANDBOOK
SNYDER: But like what Marine has been telling me lately, is that they're getting very sharp about what to gather that's edible, how to get sea salt, what are the edible plants and the edible seeds, and the revolutionary technological book for this state is A.L. Kroeber's Handbook of the California Indians, which tells you what's good to eat and how to prepare it. And also what to use for tampax: milkweed fluff . . . (laughter) Diapers made of shredded bark. . . . The whole thing is all there.

LEARY: Beautiful. . . .

WATTS: But the thing is this. I've found so many people who are the turned on type, and the circumstances and surroundings under which they live are just plain cruddy. You would think that people who have seen what you can see with the visions of psychedelics would reflect themselves in forms of life and art that would be like Persian miniatures. Because obviously Persian miniatures and Moorish arabesques are all reflecting the state of mind of people who were turned on. And they are rich and glorious beyond belief.

GINSBERG: Majestic.

WATTS: Majestic! Yeah! Well now, why doesn't it so occur. . . . It is slowly beginning to happen. . . . 'Cause I've noticed that, recently, all turned on people are becoming more colorful. They're wearing beads and gorgeous clothes and so and so forth . . . and it's gradually coming out. Because you remember the old beatnik days when everybody was in blue jeans and ponytails and no lipstick and DRAB—and CRUMMY!

SNYDER: What! (laughter)

WATTS: Now, something's beginning to happen!

SNYDER: Well, it wasn't quite that bad, but we were mostly concerned with not being consumers then . . . and so we were showing our non-consumerness.

WATTS: Yes, I know! The thing is I am using this as a symbol because the poor cons in San Quentin wear blue jeans.

SNYDER: The thing is that there are better things in the Goodwill now than there used to be.

WATTS: Yes, exactly. (laughter) But the thing is that now I see it beginning to happen. Timothy here, instead of wearing his old— whatever he used to wear—has now got a white tunic on with gold and colorful gimp on it.

GINSBERG: Gimp?

WATTS: Yes, and it's very beautiful, and he's wearing a necklace and all that kind of thing, and color is at last coming into the scene.

SNYDER: That's going back before the Roundheads, and before Cromwell. . . .

WATTS: Yes, it is.

LEARY: Let's get practical here, I think we're all concerned about the increasing number of people who are dropping out and wondering where to go from there. Now let's come up some practical suggestions which we might hope could unfold in the next few months.

BUSH, FARM, CITY

SNYDER: There's three categories: wilderness, rural, and urban. Like there's gonna be bush people, farm people and city people. Bush tribes, farm tribes, and city tribes.

LEARY: Beautiful. That makes immediate sense to myself. How about beach people?

VOICE FROM AUDIENCE: Let me throw in a word . . . the word is evil and technology. Somehow they come together, and when there is an increase in technology, and technological facility, there is an increase in what we usually call human evil.

SNYDER: I wouldn't agree with that . . . no, there's all kinds of non-evil technologies. Like, neolithic obsidian flaking is technology.

VOICE FROM AUDIENCE: But in its advanced state it produces evil.
. . .

WATTS: Yes, but what you mean, I think, is this: When you go back to the great myths about the origin of evil, actually the Hebrew words which say good and evil as the knowledge of good and evil being the result of eating the fruit of the tree of knowledge. . . .

ANALYTICAL LAG

WATTS: These words mean advantageous and disadvantageous and they're words connected with technical skills. And the whole idea is this, which you find reflected in the Taoist philosophy, that the moment you start interfering in the course of nature with a mind that is centered and one-pointed, and analyzes everything, and breaks it down into bits. . . . The moment you do that you lost contact with your original know-how . . . by means of which you now color your eyes, breathe, and beat your heart. For thousands of years mankind has lost touch with his original intelligence, and he has been absolutely fascinated by this kind of political, god-like, controlling intelligence . . . where you can go ptt-ptt-ptt-ptt

. . . and analyze things all over the place, and he has forgotten to trust his own organism. Now the whole thing is that everything is coming to be realized today. Not only through people who take psychedelics, but also through many scientists. They're realizing that this linear kind of intelligence cannot keep up with the course of nature. It can only solve trivial problems when the big problems happen too fast to be thought about in that way. So, those of us who are in some way or other—through psychedelics, through meditation, through what have you—are getting back to being able to trust our original intelligence . . . are suggesting an entirely new course for the development of civilization.

SNYDER: Well, it happens that civilization develops with the emergence of a class structure. A class structure can't survive, or can't put across its principle, and expect people to accept it . . . if they believe in themselves. If they believe, individually, one by one, that they are in some way godlike, or buddha like, or potentially illuminati. So it's almost ingrained in civilization, and Freud said this, you know "Civilization as a Neurosis," that part of the nature of civilization is that it must PUT DOWN the potential of every individual development.

PRIVATE VISIONS
SNYDER: This is the difference between that kind of society which we call civilized, and that much more ancient kind of society, which is still viable and still survives, and which we call primitive. In which everybody is potentially a chief and which everybody . . . like the Comanche or the Sioux. . . . EVERYBODY in the whole culture . . . was expected to go out and have a vision one time in his life. In other words, to leave the society to have some transcendental experience, to have a song and a totem come to him which he need tell no one, ever—and then come back and live with this double knowledge in society.

WATTS: In other words, through his having had his own isolation, his own loneliness, and his own vision, he knows that the game rules of society are fundamentally an illusion.

SNYDER: The society not only permits that, the society is built on it. . . .

WATTS: Is built on that, right!

SNYDER: And everybody has one side of his nature that has been out of it.

WATTS: That society is strong and viable which recognizes its own provisionality.

SNYDER: And no one who ever came into contact with the Plains Indians didn't think they were men! Every record of American Indians from the cavalry, the pioneers, the missionaries, the Spaniards . . . say that everyone one of these people was men. In fact, I learned something just the other day. Talking about the Uroc Indians, an early explorer up there commented on their fantastic self-confidence. He said, ". . . Every Indian has this fantastic self-confidence. And they laugh at me," he said, "they laugh at me and they say: Aren't you sorry you're not an Indian? Poor wretched Indians!" (laughs) this fellow said.

ALONE AND AT ONE

SNYDER: Well, that is because every one of them has gone out and had this vision experience . . . has been completely alone with himself, and face to face with himself . . . and has contacted powers outside of what anything the society could give him, and society expects him to contact powers outside of society . . . in those cultures.

WATTS: Yes, every healthy culture does. Every healthy culture provides for there being non-joiners. Sanyassi, hermits, drop-outs too. . . . Every healthy society has to tolerate this. . . .

SNYDER: A society like the Comanche or the Sioux demands that everybody go out there and have this vision, and incorporates and ritualizes it within the culture. Then a society like India, a step more civilized, permits some individuals to have these visions, but doesn't demand it of everyone. And then later it becomes purely eccentric.

LEARY: We often wonder why some people are more ready to drop out than others. It may be explained by the theory of reincarnation. The people that don't want to drop out can't conceive of living on this planet outside the prop television studio, are just unlucky enough to have been born into this sort of thing . . . maybe the first or second time. They're still entranced by all of the manmade props. But there's no question that we should consider how more and more people, who are ready to drop out, can drop out.

WATTS: If there is value in being a drop-out . . . that is to say, being an outsider. . . . You can only appreciate and realize this value, if there are in contrast with you insiders and squares. The two are mutually supportive.

LEARY: Yeah, if someone says to me, "I just can't conceive of dropping out . . ." I can say, "Well, you're having fun with this go around . . . fine! We've all done it many times in the past."

GINSBERG: The whole thing is too big because it doesn't say drop out of WHAT precisely. What everybody is dealing with is people, it's not dealing with institutions. It's dealing with them but also dealing with people. Working with and including the police.

SNYDER: If you're going to talk this way you have to be able to specifically say to somebody in Wichita, Kansas who says, "I'm going to drop out. How do you advise me to stay living around here in this area which I like?"

LEARY: Let's be less historical now for awhile and let's be very practical about ways in which people who want to find the tribal way. . . . How can they do it . . . what do you tell them?

SNYDER: Well, this is what I've been telling kids all over Michigan and Kansas. For example, I tell them first of all: "Do you want to live here, or do you want to go someplace else?"

LEARY: Good!

LAND, WATER AND CLOUDS
SNYDER: All right, say I want to stay where I am. I say, okay, get in touch with the Indian culture here. Find out what was here before. Find out what the mythologies were. Find out what the local deities were. You can get all of this out of books. Go and look at your local archaeological sites. Pay a reverent visit to the local American Indian tombs, and also the tombs of the early American settlers. Find out what your original ecology was. Is it short grass prairie, or long grass prairie here? Go out and live on the land for a while. Set up a tent and camp out and watch the land and get a sense of what the climate here is. Because, since you've been living in a house all your life, you probably don't know what the climate is.

LEARY: Beautiful.

SNYDER: Then decide how you want to make your living here. Do you want to be a farmer, or do you want to be a hunter and food gatherer? You know, start from the ground up, and you can do it in any part of this country today . . . cities and all. . . . For this continent I took it back to the Indians. Find out what the Indians were up to in your own area. Whether it's Utah, or Kansas, or New Jersey.

LEARY: That is a stroke of cellular revelation and genius, Gary. That's one of the wisest things I've heard anyone say in years. Exactly how it should be done. I do see the need for transitions, though, and you say that there will be city people as well as country people and mountain people. . . . I would suggest that for the next year or two or three, which are gonna be nervous, transitional, mutational years—where things are gonna happen very fast, by the way—the transition could be facilitated if every city set up little meditation rooms, little shrine rooms, where the people in transition, dropping out, could meet and meditate together. It's already happening at the Psychedelic Shop, it's happening in New York. I see no reason though why there shouldn't be ten or fifteen or twenty such places in San Francisco.

SNYDER: There already are.

THE ENERGY TO CREATE
LEARY: I know, but let's encourage that. I was just in Seattle and I was urging the people there. Hundreds of them crowd into coffee shops, and there is this beautiful energy. They are liberated people, these kids, but they don't know where to go. They don't need leadership, but they need, I think, a variety of suggestions from people who have thought about this, giving them the options to move in any direction. The different meditation rooms can have different styles. One can be Zen, one can be macrobiotic, one can be bhahte chanting, once can be rock and roll psychedelic, one can be lights. If we learn anything from our cells, we learn that God delights in variety. The more of these we can encourage, people would meet in these places, and AUTOMATICALLY tribal groups would develop and new matings would occur, and the city would be seen for many as transitional . . . and they get started. They may save up a little money, and then they head out and find the Indian totem wherever they go.

A MAGIC GEOGRAPHY

SNYDER: Well, the Indian totem is right under your ground in the city, is right under your feet. Just like when you become initiated into the Haineph pueblo, which is near Albuquerque, you learn the magic geography of your region; and part of that means going to the center of Albuquerque and being told: There is a spring here at a certain street, and its name is such and such. And that's in a street corner in downtown Albuquerque. But they have that geography intact, you know. They haven't forgotten it. Long after Albuquerque is gone, somebody'll be coming here, saying there's a spring here and it'll be there, probably.

LEARY: Tremont Street in Boston means "three hills."

GINSBERG: There's a stream under Greenwich Village.

VOICE FROM AUDIENCE: Gary, what do you think of rejecting the week as a measure of time; as a sort of absurd, civilized measure of time, and replacing it with a month, which is a natural time cycle?

LEARY: What is the time cycle?

SNYDER: The week, the seven day week. Well, the seven day week is based on the Old Testament theory that the world was created in seven days, you know. So you don't need it, particularly.

VOICE FROM AUDIENCE: Right. It seems to me a formal rejection of it and a cycling of social events around the idea of monthly cycle. . . .

HOLY DAY!

WATTS: I don't agree with that, because . . . everywhere that this week thing has spread, people have adopted it, where they didn't have this time rhythm before. But people have not understood the real meaning of the week, which is that every seventh day is a day to goof off. It's to turn out of the whole thing. The rules are abrogated. "The six days thou shalt labor, and do all that thou has to do. The seventh day thou shalt keep holy." HOLY DAY! and this means holiday. It means instead of a day for laying on rationality and preaching and making everybody feel guilty because they didn't operate properly the other six days.

LEARY: You turn on.

WATTS: The seventh day is the day. . . . Yes, absolutely, to go crazy. . . . Because if you can't afford a little corner of craziness in your life, you're like a steel bridge that has no give. You're so rigid you're going to collapse in the first wind.

LEARY: There is also some neuro-pharmacological evidence in support of the weekly cycle. That is, you can only have a full-scale LSD session about once a week. And when they said in Genesis— "On the seventh day He rested," it makes very modern sense.

GINSBERG: You can interpret it psychedelically, but that's like new criticism. . . . (laughter) You can actually LIKE new criticism. . . .

LEARY: I want you to be very loving to me for the rest of . . . and the tape will be witness . . . whether Allen is loving or not to me, for the rest of this evening.

GINSBERG: That's all right, I can always use a Big Brother. . . .

WATTS: May I point out, this has directly to do with what we've been talking about.

GINSBERG: But I was just getting paranoid of you interpreting the Old Testament as a prophecy of LSD. That's what I was THINK-ING.

LEARY: My foot has often led to other people's paranoias at the time.

WATTS: One day in seven, one seventh, is the day of the drop out.

SNYDER: That's not enough. (laughter)

WATTS: Now wait a minute. You're going too fast, Gary.

VOICE FROM AUDIENCE: Gary, the first six days of the week you drop out, and the seventh day you work.

SNYDER: Baby, we've gotta get away from this distinction between work and play. That's the whole thing, really. Like this one day in seven thing, the reason I don't agree with it is that it implies that making the world was a job.

WATTS: Oh, that's perfectly true. I entirely agree with you on that.

A BAD SCENE

SNYDER: And any universe that is worth creating isn't any job to create. You dig it. I don't sympathize with his fatigue at all. . . . He must have made a bad scene. (chuckles)

WATTS: You are talking on a different level than we're discussing at the moment. You are talking from the point of view where from the very deepest vision everything that happens is okay, and everything is play.

SNYDER: Well, I wasn't really talking from that vision.

WATTS: Well, that's where you really are. Now, I'm going one level below this, and saying. . . .

SNYDER: What I'm saying is if you do enjoy what you're doing, it's not work.

WATTS: That's true. That's my philosophy: that I get paid for playing. Now, the thing is, though, that just as talking on a little bit lower level . . . now—one day in seven is for goofing off . . . and that's a certain less percentage. So in a culture, if the culture is to be healthy, there has to be a substantial but, nevertheless, minority percentage of people who are not involved in the rat race. And this is the thing that it seems to me is coming out of this. We cannot possibly expect that everybody in the United States of America will drop out. But it is entirely important for the welfare of the United States that a certain number of people, a certain percentage, should drop out. Just as one day in seven should be a holiday.

VOICE FROM AUDIENCE: That's the baby that's being born. That's the baby that's being born NOW. The problem that we have to deal with is how to get that baby out easily.

LEARY: I think we must be more practical than we have been, because there are hundreds of people who are very interested in what we are talking about in the most A-B-C practical sense like: What do I do tomorrow!

WATTS: Right!

BIBLIOGRAPHY

Alpert, Richard, Timothy Leary, and Ralph Metzner. *The Psychedelic Experience.* Citadel Underground, 1992.

Amburn, Ellis. *Subterranean Kerouac: The Hidden Life of Jack Kerouac.* St. Martin's Griffin, 1998.

Artaud, Antonin. *The Peyote Dance.* Farrar, Straus and Giroux, 1976.

Baker, Deborah. *A Blue Hand: The Beats in India.* Penguin, 2008.

Ball, Gordon. *Allen Ginsberg Journals, Early Fifties, Early Sixties.* Grove Press, 1977.

———. *66 Frames.* Coffee House Press, 1999.

Blake, William. *Collected Poems.* Routledge Classics, 2002.

Blum, Richard (and associates). *Utopiates: The Use & Users of LSD 25.,* Atherton Press, 1970.

Burroughs, William. *The Soft Machine.* Grove Press, 1966.

———. *The Yage Letters Redux.* City Lights Books, 2006.

Carter, David, ed. *Allen Ginsberg Spontaneous Mind: Selected Interviews 1958–1996.* HarperCollins, 2001.

Charters, Ann. *Kerouac: A Biography.* St. Martin's, 1973.

Chesterton, Gilbert Keith. *William Blake.* Cosimo Classics, 2005.

Clark, Tom. *Charles Olson: The Allegory of a Poet's Life.* North Atlantic Books, 2000.

Dorje, Gyurme (translator). *The Tibetan Book of the Dead.* Penguin, 2005.

Forte, Robert. *Timothy Leary: Outside Looking In.* Park Street Press, 1999.

Friedman, B.H. *Tripping: A Memoir.* Provincetown Arts Press, 2006.

Fuller, John G. *The Day of St. Anthony's Fire.* Macmillan, 1968.

Ginsberg, Allen. *Collected Poems 1947–1980.* Harper & Row, 1984.

———. *Indian Journals.* Grove Press, 1970.

Greenfield, Robert. *Timothy Leary: A Biography.* Harcourt, 2006.

Grob, Charles, S. *Hallucinogens: A Reader.* Tarcher Putnam, 2002.

Higgs, John. *I Have America Surrounded.* Barricade Books, 2006.

Hillman, D.C.A. *The Chemical Muse: Drug Use and the Roots of Western Civilization.* Thomas Dunne Books, 2008.

Hofmann, Albert. *LSD My Problem Child: Reflections on Sacred Drugs, Mysticism and Science.* MAPS.org, 2009.

Horowitz, Michael and Palmer, Cynthia. *Moksha: Aldous Huxley's Classic Writings on Psychedelics and the Visionary Experience.* Park Street Press, 1999.

Huxley, Aldous. *The Doors of Perception & Heaven and Hell.* Harper Perennial Modern Classics, 2004.

James, William. *The Varieties of Religious Experience: A Study in Human Nature.* Modern Library, 1994.

Kerouac, Jack. *On the Road: The Original Scroll.* Viking, 2007.

Kramer, Jane. *Allen Ginsberg in America.* Fromm International, 1997.

Lattin, Don. *The Harvard Psychedelic Club: How Timothy Leary, Ram Dass, Huston Smith, and Andrew Weil Killed the Fifties and Ushered In a New Age for America.* HarperCollins, 2010.

Leary, Timothy. *Flashbacks.* Jeremy P. Tarcher, Inc., 1990.

———. *The Fugitive Philosopher.* Ronin Publishing, 2007.

———. *High Priest.* College Notes & Texts, 1968.

———. *Jail Notes.* Grove Press, 1970.

———. *Leary on Drugs.* RE/Search Publications, 2008.

———. *The Politics of Ecstasy.* Ronin, 1998.

Lee, Martin A. and Shlain, Bruce. *Acid Dreams. The Complete Social History of LSD: The CIA, The Sixties, and Beyond.* Grove Press, 1985.

Maher, Paul. *Kerouac: The Definitive Biography.* Taylor Trade Publishing, 2004.

McCleary, John Bassett. *The Hippie Dictionary.* Ten Speed Press, 2004.

McNally, Dennis. *A Long Strange Trip: The Inside History of the Grateful Dead.* Broadway, 2002.

———. *Jack Kerouac, The Beat Generation, and America.* Da Capo, 2003.

Miles, Barry. *The Beat Hotel.* Grove Press, 2000.

———. *Hippie.* Sterling, 2005.

———. *Ginsberg: A Biography.* Simon & Schuster, 1989.

———. *El Hombre Invisible: A Portrait of William Burroughs.* Hyperion, 1993.

Morgan, Bill and Juanita Plimpton-Lieberman, eds. *The Book of Martyrdom & Artifice.* Da Capo, 2006.

Morgan, Bill. *I Celebrate Myself: The Somewhat Private Life of Allen Ginsberg*. Penguin, 2006.
————. *The Letters of Allen Ginsberg*. Da Capo, 2008.
Morgan, Ted. *Literary Outlaw: The Life and Times of William S. Burroughs*. Henry Holt, 1988.
Newland, Constance A., *Myself and I*. Signet, 1962.
Olson, James S. *Historical Dictionary of the 1960s*. Greenwood Press, 1999.
Paz, Octavio. *Alternating Current*. Arcade Publishing, 1991.
Perry, Charles. *The Haight Ashbury: A History*. Vintage, 1985.
Plummer, William. *The Holy Goof: A Biography of Neal Cassady*. Thunder's Mouth Press, 1981.
Romaine, Suzanne. *Communicating Gender*. Lawrence Erlbaum Associates, 1999.
Schou, Nicholas. *Orange Sunshine: The Brotherhood of Eternal Love and Its Quest to Spread Peace, Love, and Acid to the World*. Thomas Dunne Books, 2010.
Schultes, Richard Evans. *Where the Gods Reign: Plants and Peoples of the Columbian Amazon*. Synergetic Press, 1990.
Silesky, Barry. *Ferlinghetti: The Artist in His Time*. Warner Books, 1990.
Smith, Grover, ed. *The Letters of Aldous Huxley*. Harper & Row, 1969.
Stevens, Jay. *Storming Heaven: LSD and the American Dream*. Harper & Row, 1987.
Torgoff, Martin. *Can't Find My Way Home: America in the Great Stoned Age, 1945–2000*. Simon & Schuster, 2004.
Wolfe, Tom. *The Electric Kool-Aid Acid Test*. Picador, 1968.
Yeats, W.B. *A Vision*. Macmillan, 1937.

Other Sources
Harvard Crimson, back issues online at www.thecrimson.com.
Harvard Review, Drugs and the Mind issue, Summer 1963, Vol. 1 No. 4.
Look Magazine, "The Strange Case of the Harvard Drug Scandal," Andrew T. Weil, November 5, 1963.
New York Times Magazine, "Albert Hofmann: Day Tripper," Dec. 28, 2008
Olson: The Journal of the Charles Olson Archives #3. University of Connecticut Library.

Reality Studio: A William S. Burroughs Community, Timothy Leary on William Burroughs, Brion Gysin, and Bou Saada, October 17, 1989.

San Francisco Oracle #7, The Houseboat Summit, February 1967.

Stolaroff Collection, Laura Huxley's Letter on Aldous' Passing, The Vaults of Erowid, July, 2009.

Time Magazine, St. Anthony's Fire article, Sept. 10, 1951.

Whole Earth Review, "No More Bagels: An Interview with Allen Ginsberg," Steve Silberman, September 1987.

THANKS AND APPRECIATIONS

Many of the details of the lives of Allen Ginsberg and Timothy Leary have been well documented in numerous interviews, articles, books, and biographies. I am indebted to the biographers, journalists, academics, and filmmakers who have provided information, insights and inspiration for my work. In addition to published work, I am deeply indebted to the special collections department at Stanford University for allowing me access to Allen Ginsberg's archives. Those archives planted the initial seed of this book in my mind back in the mid-1990s and provided the majority of the unpublished source material, mainly by way of personal letters. I am also thankful to the Berg Collection at the New York Public Library for access to its William S. Burroughs archive and to James Grauerholz for granting that permission. Thanks also to Archives & Special Collections at the Thomas J. Dodd Research Center at University of Connecticut for allowing me to use materials from their Charles Olson Research Collection.

Many individuals have helped in countless ways during the writing of this book. Thank you to Bill Morgan for providing insights and clarification on his Allen Ginsberg books and research. Thank you to Michael Horowitz and Denis Berry for allowing me to access Timothy Leary materials at the Berg Collection. Thank you to John Higgs for additional insights into his Timothy Leary biography, *I Have America Surrounded*. Thank you to Ralph Metzner for insight into the "O'Donell" incident in *High Priest* and to Don Lattin for referring me to Dr. Metzner. Thank you to Steve Silberman and the Beat Generation discussion group at The Well for their enthusiasm and for sharing information, and to David Gans for introducing me to The Well and for his vocal support of my writing.

Without a doubt, Richard Greenfield's *Timothy Leary: A Biography* has been the most useful and comprehensive secondary source of information on Timothy Leary. I am thankful to Mr. Greenfield for his exhaustive research and for providing such a detailed portrait of this complicated man.

Thank you to Elaine Katzenberger at City Lights for her interest and support of this book from its early stages through to publication and for her invaluable editorial suggestions. Simply put, I couldn't imagine a better home for *White Hand Society* than City

Lights. Thanks, also, to Maia Ipp of City Lights for her enthusiasm for this book, Lawrence Ferlinghetti for sharing memories of his visit to Leary in prison, and to Sarah Silverman, Stacey Lewis, and everyone at City Lights who worked to bring it to life. Thank you to my agent Linda Roghaar of the Linda Roghaar Literary Agency for her great efforts on my behalf. Thank you to everyone at BOA Editions for their support of my writing and for believing in my literary career. Thank you to the members of the Conners family, the Westervelt family, and all of my family—blood and extended—who teach and amaze me in their own ways.

Finally, eternal thanks to my wife Karen for her love and support and to my children, Whitman, Max, and Kane, for encouraging my obsessions and making each day a new trip.

ABOUT THE AUTHOR

Peter Conners' previous books include the memoir *Growing Up Dead: The Hallucinated Confessions of a Teenage Deadhead*, as well as the poetry collection *Of Whiskey & Winter* and the novella *Emily Ate the Wind*. He lives with his family in Rochester, NY. He is Publisher of the not-for-profit literary publisher BOA Editions, Ltd.

For more information visit: www.peterconners.com